# ART, POPULAR CULTURE, AND THE CLASSICAL IDEAL IN THE 1930s: TWO CLASSIC FILMS

## A Study of Roman Scandals and Christopher Strong

## by David Soren

Midnight Marquee Press, Inc.
Baltimore, Maryland, USA

I would like to thank my wife Noelle Soren for assistance in the preparation of the visuals for this volume. Susan Svehla is responsible for the beautiful layout and additional visual material. The material included here is taken from lectures over the course of 37-years of teaching at the Universities of Missouri and Arizona.

Special thanks to Sally Summer
and the entire Summer family for their help
in preparing this book
and also for permitting the use the unfinished autobiography of Dorothy Arzner.

ISBN 978-1-936168-04-0
Library of Congress Catalog Card Number 2010926957
Manufactured in the United States of America
First Printing June 2010

# TABLE OF CONTENTS

## Part One

## Appreciating Roman Scandals (1933)

## Part Two

## Appreciating Christopher Strong (1933)

## Dorothy Arzner's Other Films

## Part Three

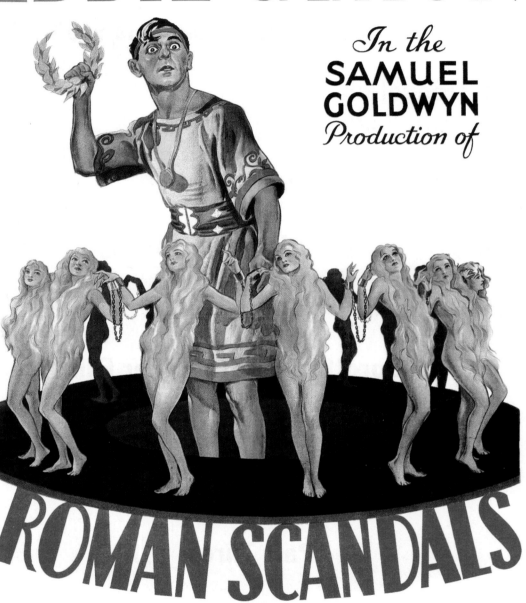

# APPRECIATING ROMAN SCANDALS (1933)
# INTRODUCTION

Several years ago a student came up to me on the first day of my University of Arizona course *Art and the Classical Ideal in the 1930s* and made a statement that shocked me. He said: "I've never seen a movie in black and white before. And I don't watch those old movies because there are too many references in them that I don't understand." This is not an unusual response from today's students, and truthfully, I don't understand why they enjoy the entertainment that *they* do.

Each generation finds it difficult to understand the previous generation. Yet if history has taught us anything, it is the importance in studying the past to learn about the great men and women that have contributed to the creation of our modern world. And it is equally important to use their accumulated wisdom, as well as learning from the errors in judgment that they had made as they traveled that path to enlightenment.

It is especially important to study the 1930s, a time not so unlike our own—an economic depression that caused massive unemployment, wiped out life savings and threatened the hopes of the young for a chance at the American dream. It was a time filled with corruption in the United States Senate and House of Representatives—private interests were able to lobby individual Senators and Representatives through contributions to campaigns as well as well as deals made under the table.

It was a time when the new medium of radio contained popular political leaders, even demagogues, who ranted against the established authority and embraced varying agendas. These groups, depending on your point of view, were seeking to either enlighten or to inflame the citizenry to action often through powerful ministries, which reached audiences of up to 40 million people across America. These were exemplified by such figures as Billy Sunday and Father Charles Coughlin, who is known as the "father of hate radio." Sunday had been a professional baseball player who became an evangelist determined to bring about Prohibition and stop what he termed the evils of drink. He amassed an enormous amount of wealth through his radio programs but was, despite modern arguments to the contrary, never pub-

**Father Charles Coughlin, "father of hate radio"**

everything streamlined, curvy and blonde was "in." Anyone unfamiliar with the 1930s can nonetheless instantly recognize that the hairstyles, costumes and sets have a particular look to them.

But how can young people better appreciate what was going on in this era if they don't understand and appreciate much of the jargon and many of the references? One place to start is by viewing the films discussed in this book. By reading the essays and watching the films, younger readers (and that means almost anyone besides myself) may gain a greater appreciation for the 1930s and will also enjoy the movies more than by simply watching it *a priori* (without any background or experience, and without understanding fully what these films once communicated to their popular audience). It helps to have the 1930s explained by an old person such as myself so you can then experience the movies again *a posteriori* (after learning more background information to prepare yourself).

licly exposed in any scandal. In the days preceding WWII, Coughlin often urged his listeners to support Mussolini's fascism and would also engage in anti-Jewish rhetoric.

These individuals often crossed the line between religious programming and political action programming, a line which we continue to find controversial today, with large numbers of proponents on either side of the issue regarding the separation of church and state. At the time, Republicans generally favored a *laissez faire* approach to solving the economic crisis (embodied by President Herbert Hoover), while Democrats under Hoover's successor Franklin D. Roosevelt were willing to try bold methods, some of which ultimately were declared unconstitutional by the Supreme Court, in their quest to jump-start the economy.

The 1930s were a time of contrasts. At a time when Americans had less money than at any time in their history, most movies revealed the obsession of the American people with elegance, wealth and beautiful people, so that an alien from Mars seeing most of these films would imagine that the society that had made them was entirely wealthy and not in the depths of the Depression.

The 1930s was also an era of innovation in technology and design, when form began to follow function and

Most of my students, rather unhappy about the required memorizing of dates for their college courses, believe that I am old enough to have lived through not only the 1930s, but even the Neolithic Period and Early Bronze Age and that during my youth I was a hunter-gatherer, who eventually learned to make hand-coiled pots in front of my cave. I'm not that old, but I am nearly that old, and I remember enough, and have looked into the history of the 1930s enough, to offer these essays of help. The 1930s were tragic, elegant, fascinating and fun. Enjoy discovering them *a posteriori* through the magic of the movies and the crutch of this book.

# ROMAN SCANDALS

## THE PLOT

Young Eddie (Eddie Cantor) lives in a graft-filled town named West Rome, Oklahoma where he is employed as a delivery boy for Mr. Cooper's grocery store but he gives away so much food to people and animals from his tiny income that he ends up owing the storeowner each time a paycheck comes around. Allowed to sleep in the local museum by a friendly guard, he also hangs his laundry there, until he is caught sleeping late by the corrupt local officials, who are the Mayor (Harry Holman), Chief of Police Charles Pratt (Charles C. Wilson) and evil would-be philanthropist and know-it-all Warren Finlay Cooper (Willard Robertson), who takes a particular delight in building jails and throwing homeowners and renters into the street. Cooper's latest plot is to donate land for the new city jail and then divide up the contractor fees among his cronies: the mayor and chief of police.

Despite being innocent to the point of eccentricity, Eddie is beloved by the poor and kind people in town. However when an official car containing the corrupt authorities crashes into Eddie's horse-drawn cart, Eddie becomes dazed and imagines that at the town limit he suddenly has lost his shoes in favor of sandals and that he has been transported to the outskirts of ancient Rome sometime during the Roman empire [31 B.C.–A.D. 476].

Accosted immediately by Roman soldiers, Eddie is hauled off to the slave market where he is sold to the people's champion Josephus (David Manners), who buys him to give him his freedom. But Eddie likes Josephus and laments that he cannot even hold a job as a slave. So he follows Josephus and tries to help him. When the Briton princess Sylvia (beautiful 1930s blonde Gloria Stuart) is brought to Rome in the emperor Valerius' (Edward Arnold) Roman triumphal procession, Eddie tries to save her because he thinks she is looking straight at him, when in fact she is glancing at the handsome Josephus. Jailed for his actions, Eddie is given a laughing potion by a fellow prisoner and manages ultimately to amuse the Roman emperor Valerius, who spares his life but makes him official food taster in the palace, a job with no future as someone always seems eager to try to poison the emperor.

Cast: Eddie Cantor (Eddie aka Oedipus); Ruth Etting (Olga); Gloria Stuart (Princess Sylvia); David Manners (Josephus); Verree Teasdale (Empress Agrippa); Edward Arnold (Emperor Valerius); Alan Mowbray (Majordomo); Charles C. Wilson (Police Chief Charles Pratt); Harry Holman (Mayor of West Rome); John [aka Jack] Rutherford (Manius); Willard Robertson (Warren Finley Cooper); Uncredited parts include: Lucille Ball (in her film debut); Billy Barty; Harry Cording; Richard Alexander; Charles Arnt; Frank Austin; Stanley Blystone; June Gale; Jane Darwell; Francis Ford; Paulette Goddard; Noble Johnson

Credits: Directed by Frank Tuttle; Art and Set Decoration by Richard Day; Story by George S. Kaufman and Robert E. Sherwood; Screenplay by William Anthony McGuire, Nat Perrin, Arthur Sheekman; Produced by Samuel Goldwyn; Music by Alfred Newman; Photographed by Gregg Toland, Ray June; Edited by Stuart Heisler; Costumes by John W. Harkrider; Choreography by Busby Berkeley; Songs by Al Dubin and Harry Warren; Released December 29, 1933; Premiered Los Angeles, November 27, 1933; Premiered New York, December 25, 1933; Filmed on location at Samuel Goldwyn Studios; Black and White; 35mm; 10 Reels; Mono; 92 Minutes; Filmed July 1933 through October 17, 1933; Remake of *Vamping Venus*, 1928

**Eddie Cantor sings "Build a Little House" in *Roman Scandals*.**

documents proving not the corruption of the emperor of ancient Rome, but rather of the town officials and self-proclaimed leading citizen Cooper. The police chief has dropped the check for the payoff from Cooper and Eddie has found it. All the corrupt officials are rounded up and the citizens of West Rome, who have been thrown out on the street, have their homes saved. Eddie has his face posted all over town so that all may pay their respects to the local hero and even dogs are observed licking the image!

Valerius, of course, proves to be evil and corrupt, just like the West Rome, Oklahoma politicians, and, in addition, the empress Agrippa (Verree Teasdale) wishes to conspire with Eddie and the palace chef to serve the emperor poisoned nightingales. She warns Eddie: "The one without the parsley is the one without the poison." But Eddie nearly is poisoned himself because he cannot remember the phrase and because an observant slave adds in the missing parsley before the food is served to Valerius. Eventually, the emperor plans to do away with Eddie, Sylvia and Josephus, who has now become Sylvia's lover. The lovers flee the palace by chariot and head for Ostia, and ultimate escape by sea, but the emperor's chariots follow in hot pursuit while Eddie, in his own chariot, attempts to divert them and to keep hold of documents proving imperial corruption in ancient Rome. After a wild chase, Eddie's chariot falls apart completely and plunges over a cliff. He wakes up to find himself back in West Rome, Oklahoma at the original crash site of his cart. He also finds that in the confusion of the crash he gets inadvertently in possession of

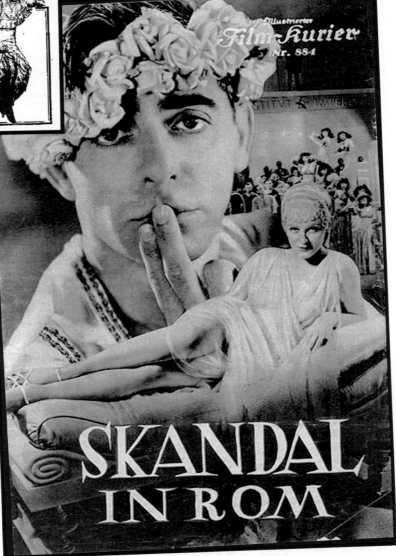

**A Foreign ad for *Roman Scandals* features Eddie Cantor**

8

## INTRODUCTION TO EDDIE CANTOR

When *Roman Scandals* was first shown for the end of the Christmas and holiday season of 1933, it was appreciated as amusing light family entertainment and a successful vehicle for its enormously popular and enduring star Eddie Cantor and his character known generally to the public as "The Kid." The Kid had already been featured in a Broadway show and later the silent movie known as *Kid Boots* (1926), and the Samuel Goldwyn talking films *Whoopee!* (1930), *Palmy Days* (1931) and *The Kid from Spain* (1932). The Kid was usually perceived by audiences of the time as a character containing something of Cantor himself, the orphaned offspring of a Jewish immigrant family. He played a Jew in the American West in *Whoopee!* and a Jew pretending to be a Spaniard in *The Kid from Spain*.

Later on he would portray a kid from Brooklyn ending up in Egypt in *Kid Millions*, and a kid transported to ancient Baghdad in *Ali Baba Goes to Town* (1937), by which time he could barely pass for a juvenile any longer! The Kid was innocent, kindhearted and considerate of others, but also a perpetual wise guy, who was always outsmarted by others until eventually his honesty and integrity somehow helped him to triumph.

Eddie Cantor was highly successful on Broadway, in the new medium of radio, on records and in film, and was, at the time that *Roman Scandals* was made, elected president of the newly formed Screen Actors Guild. In short, he was at the apex of his career. The public had come to expect that Eddie, one of America's giants of the entertainment business, would star in one musical film per year and he was ardent about making that film as entertaining as possible and filling it with lots of the sure fire gags and vaudeville routines, for which he was known.

Thus, the film was intended as nothing more than blockbuster entertainment and it quickly became United Artists' top film of the whole year and one of the 15 highest grossing movies of 1934. However, as an archaeologist and historian, I believe that this film should be viewed not just as popular entertainment, but as a unique cultural artifact, reflecting many important characteristics of its time and place. Like another important Eddie Cantor vehicle, *Ali Baba Goes to Town* (1937), which brought Franklin Roosevelt's New Deal to ancient Baghdad and is equally worthy of review by historians, *Roman Scandals* views a remote place and time (ancient imperial Rome) through the prism of modern American society (the heart of the Great Depression). In order to understand what life was like in American when the Depression was at its most frightening and how Americans responded to it, *Roman Scandals* should be required viewing.

Its star Eddie Cantor was already not only an American icon, but also a symbol for optimism during the Depression, especially since he had lost everything in the stock market crash of 1929, and still laughed it off and wrote a humorous short book about it entitled *Caught Short*. But Cantor's life had been hard from the very start and Americans knew about his struggles for success from articles in movie magazines and newspapers. Cantor had been orphaned while still a tiny child and grew up on the Lower East Side in New York. He eked out a living doing vaudeville performances and eventually became one of the premiere attractions of the *Ziegfeld Follies*, the most lavish and popular entertainment in New York. He was raised by his maternal grandmother, Esther Lazarowitz Kantrowitz, who helped keep little Israel Iskowitz off the streets. His name was unofficially changed to Kantrowitz in public school to facilitate his living situation and eventually it became shortened to Cantor as he sought a career in entertainment. His girlfriend Ida Tobias nicknamed him Eddie and a entertainment legend was born.

As he grew to manhood, it was evident that Eddie could do better than many others. He had a rather weak, high-pitched and frail-sounding singing voice and he wasn't much of a tap dancer either but rather more of a hoofer. Nonetheless he had an engagingly mannered style, which greatly appealed to Americans who saw him as energetic and enthusiastic, featuring his prancing around the stage on tiptoes singing, clapping his hands together and rolling his banjo eyes, leading to his popular epithets "Banjo Eyes" and "The Apostle of Pep." Particularly delightful was his stage, radio and screen persona as "The Kid," a character drawn from his real life as an undersized waif on the streets of the Lower East Side of New York City.

In *Roman Scandals*, his kid character is a genial soul, whom everyone likes but who is an orphan with no money. A guard allows him to sleep in the public museum where he innocently hangs his laundry, which he intends to take it down before the museum opens. He works in Cooper's grocery store but his philanthropy to both people and animals leaves him perpetually in debt to Mr. Cooper.

Cantor's wide-eyed innocence on the screen differed from the savvy ex-street kid he actually was, but it provided an opportunity to draw him into plot convolutions his character wasn't intended to understand fully and above all it allowed him to be drawn into sexual situations from which he constantly tried to escape in order to defend his virture. In *The Kid from Spain* (1932), the predecessor to *Roman Scandals*, Cantor was again the wide-eyed

innocent, seduced by Lyda Roberti, a man-crazy "Mexican" (though actually Polish) blonde bombshell. In the early Cantor films, his character starts with total innocence but is led quickly into a world of predatory or shocked women, which always leaves the viewer with a feeling that he has seen something naughty. Such scenes also gave Cantor a chance to roll his banjo eyes and wink to the audience that even though his character doesn't know what's going on, he does. Much of his comedy is involved with leading the audience along to see a naughty situation while pretending he actually knows nothing about what is being revealed. This was an essential part of his show business persona or what we used to call in vaudeville his "mask." Many great comedians project this same mask—Jack Benny being cheap, Jim Carrey being wild and crazy, Mike Meyers being a swinging idiot secret agent, Adam Sandler (before he took on more mature parts) being the innocent kid in the Cantor tradition. His "Canteen Boy" persona on the TV comedy series *Saturday Night Live* is an example of the Cantor character or mask taken to extremes! We know that these comedians know what they are doing but we suspend belief and enjoy their pretense.

Cantor's distinctive delivery in films was much the same as his delivery on stage. Feeling that the most essential thing was for the viewer to make sure and actually hear his joke, Cantor always enunciated extremely clearly and gestured to punctuate each key thought. Years of working with bad microphones, no microphones and poor sound recording had made him this way and it became a trademark, as did his prancing around the stage on tiptoes when singing, clapping his hands together and rolling his eyes. Cantor's distinctive style made him popular with vaudeville impersonators and made him a success in every field of show business he undertook: records, silent films, the Broadway stage, the Ziegfeld Follies, radio, television and sound films. At the end of his life he was such a success on television on *The Colgate Comedy Hour* and with his frequent guest appearances and cameos on other programs, that he literally worked himself to death, remaining in high demand even into his 70s. His unflagging optimism had seen him rise from being totally wiped out in 1929 to earning $450,000 by

Eddie Cantor and Lyda Roberti on the cover of *Picturegoer* magazine promote *The Kid from Spain*.

1933 and soon thereafter becoming a millionaire again. It is not an exaggeration to say that his optimism helped save America and Franklin Delano Roosevelt's plan for the country and he was also a driving force in support of the American effort in WWII, in USO tours, in standing up for and protecting actors' rights, and in founding the March of Dimes, which organized school children across the country to collect money to fight polio. The March of Dimes, established in 1938, was a play on a popular newsreel program called *The March of Time*, shown before the main feature in movie theaters.

When Eddie urges the people of West Rome, Oklahoma to survive in the street because it is "already furnished" and to get together and "build a little home," he is speaking as the honest, generous, down on his luck, optimistic Everyman that FDR wanted to popularize in the public mind in order to prevent the country from a plunge into anarchy. Eddie was a revered major American force and a critically important role model in those Depression years. The fact that he has become so completely and undeservedly forgotten and unknown today is a testament to changing modern tastes. He wasn't a handsome leading man and he did not excel at any one thing but his body of work, when presented to young audiences, is appreciated

by many both because it is still very funny in a slightly naughty yet essentially innocent way and above all because it is historically significant satire. The more most people learn about Eddie Cantor the more they appreciate his comedy and his contributions.

In *Roman Scandals*, The Kid, Eddie, is caught sleeping in the public museum and thrown out of town by a corrupt mayor, developer and police chief who are engaging in graft and secret deals. As he is leaving his horse-drawn cart has a crash with the mayor's car and he is thrown to the ground. After that he is escorted to the city limits where he suddenly finds himself transported back into ancient Rome and the time of the so-called emperor Valerius (Edward Arnold) who has just won major victories against the Britons and captured their princess Sylvia (lovely Gloria Stuart). Eddie has to change his name to Oedipus or Eddipus because there is no such name as Eddie in Latin and he becomes the personal slave of Josephus (David Manners) who is an enemy of Valerius and spokesman for the common man. Josephus, Oedipus and Sylvia become the champions of justice in the corrupt world of ancient imperial Rome, which is constantly paralleled to the world of 1933 America and its Great Depression.

## Galaxy Of Stars To Help Eddie Cantor In Starting March Of Dimes' Campaign Over Networks Tonight; On KFYO At 10 O'Clock

A galaxy of star performers from radio, stage and screen, topped by Eddie Cantor, will be heard over Station KFYO and America's three major networks, Mutual Broadcasting, Columbia Broadcasting System, and National Broadcasting company tonight from 10 to 11, in connection with the annual "March of Dimes" campaign for the National Foundation for Infantile Paralysis.

The broadcast will originate in Hollywood and New York. A partial list of celebrities scheduled to appear before the microphone includes Jack Benny, George Jessel, Jimmie Fidler, Goodman Ace, Deanna Durbin, Tyrone Power, Lanny Ross, Fred Allen, Walter Winchell, Edwin C. Hill, Burns and Allen, Lawrence Tibett, John Charles Thomas, Charles Butterworth, Ben Bernie, "Fibber McGee," Nelson Eddy, Joe Penner, Bing Crosby, Rudy Vallee, Lily Pons, Andre Kostelanetz, Jeanette MacDonald, Jack Haley, Edward G. Robinson, Amos 'n' Andy, Orson Welles, Lowell Thomas, Major Edward Bowes, Bob Ripley, Richard Crooks, Gladys Swarthout, Jascha Heifetz, Cecil B. DeMille, Erno Rapee, H. V. Kaltenborn and Beniamino Gigli.

Last year Cantor, chairman of the "March of Dimes" committee, collected over $85,000, a silver tide which actually swamped The White House.

### EDDIE CANTOR

"Johnson Family" roster, and he is the liveliest, bouncing member of this popular Mutual network show. The newcomer's father is Jimmy Scribner, creator of the Johnson Family." The new Chicazola star was born in Cincinnati January 11. Mother, baby and father are doing fine.

The program is aired over KFYO daily at 4:15 p. m.

## ROMAN SCANDALS
## AND THE GREAT DEPRESSION

*Roman Scandals* was intended as escapist fare to provide an optimistic feeling as the Depression was striking fear into the hearts of Americans and forcing staggering unemployment, thus far much worse than the reported 10 to 15% figures we are approaching nationally during the present major recession of 2009-2011 when this book is being published for the first time. Just as in America in 1933, the ancient Rome of Oedipus is full of corrupt officials but Oedipus offers hope and faith in the common man to save the day. *Roman Scandals* supported President Franklin Roosevelt's attempt to urge people not to abandon hope but instead to give time for FDR's Brain Trust and New Deal to save the country through stimulus programs such as the CCC (Civilian Conservation Corps) and the WPA (Works Progress Administration). These organizations were designed to provide basic support money for starving, unemployed families and to help the country's deteriorating infrastructure of public works.

Business owners in 1933 were encouraged to pitch in, keep people employed, and display in their shops emblems of the National Recovery Administration such as "We do our part!," featuring a blue American Thunderbird, the legendary bird of power of the Native American people of the Pacific Northwest, and more generally a symbol of power and strength. However, while the upper part of the logo is a Thunderbird, the rest of the figure resembles an eagle clutching lightning—this was an ancient Greek and Roman symbol of the power of the Greek god Zeus or the Roman Jupiter and had also been adapted by the Nazis as

one of their prominent logos at the same time. The eagle is also clutching a notched gear, a symbol of recovering American industry but also resembling a Roman laurel wreath, which may have been its initial inspiration for the eagle's designer Hugh Samuel Johnson, who was also the head of the NRA.

FDR's fireside chats on the radio and his powerfully confident, self-assured voice helped to keep America going while the New Deal began to resurrect the country from the ashes. He projected a sense of reassurance

**FDR gives a Fireside Chat.**

and physical power and what the newspaperman H.L. Mencken mockingly referred to as his "Christian Science smile." Conservative critics in modern times, the strongest among them being Rush Limbaugh and Sean Hannity, have stated that only WWII beginning in December, 1941, was able to turn around the Great Depression but economic statistics clearly show that FDR's programs were effective, particularly in the first phase of the New Deal shortly after he took office and that eventually public confidence began to turn revive. FDR did not end the Depression but he did help to stop its downward spiral of the Herbert Hoover presidency.

Along with FDR, Eddie Cantor did a great deal to restore faith in America through his escapist and optimistic films and his writings, particularly his small books produced during the Depression to raise spirits. His reassuring voice also provided entertainment and encouragement on the radio where he was perhaps the most important American star. Despite being on radio as early as 1922, he hit his stride on *The Chase and Sanborn Hour* beginning on September 13, 1931. He was soon the highest paid radio entertainer with an enormous following in every stratum of society. If he introduced a song and it was good it would sell phenomenally. In 1934, for example, he introduced "Santa Claus is Coming to Town," which became a gigantic hit overnight and sold 400,000 records in one month and 100,000 copies of sheet music!

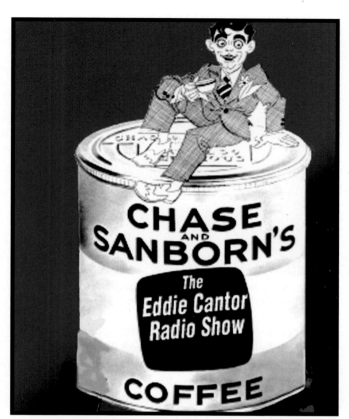

And the song is still popular today. That's how big he was in the 1930s.

Eddie was beloved also because he had resurrected himself from the ashes and he argued on his radio show that the average American could also do this by applying himself. He kept faith with America and with his president. Eddie's message of hope entertained through comedy, gave an appearance of normalcy, and made fun of the Depression. Together with FDR's more serious approach to problem solving, the two men packed an effective one-two punch. *Roman Scandals*, released December 29, 1933, was designed as a package of New Year's optimism for 1934 and a complement to the New Deal. With radio, movies, records and shows, Eddie became a Depression-era media megastar and FDR the first real media president, succeeding Herbert Hoover (1929-1933) who was not media savvy. Hoover, who essentially had supported the big business policies of buying stocks with no margin, had no answer for the ills of the country other than hoping that the ship of state would somehow right itself by trusting in big business and opposing government regulation. He also had the misfortune of being president when the corruption and mismanagement in business and politics had reached a head, culminating in the great stock market crash of October 1929, followed by years of a growing unemployment so bad that many people were

Many families lost their homes and were forced to live in their automobiles during the Great Depression.

into their own cars. The impromptu communities in the city dumps were quickly dubbed Hoovervilles.

In the beginning of *Roman Scandals* we see a community of people ejected from their homes and living on the street. It could easily have been depicted as an expression of grief and hardship but is instead turned into a place of communal help and support and pure joy, very different from the harsh realities people were facing outside the theater. Living outside in the open air might have its advantages, if one believes the populist rhetoric of the film's opening tune "Build a Little Home":

> It's not a palace or a poorhouse
> But the rent is absolutely free.
> And it's my house, but it's your house,
> If you'll come and stay with me.
> With a carpet on the floor,
> Made of buttercups and clover,
> All our troubles will be over,
> When we build a little home.

forced to live outdoors near city dumps where they might find discarded food or meals brought in by concerned citizens who were still employed. Others lined up to survive by being fed at breadlines or soup kitchens after being forced out of their homes to live in tents or move

Turning horrifying reality (with which the audience could all too readily identify) into optimism is one of the

Shanty towns grew up near trash dumps as homeless families tried to survive on the garbage heaps.

One reason that movies remained popular throughout the '30s was their cheap cost of attendance, perhaps a quarter at times with frequent discounts and offers of giveaway prizes such as Depression Modern glass for the home. Especially popular was Bank Night, a concept invented by 20th Century Fox booking agent Charles U.

very first things that the movie does to lighten the burden of its audience:

> You'll always have a roof above you,
> As long as there's a sky.
> And if you have someone to love you,
> You're sure of getting by.
> You don't need a lot of log and stone,
> Build a home on happiness alone.

In *Roman Scandals* the "Build a Little House" number features families living outdoors.

Yeager in Denver, Colorado whereby you signed your name in a book and got a number which was drawn by lot on Bank Night and you might win cash prizes. Bank Night quickly became a staple of movie theaters in the Depression and they offered tangible hope of escaping one's financial predicament which was further bolstered by the abundant escapist film fair such as *King Kong* or the various Busby Berkeley fantastic musicals such as *42nd Street*, *Golddiggers of 1933* and *Roman Scandals*. There were of course also realistic movies that depicted the horrors of contemporary life, such as William Wellman's *Wild Boys of the Road* or King Vidor's *Our Daily Bread*, but these were not the films that mass audiences, craving cheap entertainment and escape, sought.

In the 1930s glass giveaways in movie theaters were common and cheap, streamlined looking glass came to be known as Depression Glass and is still highly collected today.

## THE DEPRESSION MODERN-STYLE

*Roman Scandals* was designed in a new style expressly concocted for dealing with the Great Depression; it has come to be known as Depression Modern, thanks to its chronicler Martin Greif. It reflected a desire to do away with the cluttered and expensive Greek or Roman classical look with elaborately carved and expensive columns and moldings and replace it with a more modern, streamlined design that showed the influence of airplanes and ocean liners, those wonders of the age which could be both beautiful and functional. The idea that beautiful form could follow function became dominant and there was also the notion that streamlining with modern materials such as chromium looked toward a future world, which would solve the problems of this world through science. And the use of light wood such as bleached maple for furniture plus light colors would reflect what was called a "sunny disposish" (sunny disposition), a term popularized first in the 1926 Broadway musical *Americana*.

Along with the classical art or *Beaux-Arts* style (classical fine art style taught at the *Ecole des Beaux-Arts* in Paris) which had now become out of fashion, another art movement known as Art Deco also fell by the wayside increasingly by the time *Roman Scandals* was made. Deco largely involved the use of sumptuous materials, many angular or non-traditional forms and stepped pyramids. It had become popular at an exhibition known as *L'Exposition des Arts Decoratifs* in Paris in 1925 and it was influenced by the angular Cubist art of Pablo Picasso, modern streamlining and even the discovery of King Tut's tomb in the Valley of the Kings in Egypt, as well as other movements and ideas of the period between 1895 and 1925. In America, Deco forms were reproduced all across the main streets of America in a style which

Originally a gas station ca. 1936 in Tucson, Arizona, this building imitates the balloon tethering top of the Empire State Building of New York City and adds the typical curvilinear sweep of the Depression Modern Style along with the stepped look borrowed from Art Deco.

has come to be termed Cut-Rate Deco or Modernistic, featuring glazed tiles slapped onto buildings decorated with volutes, non-historical ornament and garish colors. But by 1933 all that was going out of vogue. The stepped pyramid look remained but got more curvilinear and the

The Chance House, ca. 1939, in Centralia, Missouri features horizontal chrome streamlining, plus a curvilinear dining room with bleached maple furniture. It is a superlative example of the Depression Modern-Style.

streamlining stayed popular but overall simplification meant restfulness and beauty.

As Depression Modern grew in popularity, it also emphasized lightness and solar imagery. This emphasis had come from the development of such European spas as the Auguste Rollier Heliotherapy Clinic in Switzerland, which had been established as in 1903 and became widely known by the 1920s. Rollier reported having great success in treating dreaded diseases such as tuberculosis by exposing people to the sun and ultra-violet light in strong but measured doses. In 1911 for example, he treated 369 cases of tuberculosis with exposure to the sun and of these 284 were healed and 48 improved. Treatment continued until the body was well tanned. Thus a gently tanned body became described as a "healthy tan" because it was believed to be so. Statistics claiming vast improvements in treating various diseases were provided and the solar cult was born. Revealing bathing suits for women allowed more exposure of the sun's rays and looked good too.

Pioneer women's swimmer Annette Kellerman of Australia had developed the Unitard or one-piece women's bathing suit by 1907, claiming that it was healthier for the body because it provided women more flexibility in the water. She was promptly arrested on a Boston beach, but after her court trial and Rollier's discoveries, the simpler one-piece suit had arrived to stay and now had a justification for existing. Blonde solar bursts were displayed widely on cigarette cases and were used inside theaters such as the 1932 Radio City Music Hall in New

Annette Kellerman poses in her shocking one-piece swimsuit.

their bustles (formed with crinoline or stiff fabric hiding female posteriors), and employed cosmetics so they could become what Elizabeth Arden would call "women fresh as posies," boyish, slender-bodied pals to the males. They began to do things that shocked their parents since they were able to escape from the watchful eyes of their community and go to petting parties in automobiles that could take them far away into the country.

These female companions, embodied in the movies and on the stage by the likes of Clara Bow, Sally O'Neill, Marjorie "Babe" Kane, Helen Kane, Frances White and Jane Green, came to be referred to as flappers, as if they were ducklings just learning to fly. The ideal flappers were typically slim and flat-chested brunettes with short hair and cloche hats (usually bell-shaped, close fitting felt hats over short dark hair) invented by Parisian Caroline Reboux or short-skirted clothing styles popularized in Paris by such designers as Coco Chanel. The hugely broad-brimmed hats of the 1910s popularized by vaudeville stars such as Reine Davies were out of fashion now and bobbed hair and pouty lips were in. The girls were boyish but sometimes spoke their minds, often uttering phrases that would shock their parents by "being flip" and talking about sex openly, drinking during Prohibition at speakeasies, smoking and listening not to the gentle

York City. Before Rollier, Rudyard Kipling had written: "Only mad dogs and Englishmen go out in the noonday sun." And later this became a popular song by England's Noel Coward with the same title, but now the solar cult had arrived and the blonde look was in. Even F. Scott Fitzgerald wrote about the cult of the sun and feminine beauty as women exposed their bodies on the French Riviera in *Tender is the Night* (1934). The solar cult also was exploited in publicity for the development of Florida and California, the sun states, and after the solar cult took hold, these two states had the most rapid growth rate of any state in the union between 1920 and 1940.

Along with streamlined forms and blonde, solar imagery, curves were in fashion too. In this time of Depression, hard edges such as had been popular in the Cubist art of Pablo Picasso and Georges Braque in the 1910s and 1920s were out. They were replaced by curvilinear forms and were reflected in the changing look of women. In 1920 the 19th Amendment gave women the right to vote but they were not fully emancipated even though they were progressing into a new perception of themselves. They wore lighter clothing, discarding their hoop skirts (flared out with stiffeners such as baleen or whale bone) and

Silent screen siren Louise Brooks was the quintessential flapper.

classical music of the piano and pianoforte but rather to new hot jazz or jass music played on the saxophone by groups like The Six Brown Brothers. It wasn't opera, or even operetta or violin that was listened to so much by the young, but rather popular music with a raucous beat that had evolved out of what was termed "Negro music" such as blues, jazz and ragtime and was featured by white performers such as Marion Harris, the Boswell Sisters, Fred Waring, George Olsen and Ruth Etting. When the Boswells started slurring their lyrics and syncopating their rhythms many radio listeners found these musical variations low class and shocking!

**Clara Bow on the cover of** *Motion Picture Classic* **fan mag, 1927**

By 1920, although women were voting nationwide, they weren't yet fully emancipated social equals. They were generally limited in the jobs they might take such as librarian, nurse and schoolteacher, and they were expected to give up their careers for the man they loved when they got married—because having a working wife was a sign of male failure. Women who wanted careers instead of men or careers with men were viewed as strange and these anti-feminist attitudes were reinforced by the rising profession of psychiatry and the teachings of Charles Darwin and Sigmund Freud. It may seem bizarre that evolutionists supported the idea of the natural inferiority of women but they did. Darwin believed that

**The Dolly Sisters in the 1910s were vaudeville and Broadway dancers and international fashion plates who pioneered the slender and short-haired look for women, anticipating the flapper era.**

women were biologically and intellectually inferior to men, and some evolutionists, buoyed by the teachings of Freud, argued that women were a separate and inferior psychological species from men, known as *homo parietalis* as opposed to the *homo frontalis* of the males. Thus men had primacy or frontality and women were parietal and perhaps functioning from a different and less important lobe of the brain, behind the frontal lobe. Since this was sometimes also taught in school, women could become conditioned to believe in their own inferiority because their preeminent scientists of the time said they were. Thus the 1920s could be a confusing time for women, having become emancipated in many ways while still being limited in their social possibilities and in their self evaluation.

In the 1920s girls who fit into the flapper mode were said to have "It," an idea put forward in *Cosmopolitan* magazine by the British interpreter of the American scene Elinor Glyn; such women said titillating things, could wear exotic clothing items and accessories and yet were great companions for males escorting them to parties. They wore lighter garments of silk and rayon and threw away their corsets, preferring to wear clothing that might be as much as 1/10th as heavy as their older wear with whale-bone supports. For Elinor, the most typical symbol of the 1920s woman was Clara Bow, that redheaded bundle of energy whose iconic popularity soared at the time. Celebrating Clara in 1925, the magazine *Vanity Fair* wrote:

> In one person, in one pose, we have the *genus* American girl, refined, washed, manicured, pedicured, permanent-waved and exalted herewith… Do you wonder that for the nonce she is almost the most popular of the movie stars?

It may seem to modern eyes that these Charleston or Black Bottom dancing girls had jettisoned their self-control along with their corsets. But, as we have suggested, the flapper was not totally free. This becomes clear when we observe how comedian and director Charlie Chaplin described his ideal 1920s woman:

1. When in my company, she never admires other men.

18

**By the time *Roman Scandals* was filmed the blonde look was taking over and curves were back in style. (Photofest)**

2.  If I am obliged to leave her in order to keep another engagement, her disappointment is always keen enough to be flattering to me, but never quite keen enough to keep me from going where I am going

3.  Her diamond bracelets never need cleaning.

4.  Her shoulders are never shiny

5.  She never takes advantage of a voluptuous situation to narrow her eyes.

6.  She always reads all of the Sunday papers (the funny sheet first) but, having read them, she refolds them neatly and leaves them as they were.

7.  She knows the words of no popular dance music, or, if she does, never sings them in my ear when dancing.

8.  She uses only a faint eau de toilette during the day, but sprays herself plentifully with L'Heure Bleue upon retiring.

9.  I am not exactly in love with her, but

10. She is entirely in love with me.

Clara Bow's star faded sharply as the '30s and a new view of women appeared. Bow tried to adapt to the changing times, appearing as a full-figure '30s bombshell, but her reign was over as she fell victim to alleged and sometimes untrue scandals that further damaged her already tarnished reputation for unrestrained sexuality. In America, however, when someone gets enormously popular for a time, there is usually an eventual backlash. This is true for everything from The Dixie Chicks to The Spice Girls to the Bee Gees to George W. Bush to Barack Obama and on and on. More than anything, Clara Bow succumbed to the American desire to search for the latest vogue. Clara became yesterday's trend and was quickly discarded like an old VHS cassette.

By the time of *Roman Scandals*, the blonde look was taking over. And the curvilinear look. And the rounded look. Women plucked out their eyebrows and painted in a curve of beauty. The Art Deco hard-edged, crystalline rhombic look was out. The simplified, curvilinear, streamlined, blonde look was in. Actresses such as Mae West, Jean Harlow, Alice Faye, Marion Davies, Shirley Temple and my particular favorite Ann Sothern filled the

19

Ginger Rogers and Fred Astaire—"She gave him sex and he gave her class."

bill now. And of course in *Roman Scandals* it was Gloria Stuart as the epitome of blonde pulchritude.

Among the stars that best exemplified the Depression Modern-style were the dancing team of Fred Astaire and Ginger Rogers. The pencil thin Fred appeared streamlined, like a Depression Modern-accent, and the curvilinear blonde, round-faced Ginger was the ideal of the '30s female look. He was plain in appearance, yet appeared streamlined. She spoke in a hard-boiled manner, yet appeared especially elegant and less working-class when she danced with Fred. Katharine Hepburn put it simply: "She gives him sex and he gives her class." And that was the secret of their success, plus the fact that Astaire, choreographing with Hermes Pan at RKO Pictures, managed to dance in curvilinear sweeping and elegant movements which embodied the style of the time. Astaire and Rogers dancing on Bakelite floors, making synchronized curvilinear movements, became one of the iconic images of the Depression Modern-style. And let us

not forget the "third" dancer between them, the beautiful flowing, sweeping gowns that Ginger wore and which were incorporated into the graceful flowing movements of the dance. Never was this more apparent than in the slow-motion dance sequence from *Carefree* (1938). In that sequence the gown, Astaire and Rogers, and even Ginger's scarf all come together amid typical RKO Depression Modern-design.

The look of the art of the 1930s had already been espoused by a forgotten but influential industrial designer (the term barely existed before he developed it) from Paris named Raymond Loewy. Loewy was a great admirer of simplification. The computer font now known as Broadway was originally largely his invention as he campaigned to streamline and simplify lettering and to improve clarity and readability in all products being sold to the public. He admired the airplane wing and urged its idea of "form follows function" be applied to art and interior design and commercial products. "Like an airplane wing, there

**Raymond Loewy**

sion, Loewy felt, called out for a style of reason, which would provide an opportunity to relax from the pressures of complicated modern life. Being simple was being more modern. And so furniture became light-colored, featuring bleached maple wood, streamlining and restful curves.

Architect and designer Walter Dorwin Teague (1883-1960) commented that the Depression Modern-style was a desire to hark back to earlier times when life was simpler and in particular to embrace ancient Greek and Roman ideas, celebrating cultures which exemplified great beauty, culture and mystery. America had been born during the Neo-Classical Period in Europe and reflected many of the styles then popular in England and France so that

should be nothing about a work of art that needs to be added and nothing that must be taken away." Loewy's ideas and those of interior designer Donald Deskey and Russell Wright swept across the country helping to produce the Depression Modern-style with its blondness, curve of beauty, streamlined quality and use of traditional and ultra-modern materials in combination. The Depres-

The Packard Motor Company hired the Marion Morgan Dancers to help promote their new 1927 Packard 343. Here a dancer becomes a living hood ornament for the Packard.

this legacy resonated much more deeply in America in the '30s than it does now. In the world of dance Isadora Duncan had expressed the importance of going back to the classical Greek and Roman world for inspiration and to draw on that world to create modern forms for the dance. Her ideas were extremely influential in Europe and spread to America through numerous disciples such as Marion Morgan, who brought Isadora's theories into the movies in the later 1920s.

**Donald Deskey designed this sofa for Radio City Music Hall.**

## THE 1930s AND THE CLASSICAL IDEAL

As the vogue for things both classical and at the same time ultra-modern spread, modern materials were given Greek and Latin prefixes, attempting to get back to the roots of classical civilization on which America was founded, using Roman law and Roman architecture so much admired by Thomas Jefferson and brought by him to Virginia. Greek and Roman sculpture had been used in the 1830s by nationally prominent sculptors such as Horatio Greenough to immortalize American patriots like George Washington, and Greek and Latin were used to promote and clarify our national identity. Many examples of this classical influence on America exist. One may cite the Latin phrase *e pluribus unum* ("out of many one"), placed on our national seal in 1776 along with the Greek eagle of Zeus. There is also the naming of Philadelphia in 1701 by Quaker William Penn as the settlement of brotherly love, from two words in ancient Greek, *phileo* "to love" and *adelfos* or "brother." There was the founding of Cincinnati in 1790, named for the Roman republican military hero Cincinnatus, who left his plow to save the Roman republic from the enemy Aequi and Sabine tribes.

**Horatio Greenough's statue of George Washington**

This classical influence persisted through many years in America. The Lincoln Memorial in Washington made in 1922 is an homage to the Parthenon, that famous temple of ancient Athens from the 440s BCE., while the Jefferson Memorial made in 1934 was an homage to the Pantheon, most famous temple of ancient Rome, built in the 130s A.D. by the emperor Hadrian, and the examples go on and on.

As new and seemingly miraculous fibers and plastics appeared on the market, classical Greek and Roman words were brought in to identify them as wondrous inventions that would simplify our lives and would be worthy of ancient Greece and Rome. Herculon was a stain-resistant synthetic textile fiber that was imbued with the name, and supposedly the properties, of the Greek hero Herakles or his Roman name Hercules. Cellophane, from the Greek verb to appear and the Latin noun for a cell or small enclosure, was invented by the Swiss chemist Jacques E. Brandenberger, but it was not until 1927, when the Dupont Company was able to make it moisture proof, that its sales went through the roof. The vogue for cellophane in the early '30s was enormous and one Eddie Cantor joke used in *Roman Scandals* in the song "Keep Young and Beautiful" suggests that women could ensure staying fresh and young by wearing a bathing suit of cellophane. Its transparent qualities would of course drive a male "half insane" as the song suggests. Another company made a heater called Duo-Therm, a term which came from two Latin words that suggested double heating capabilities. So a major part of the '30s streamlining, simplification and reduction to essentials was also designed to go back in time to ancient classical and American roots!

The place where these Depression Modern-ideas crystallized and reached a massive audience of artists and designers was the Chicago Century of Progress, held for the purpose of celebrating the 100th anniversary of the incorporation of the city of Chicago. Never mind that Chicago was a corrupt, crime-ridden, gangster-filled "tod-

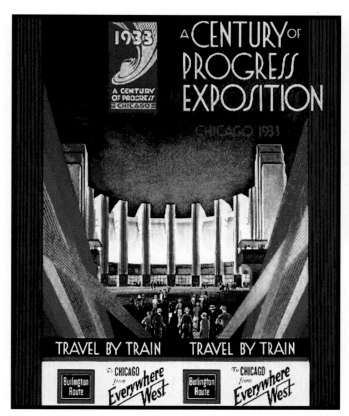

**Display of Bakelite jewelry**

dlin' town." This was a celebration of what science could do for our future world once this Depression was licked. We would see a time where design was brought to bear on improving the quality of our life from homes to airplanes to baby-nurturing incubators, all proudly displayed at the Exposition! On May 27, 1933 the fair opened and its influence was at its zenith as *Roman Scandals* was being filmed. The fair closed in October 1934. Its motto was "Science Finds, Industry Applies, Man Conforms."

*Roman Scandals* was one of the first films to fully reflect the Depression Modern-style, which also involved the extensive use of plastics and such elements as highly polished Bakelite floors. Bakelite was a plastic invented by the amazing Belgian scientist Leo Baekland. He was the son of an illiterate shoemaker, but he was determined to rise above his station ever since he read the *Autobiography of Benjamin Franklin* when he was just eight years old. Dedicating himself to work-

**Nitrogen Dioxide Gas Caused Blast In Cleveland Clinic**

(By The Associated Press)
CLEVELAND May 20—Nitrogen Dioxide formed from the decomposition of the nitrocellulose X-ray films caused the deaths of the 124 men and women in the Cleveland Clinic disaster last Wednesday, Dr. William E. Tower, co-founder of the Clinic and one of its directors declared late-to-day.

This was the first official statement to come from a director of the clinic regarding the actual cause of the deaths.

ing hard and pursuing his dreams, as Franklin had encouraged, he earned a doctorate from the University of Ghent and ended up marrying his professor's daughter! After winning a fellowship to Columbia University in New York City, he initially used his chemistry abilities to invent a new kind of photographic paper for film magnate George Eastman; it was called Velox. But his greatest discovery was yet to come.

He added heat and pressure to a toxic, colorless, crystalline solid known as Phenol and mixed it with formaldehyde, using wood flour as a filler. The result was a powerful synthetic plastic, the finest ever made. Being electrically non-conductive and resistant to heat, it was still malleable enough in the forming stage to be used for everything from dance floors to telephones, bracelets and even radios. Invented in 1907, it was developed through the 1920s and became one of the major symbols of the capabilities of science to enhance modern life. One dramatic improvement was in the production of billiard balls, which had originally been made of nitrocellulose (later known as celluloid), invented by John Wesley Hyatt in 1869. The processing of this simple industrial plastic was often volatile, resulting in explosions in the factory resulting from the sudden release of nitrogen dioxide, and rumors persist to this day that energetic games of pool could cause the celluloid billiard balls to explode in the players' faces! There are no definite recorded cases of this phenomenon happening but nonetheless Celluloid was dangerous and Bakelite was much safer to produce.

## RICHARD DAY AND THE "BOTH- AND- STYLE"

With the Depression Modern-Style in full swing, *Roman Scandals* employed another artistic idea that superbly complemented the film. Since the idea of the film was to combine a view of the ancient world of Rome with modern ideas from the 1930s, a special style of art or "look" for the film was developed by art director Richard Day (1896-1972). Day had begun his career working in silent films for Erich Von Stroheim, considered the most difficult director to work for and the most demanding for artistic visuals. Day had a reputation for imaginative design and an ability to reflect on film the hottest trends, while still giving them his own unique look. He worked on more than 300 films in his career, including numerous blockbusters, and earned 20 Academy Award nominations, winning seven golden statues for films such as *On the Waterfront* (1954), *A Streetcar Named Desire* (1952), *How Green Was My Valley* (1942) and *The Dark Angel* (1935).

For *Roman Scandals*, Day elected to go with what has come to be known in art history as the "Both- and-Style." This was a style that combined the desired artistic form with a more traditional style. It had developed particularly in New York City in the 1910s with the demand for skyscrapers and the need to provide striking designs for them. Thus in New York one could have a building that both had the form of a skyscraper and the style of

**The Roman Colosseum**

Art Deco (i.e. The Chrysler Building of 1928 by William Van Alen). Or you could have a building that was both a skyscraper and Depression Modern Streamlined design (The Empire State building of 1930 by Shreve, Lamb and Harmon). One could even have skyscrapers that were both a skyscraper and Gothic such as Cass Gilbert's F.W. Woolworth Building of 1913. For *Roman Scandals*, Day took the decision to present director Frank Tuttle with set design that was in form Ancient Roman and in style Depression Modern.

Thus, in the slave market sequence, designed in consultation with choreographer and special sequence director Busby Berkeley, Day needed to meet several requirements that Berkeley required for his dance sequence: a stepped but rounded set centerpiece that resembled a huge birthday cake. Day provided this stepped look, which was in popular use at the Chicago Century of Progress. The stepped look had already been popular in Art Deco where it had developed out of ancient Mayan stepped pyramids such as the one at Uxmal. The look also borrowed from Mesopotamian ziggurats such as that of Ur, and Egyptian stepped pyramids of the Old Kingdom such as that at Saqqara. The stepped look swept America and was commonly used in conjunction with metal and neon signs to advertise such things as Buick car dealerships. Berkeley enjoyed using the rounded step look so that he could spread out beautiful girls on all the levels and have them do various

**Busby Berkeley used a stepped structure to showcase his beautiful dancers.**

**Neon sign in early Depression Modern-style with stepped pyramid look carried over from Art Deco. Boonville, Missouri (ca. 1934).**

rhythmic movements with their legs and arms while he photographed them from overhead way up at the very top of the studio.

Day came up with the concept of taking the classical column and architrave and simplifying and streamlining them according to Depression Modern guidelines. Thus original Roman columns of Ionic form normally featured individual drums, a fluted column shaft, and a separate capital at the top of the shaft, which sported spiral-form volutes, the capital being decorated with elaborate moldings. Keeping the basic form of the Roman Ionic column, Day streamlined it into something much more Depression Modern looking, eliminating the flutes, column drums and capital moldings, and blending the shaft into the capital. The Roman sets designed for the film were a symphony of Bakelite and other synthetic materials, which were sometimes transparent and sometimes translucent, while the architraves located above the Ionic columns were emphasized horizontally with chromium-looking strips. It was the fashion in the Depression Modern-style to use chromium stripping to emphasize the horizontal stream-lined look and Day knew that the ancient Romans, when they made Ionic architraves, had horizontal accents called *fasciae* or banded divisions. Brilliantly, he took this an-cient idea of *fasciae* and streamlined it into a '30s look that preserved the integrity of the original ancient idea. Day also made the architrave curvilinear in the '30s style but the ancient Romans, particularly in the time of the emperor Hadrian (ruling A.D. 117-138), were also fond of curved perimeters of Ionic columns. This illustrates how clever Day was at creating his Both- and- Style and integrating the ancient Roman forms with the Depression Modern-style.

The Ionic columns of Day's set have no flutes but rather are simplified and streamlined but this was a technique that was also embraced by ancient Romans as well as by Neo-Classical architects in the 18th and 19th centuries, among them Thomas Jefferson, who also admired the look of simplification of the fluted ancient Roman column. The Ionic capitals of Day rise up more directly as if growing up from the column shafts, in contrast to the more elaborately molded ancient Roman Ionic columns. But through this combination of old and new, Day successfully creates a feeling that is simultane-ously Roman and modern. In short, it is very clever set design, which enhances the basic premise of the film, using ancient Rome to make a satirical comparison to modern American life. That is exactly the sort of concept that made Day a designer in enormous demand. He had a limited budget with this Goldwyn film but he managed to use it ingeniously.

**Chorus girls pose by a classical column in this studio shot from *Roman Scandal*s.**

## BUSBY BERKELY

While we are on the subject of Richard Day's designs and his collaboration with Busby Berkeley for the musi-cal production numbers in *Roman Scandals*, we should note that much has been made of the lurid sexuality and even torture displayed in the early musical sequence in the film featuring the song *No More Love* sung by Olga, the emperor's favorite, played by Ruth Etting. In this

**Bernice Claire**

found themselves scrambling back to New York or having to eventually go abroad for work. One of the saddest situations was the case of Bernice Claire, the stunningly beautiful, talented and vocally gifted light opera star of Broadway who arrived in Hollywood at age 22, just in time to see her film career evaporate as musicals failed to attract an audience after she had been an initial success.

Unsuccessfully trying to make it as a dramatic actress in non-musical films, her career immediately hit the skids and a major American talent has become forgotten. Readers are encouraged to track down her now obscure movie roles, such as *Spring is Here*, to appreciate what a remarkable ingénue and talent she was. By the time musicals revived new faces were on the scene and she was "replaced" by Jeanette MacDonald, a fine actress and soprano in her own right, who became famous in duets with co-star Nelson Eddy. But for those who have ever seen the forgotten Bernice Claire, in duet with Alexander Gray, there is no comparison. The two were "the" light opera screen stars of 1930. By 1931 they were out of vogue. Still, her rendition of the classic tune "With a Song in My Heart" in *Spring is Here* is a high-water mark of the early musical.

Busby Berkeley brought to *Roman Scandals* a reputation for making his dance numbers more cinematic than other choreographers. Almost single-handedly Berkeley resurrected the movie musical by taking it away from its stagebound origins and producing musical numbers that were more purely cinematic. Often he was called in not as the director of the entire picture but rather as the person who would do the musical production numbers. This was the case with *Roman Scandals*, whose director was the competent Frank Tuttle. With his films for 1933 such

sequence the upper tier of the large birthday cake-shaped stepped-centerpiece is occupied by naked, chained girls with long, flowing blonde tresses. This is clearly not the brainchild of Richard Day but rather of that mad genius of the early talkie musical, Busby Berkeley. Already famed for his imaginative choreography on the New York stage and schooled as a professional drillmaster in the U.S. Army, Berkeley went to work for Samuel Goldwyn lending his unique concepts to sound film.

By 1933, the Hollywood musical was all but dead. A huge number of musicals had been released between 1929 and 1931 and they were essentially filmed stage plays with little that was cinematic. They were mostly photographed on what was shown to be a stage, with a large audience clearly seen in front. There were few close-ups, lots of sloppy choreography with chorines often spotted slipping and even sometimes falling, and little more than two-shots being used by the directors. Many young stars, who were making their way from Broadway to the musical movie, were at first hits, but were soon quickly stopped in their tracks with the utter collapse of the musical in popularity. It had seemed that Bessie Love, Charley King and Nick Lucas would go on to become huge stars doing musicals but they suddenly

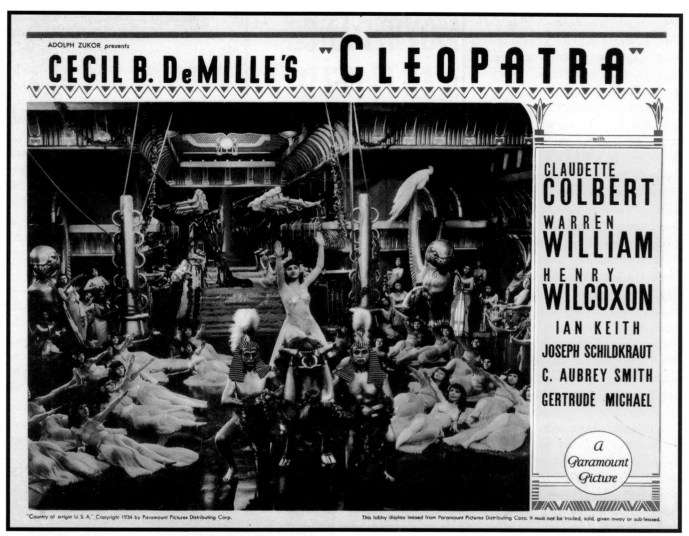

ADOLPH ZUKOR presents

# CECIL B. DeMILLE'S "CLEOPATRA"

with

CLAUDETTE COLBERT
WARREN WILLIAM
HENRY WILCOXON
IAN KEITH
JOSEPH SCHILDKRAUT
C. AUBREY SMITH
GERTRUDE MICHAEL

a Paramount Picture

"Country of origin U.S.A." Copyright 1934 by Paramount Pictures Distributing Corp.

This lobby display leased from Paramount Pictures Distributing Corp. It must not be traded, sold, given away or sub-leased.

as *Roman Scandals*, *42nd Street*, and *The Golddiggers of 1933*, Busby brought audiences back to see musicals with something that was new and different. His concept was to take a musical number and start it as if it were being presented in real time, usually on a stage in a theater with an audience. Quickly he would change from the stage-bound setup to include multiple setups that could never have been presented on any one stage at one time. He often employed special effects and used multiple viewpoints that could never be glimpsed by a stationary audience.

Berkeley also drew on his younger days as an army drill sergeant by marching his chorines through intricate interweaving patterns, often shooting them from above or in extreme close-ups. His sequences could be highly sexual but in fantasy films they were set in ancient places such as Rome or Baghdad and so Busby could therefore get away with depicting sexual torture and debauchery because it was "historical." *Roman Scandals* was a spoof of such Cecil B. De Mille Paramount Pictures epics about

ancient Rome that were doing exactly the same thing. *Sign of the Cross* (1932), made by De Mille, featured an elaborate sequence in the Colosseum in Rome, which combined sex, depravity, horror and torture, all presented as acceptable to the general public because of its historicity. De Mille's films were also pre-code, including one he was in the midst of preparing with much publicity entitled *Cleopatra*, which contained a wild pleasure barge sequence full of wrestling panther women, fishing nets with scantily clad damsels and drunken orgies. After *Roman Scandals* and *Cleopatra*, the Hayes Code put an abrupt end to depictions of excess on film.

The Hayes Code had been the result of a public clamoring especially from Christian groups (particularly Catholics), which led to well-respected former chairman of the Republican National Committee and former U.S. Postmaster General Will H. Hays (1879-1954) being elected by the various Hollywood movie studios as the first president of what was to become the MPAA or Motion

Picture Association of America. On July 1, 1934, the Hollywood movie would tame down considerably but not before *Roman Scandals* pushed pre-code film to the limit.

Berkeley himself was a notorious womanizer who was not above using the casting couch to achieve his aims. In a film such as *Roman Scandals,* which required the casting of over 100 wannabe starlets, he certainly had endless opportunities. He eventually married five times and spent much of his personal life in an inebriated or quasi-inebriated state. On September 8, 1935, Berkeley, at the age of 39, drove home drunk from a Hollywood party, not noticing that he was driving on the wrong side of the road. He crashed his flashy Cadillac into several other cars, killing three people and injuring five. One woman died instantly and two later in hospital from injuries related to the crash. Since Warner Bros. needed him to continue working he was able to obtain the services of the celebrated lawyer to the stars, Jerry Giesler, who managed to get the case resolved by claiming that the tires were bad and that Berkeley was not drunk. Pat O'Brien, normally a pinnacle of integrity, was brought forth to testify that Berkeley was not drunk and he was a pivotal influence on the trial which let Berkeley off the hook in a shocking miscarriage of justice, an early example of the concept that celebrities can afford and enjoy one kind of justice which the average American cannot. It took three trials however, with the first two ending in hung juries! Giesler, by the way, achieved great fame getting Errol Flynn off the hook for statutory rape, saving gangster Bugsy Siegel from various charges and acquitting Alexander Pantages, the theater producer, for raping a 17-year-old girl. He was the go-to guy if you were famous and in a hot spot and with that reputation he became the first president of the Los Angeles Bar Association!

Berkeley was known for working in an alcoholic haze, sequestering himself in a bathtub at home with martinis, along with a pad for diagramming the most intricate fantasies. His sexual appetites allowed him to conjure up some bizarre sequences including the filming at night at Goldwyn's studio of a group of nude chorus girls with strategically arranged long blonde hair, each

## MOVIE DANCE MAN IS HELD

### Busby Berkeley Faces Two Manslaughter Charges in South

HOLLYWOOD, Cal., Sept. 13.— (UP)—Busby Berkeley, film colony dance director, was charged tonight on two counts of manslaughter after investigation of an automobile crash Sunday in which a 60-year-old woman and a girl student were killed.

The dark, slightly corpulent dance master was confined to a hospital with concussion of the brain as a result of the crash in which three cars collided and burst into flames on a seashore highway.

Bail was set at $2,500.

one chained to a gold star on his giant stepped-cake centerpiece. In the same musical sequence, the empress' favorite girl is taken away and tortured by the emperor's soldiers and forced to dance as an audience of men look on smacking their lips. The unchained slave girls are whipped into obedience. Dancing on top of the cake just above the nude chained women until she drops of exhaustion and plummets from the centerpiece, the slave girl dies in her mistress' arms. The sequence, sung by Ruth Etting and featuring the song *No More Love*, appears to be one of the first lesbian sequences in a major Hollywood film.

Berkeley's overtly sexual sequences were doing nothing more than echoing De Mille's own film excesses and in the days before the code such personal tastes could be given almost free reign without worrying about being shut down. But by the summer of 1934 it was all over.

Berkeley did not invent the new grammar of the movie musical for Samuel Goldwyn

**The tortured slave girl dies in the arms of her mistress.**

28

**Busby Berkeley and Eddie Cantor ham it up on the set of *Roman Scandals* as some of the "young and beautiful" chorus girls look on. (Photofest)**

or Warner Bros. as is popularly believed. One film had helped to give him the ideas he needed to run with to re-invent this art form. That film was *King of Jazz*, directed and conceived by the Canadian stage director John Murray Anderson. The film was designed as a tribute to Paul Whiteman, the popular orchestra leader who discovered Bing Crosby and was a titan of American popular music. He was known as the King of Jazz by a public, which really didn't understand what jazz was and used the word in the way that we would say pop today. *King of Jazz* became an excuse for Anderson to pull out all the stops in attempting to invent a way to fit the stagebound theatrical musical to the new medium of the talking picture.

Among Anderson's innovations were using multiple setups for a musical sequence, multiple vantage points for each sequence, close-ups, and even a new Technicolor process combined with

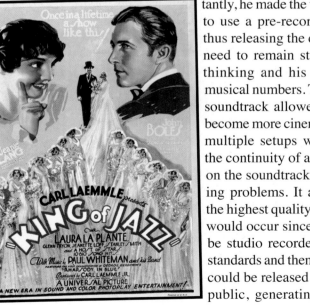

abundant special effects and lighting experiments to add colors that could not be reproduced by the current state of technical expertise, such as blue. Anderson also employed the first Technicolor animated cartoon, and, most importantly, he made the very first musical to use a pre-recorded soundtrack, thus releasing the director from the need to remain stagebound in his thinking and his presentation of musical numbers. The pre-recorded soundtrack allowed the cinema to become more cinematic, employing multiple setups without affecting the continuity of a musical number on the soundtrack or creating editing problems. It also insured that the highest quality sound recording would occur since the songs could be studio recorded to the highest standards and then these recordings could be released as records to the public, generating more revenue

Chorus girls "Keep Young and Beautiful" in the *Roman Scandals* beauty spa.

the girls notice the bulge below the waist in his tunic (!) and they chase him into a hot spa bath where he shrinks down to midget size, with the diminutive Eddie played by real-life small person Billy Barty. Tiny Eddie is chased into a cold pool where the water restores his size. In the course of his ramblings around the spa he observes women engaging in every possible beauty treatment and there are quick glimpses of topless females seen through diaphanous draperies. Such peeks were typical of the pre-code movies in which the male viewer was pretty sure he'd seen something he shouldn't but he didn't have enough screen time to be certain.

## KEEPING YOUNG AND BEAUTIFUL

The song "Keep Young and Beautiful" is a paeon to the newly burgeoning cosmetics industry and to the various beauty treatments that had suddenly become big business in America, catering to the emancipated woman and the cult of youth. The song conveys the message that one can remain perpetually beautiful and lovable through cosmetics and exercise:

> Don't fail to do your stuff, with a little
>     powder and a puff,
> Keep Young and Beautiful if you want
>     to be loved.
>
> If you're wise, exercise all the fat off.
> Take it off, off-a here, off-a there.
> When you're seen anywhere with your
>     hat off,
> Have a permanent wave in your hair.

The verse from the song further expounds on what needs to be done to avoid old age and stay in form because no male cares about a woman's brains and is only really interested in her looks:

> Cosmetics, athletics, a weighing machine
>     are part of the feminine daily routine
>     for what?
> And oceans of lotions and potions you
>     take
> To keep that old something or other
>     awake, why not?
> Even after you grow old, baby.
> You don't have to be a cold baby.

The second chorus provides more guidelines:

for the studio. The tradition of synchronizing the film to the soundtrack was born. Anderson also employed overhead shots, which had been used before by Robert Florey in the Marx Brothers musical *Cocoanuts,* made the year before in 1929.

Caught amid the backlash against movie musicals as well as the initial shock wave of the Great Depression, *King of Jazz* just about broke even but its innovations, with the exception of color, were all used by Berkeley and amplified. If Anderson had used multiple stage setups gingerly, Berkeley expanded them wildly and led his film audience totally into fantasyland. Berkeley used more close-ups, more extensive military drill-type interweaving choreography, more overhead shots and more sex. He gets and deserves tremendous credit for reviving the American musical but John Murray Anderson was an earlier pioneer who has gotten no credit for illuminating the path that Berkeley would follow and expand.

One of the major Busby Berkeley production numbers of *Roman Scandals* is "Keep Young and Beautiful" ("If You Want to Be Loved"). In it Eddie accidentally finds himself in the midst of a Roman women's beauty spa, reserved for the imperial harem, and, disguised as an Ethiopian doctor, manages to slip by undetected until

Be sure and get your man, Wrap your
   body in a coat of tan.
You'll always have your way if he loves
   you in a negligee.
Keep young and beautiful if you want
   to be loved…
You'll drive him half insane with a bath-
   ing suit of cellophane.
Keep young and beautiful if you want
   to be loved…
If using or choosing a lipstick,
Use the kind that won't leave any mark,
Use the kind that'll make both his lips
   stick,
When he kisses you in the dark!
Get him to hold you tight,
Let him get a whiff of Christmas Night…
Keep young and beautiful if you want
   to be loved…
Shake well to slenderize, Roll your eyes
   around for exercise…

These lyrics underscore the transformation in the American woman and the emphasis on what another movie of the time called *Beauty for the Asking*. It meant that so many avenues were now available for the modern woman to slenderize, firm up skin and generally remain attractive into advancing age that it was absurd not to take advantage of them. Once the turn of the century bustles, crinoline hoops and layers of petticoats had been jet-tisoned in favor of lightweight clothing and the flappers were unleashed, dramatic changes took place. But the slender pal look of the flapper was giving way in 1933 to full-figured curvilinear blonde bombshells, the physi-cal perfection of woman suggested by Auguste Rollier's Swiss clinic wherein periodic exposure to ultraviolet light allegedly achieved dramatically healthy results. Coco Chanel believed in it too as early as 1923 and soon the tanning craze was born. It was not until the 1970s that the realization came out that excessive UV exposure helps to develop melanomas.

The desire for eternal youth and the widespread use of electricity in the American home and in special salons led to all sorts of devices to promote health through science. There were machines that shook you all over, straps that rubbed along your chin (depicted in *Roman Scandals*), pogo sticks (patented first by American George Hansburg in 1919), and lotions to rub in to eliminate wrinkles or promote dimples. One leading feminine star of the era, the elegant curvilinear-blonde Constance Bennett, had her

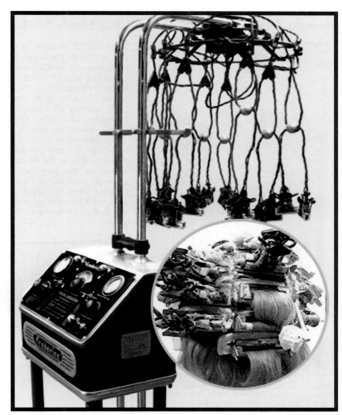

**An early permanent wave machine—women really did suffer for beauty!**

own cosmetic lines which featured ladies' compacts and all kinds of powders and lotions which literally buried the face in makeup. Once done, Constance would exclaim in her seven-minute promotional short subject how women had now achieved "the natural look." Wigs became in-creasingly popular, particularly blonde ones, and lipstick was ultra-red, advertising a non-stick quality when they were pressed into service. Fingernails got longer and more intensely red and even toenails were painted as women became more elegant, voluptuous and alluring in the 1930s. Flapper stars were out. Glamour was in.

Hairdressers and even plastic surgeons now became popular. Plastic surgery had received a considerable boost after World War I. So horrible were the injuries incurred by troops in that war that surgeons needed to go to the limits of their abilities to reconstruct the faces of the vic-tims. The techniques of Sir Harold Gillies of New Zealand were at the forefront of this progress and helped to lay the groundwork for plastic surgery in the '30s and after. "Keep Young and Beautiful" also mentions the popular-ity of the permanent wave, which began as the Marcel Wave after French hairdresser Marcel Grateau originated the idea in 1872. The wave was first produced by using a concave and convex armed tong, which was heated and

## Beauty Machine Removes Excess Flesh Without Exercise

Milady can smoke, read and gossip while this unique machine rolls off excess pounds of flesh around the hips, giving graceful curves, which fashion experts have decreed to be the coming mode. Massaging is performed by the rollers.

FASHION moguls have decreed that the boyish figure is passé, and that graceful curves are to be the coming mode. So, anticipating a need among the women, a far-sighted inventor has devised an instrument which literally rolls these curves into the body, getting rid of excess flesh without developing unsightly bundles of muscles, which exercising gave.

An important feature of the new device, however, is that developing these curves requires no work, for milady can become stylish in this new machine while reading a book, smoking a cigarette, or even gossiping. Hips, the chief point of attack, are reduced by means of rollers which massage the flesh, as illustrated in the accompanying photo.

then used, away from the scalp, to create waves in the hair. The high temperatures used however degraded the hair and unskilled practitioners burned heads.

Just a few years before *Roman Scandals* was made, a chemist name J. Baris-Woollss carried out a variety of experiments to refine and test approaches to styling and curling hair. His research investigated the effects of heat, water and alkalinity on human hair while also addressing the effects of removing oxygen, adding hydrogen and producing sulfur dioxide during the treatment. These ideas led to the development of the modern permanent wave device around 1930, which is celebrated as a new discovery in the movie.

These low-cost new devices meant that women were now able to have their hair set once a week and permed perhaps every three months. Doing this became a status symbol for middle-class women who sought to emulate the look of movie stars and the hair salon was a place to catch up on local news, even gossip. As this cult of beauty and socialization grew by the early 1930s (exemplified in movies such as *The Women*), it was constantly stated that

all of the techniques used were designed to make women look more natural, to get "back to the savage" and of course to fool men into thinking they were younger and more beautiful than they really were.

Perfumes had also dramatically risen in popularity in the flapper era of the 1920s, and by the 1930s had become essential. When Eddie Cantor sings of the power of perfume, he mentions particularly Christmas Night as the ultimate, but each woman had a favorite. Some perfumes were cheap and others were what you hoped to get as a gift from that special someone. Women researched perfume through free samples now readily available in local department stores. Such stores sprung up at the beginning of the new 20th century and were well established by 1933, featuring young attractive salesgirls attempting to convince middle-income and wealthy ladies to try various fragrances, each one of which allegedly should be worn for a certain kind of outing and would have a particular effect.

Christmas Night was also released in the USA under its

Ruth Etting, in character, promotes Christmas Night perfume on the set of *Roman Scandals*.

French name *Nuit de Noel,* which added to its exotic quality and its pretension. It was classified as a luxurious, "woody" and somehow also "oriental" fragrance that blended sweet floral essences, fresh herbs and powdery wood. It was specifically touted to be used with evening wear. Wearing this creation of the House of Caron in Paris would "put you in a Christmas mood no matter when you wore it" and it was very popular as a Christmas gift from

the time of its introduction in 1922. It was supposed to make you "anticipate Christmas feelings" no matter when you put it on for "*Nuit de Noel* heralds the magic and festivity we experience just once a year at Christmas." The House of Caron in Paris has been producing perfume since 1906. A typical ad suggests how to market their fragrance as a Christmas gift or anytime gift for your beloved. Such perfumes were considered exotic, erotic, appropriate to Christmas as a gift, and a status symbol:

> It Doesn't Have to be Christmas for You to Adore *Nuit de Noel.* What better way to show your love on Christmas than with a gift of *Nuit de Noel,* or *Christmas Night* as it's known in the U.S. and Canada? The House of Caron in France introduced this oriental scent with its rich, elaborate composition in 1922 when Europe was heady with the newfound splendors of postwar life.

Of course one reference made in "Keep Young and Beautiful" has nothing to do with cosmetics. The emphasis on athletics is strengthened by encouraging women to roll their eyes around for exercise. This is a reference to Eddie Cantor, who was famous for having banjo eyes and rolling them around to emphasize a thinly veiled sexual remark in a song that he was performing.

## EDDIE CANTOR AND THE JEWISH TRADITION IN VAUDEVILLE

Eddie Cantor was a Jewish comedian and was proud of his heritage. He donated vast sums for the founding of the Jewish state, constantly supported Jewish causes by playing numerous benefits and spoke out publicly against anti-Semitism. The tradition of Jews in the entertainment field goes back to the origins of American show business. There were few professions that Jews might initially be part of since there were frequent pogroms or state approved vicious attacks against them in Europe and especially in Russia where the word pogrom originated. Many Jews were forced to flee to America and to take such work as they were allowed to do by a non-Jewish society.

The "open" professions were limited, but in the New York area included the garment business and Jews tended to band together to help one another, which further alienated them from less socially and professionally savvy ethnic or religious groups. My own grandfather came to America from Lon-

Olga (Dennie Moore) dishes out nail polish and gossip to Sylvia Fowler (Rosalind Russell) in *The Women* (1939).

33

don and as a Jew he was helped by his people to network in the garment business and eventually became a buyer for Lit Brothers in Philadelphia. This was a frequent pattern, often set up through synagogues and Jewish social groups. Many Jewish families also demanded success and pushed children into the permitted professions with a powerful work ethic for success. The entertainment field was one of the open professions and was particularly attractive to lower-class Jews who could see it as a way out of poverty.

Jewish comedy has a particularly long tradition with the 1890s witnessing the rise of Jewish humor and comedians. As early as 1878 a team known as Burt and Leon, who were in the garment business, were having success singing Irish songs in fractured Yiddish. Florenz Ziegfeld realized that ethnic humor was funny and permitted blacks and Jews into the *Ziegfeld Follies*. Ziegfeld himself may have been Jewish or part Jewish and his protégé and common-law wife was a Polish Jew named Anna Held. Still, many Jews disguised their names so they would have a more equitable playing field in which to succeed in show business. My family name was Friedman and my grandfather was a Salamon but I was told that I could not use either name when I went on CBS TV in 1955 as a performer because I would be labeled too easily as a Jew. It wasn't only that some of the TV audience would be

**Gus Van and Joe Schenck were popular vaudevillians known for Joe's lovely tenor and piano playing and Gus' ability to sing in dialect (Yiddish, Negro, Irish, Italian) in songs that made fun of various ethnic groups.**

anti-Jew but also that generic names were better so that I wouldn't be perceived as an ethnic-only entertainer. Also I was told that a Jewish name for a singer isn't sexy. I was told the story that Sidney Liebowitz was a Brooklyn Jew who wanted to be a singer. He had no success but he changed his name to Steve Lawrence and he became a pop idol and TV and recording star. So for me Howard Friedman became Howie Davis. And this was in the early 1950s!

Even today Hispanics and Jews sometimes hide their names. Ramón Gerardo Antonio Estévez was told somewhere along the line that he'd do better as Martin Sheen. Jonathan Stuart Leibowitz decided that calling himself Jon Stewart was better for business. Of course a Jewish rock star would seem to be a paradox, until of course we find out about Gene Simmons of *Kiss* (originally Gene Klein and actually born in Israel). And so the tradition continues!

The entertainment field was one major area where Jews could flourish as writers and performers, particularly in the area of vaudeville. And in the time of *Roman Scandals* vaudeville was yielding to radio and the movies. Eddie Cantor had come out of the vaudeville tradition, which often offered 6- to 12-minute comedy sketches within a show of perhaps 12 different acts. This tradition of comedy abounds in *Roman Scandals*. An early sequence in the film shows Cantor realizing he is really back in ancient Rome. He is set upon by two Roman soldiers and the entire film simply stops at this point to allow Cantor to engage in a six-minute vaudeville routine with the soldiers which involves his thinking he is still in 1933 and not realizing that he is in ancient Rome. Finally understanding that the soldiers may put him to death so that later in time he may never be born he complains that this is not only murder but "it would be birth control."

Periodically, during the film, the action and plot stops abruptly and these typical vaudeville skits are introduced because Eddie was particularly known for them in the *Ziegfeld Follies*, often with African-American star Bert Williams playing his father, and both men in blackface. Eddie even continued this tradition into the 1950s in his early television work, particularly on *The Colgate Comedy Hour*, thus helping to introduce the vaudeville variety tradition onto television where it was taken up by such programs as *The Milton Berle Show* (*Texaco Star Theater*), *The Ed Wynn Show* and *Your Show of Shows* with Sid Caesar. In fact, Eddie's vaudeville *shtick* (a Yiddish word meaning pieces or bits) of songs, *schmaltz* (a German word meaning goose fat used for frying but by extension meaning something gooey and smeared on or something geared to tug at an audience's heartstrings), patter and short skits was so popular on radio and early

Well, Folks, Here I Come to Open the Doors of

## POLI'S MAJESTIC THEATRE

### THIS AFTERNOON AND EVENING

Mrs. Cantor presents her favorite son

# Eddie Cantor

Aided and Abetted by

### 125 — PICK OF THE WORLD ENTERTAINERS — 125

including

### LILLIAN FITZGERALD

| Cleveland Bronner | George Hale | Tot Qualters |
| Lew Hearn | LeRoy Duffield | Ingrid Solfeng |
| Joe Opp | Helen Carrington | Charlotte Woodruff |
| John Byam | Muriel DeForrest | Betty Dair |
| | Querrals Querria | |

### The Marvelous Flying Blue Devils
### Cleveland Bronner Ballet

*PLUS*

A Rare Collection of American Beauties

IN

# "Make It Snappy"

### Two Acts--27 Scenes--The Greatest Musical Show Ever Staged

Matinee Prices 50c to $2.00      Evening Prices $1.00 to $3.00

### LAST CALL—GET BUSY—DON'T GET CROWDED OUT.

television that he literally worked himself to death, suffering a series of heart attacks which may have been brought on by overwork.

Eddie always thought of himself as a vaudevillian since that is the form of show business in which he grew up and came to prominence and the *Ziegfeld Follies* in which he became particularly famous was largely a glorified form of vaudeville with more girls and more elaborate sets. Vaudeville had begun in America perhaps as early as the 1860s and had risen to prominence as family entertainment thanks to the efforts of entrepreneurs such as Tony Pastor, who featured essentially clean shows of a variety nature. Vaudeville could be almost anything entertaining with acts lasting up to perhaps 12 minutes, with the exception of a major performer, who might extend his act considerably, especially when encouraged by encores, as Al Jolson typically would do. A typical show in New York might contain dancers of various types, singers of course, stunt cyclists, performing animals, plate balancers, precocious child entertainers, opera singers, well-known sports figures acting or singing, and theatrical performers doing mini-plays with top stars such as Ethel Barrymore. Big-time vaudeville was mainly associated with New York City and particularly with the great Palace Theater on Broadway at 47th Street, but major hubs also included Chicago, which always had a slightly more rural (and New

In 1956 I joined *The Horn and Hardart Children's Hour* in Philadelphia located in WCAU CBS Studio One at City Line Avenue. I was nine, I think, one of the youngest regular cast members they had, although a youngster named Jerry Donahue had been taken by them at age five many years before. I was certainly the youngest of this bunch though. They paid for singing lessons for me, and acting coaching, and I remember that it became hard to stay in regular school, do my vaudeville shows and rehearse my parts for the show plus attend rehearsals, go to downtown singing lessons and then do the actual live performance every week. I became a team with a young and very cute girl named Cheryl and we sang songs such as "Sioux City Sue," "I'm Blue Every Sunday" and our big one. "On the Beach With You," for which they built us a beach set with parasols and brought in what looked like actual sand onto the soundstage! The one thing I really recall about the *Children's Hour* is that all the little girls were gorgeous. Unlike public school where you were around "ordinary people" as we called them in our little niche at WCAU, everyone here or nearly everyone was gorgeous and talented and smart too, because if you couldn't adapt to the vagaries of live TV you were gone in a hurry, and everything did often go wrong. *The Children's Hour*, I learned later, was the most prestigious kiddie show you could be on in Philadelphia. It had been founded by Stanley Broza (who insisted on being called Stan Lee Broza). He was a big baldheaded man with lots of energy who founded the show on radio in 1928. Since that time many famous stars got their start on it. I can remember that the Nicholas Brothers and Kitty Kallen the band singer were on. A sister show was started successfully in New York City but the Philly show was the original. By 1948 it was one of the first radio shows to successfully make the transition to TV and featured such future greats as Eddie Fisher. It was on Sundays from 11:30am to 12:30 at WCAU.

*Horn and Hardart Children's Hour* (1948)

Yorkers would often say cornier or hokier) appeal and there were big West Coast centers and numerous small time circuits too and once vaudeville fell under the control of monopolistic consolidators such as B.F. Keith and Edward Albee, entertainment was eventually controlled from coast to coast and performers were oppressed to the point where they needed to organize. Eddie Cantor was one of the driving forces that helped performers less advantaged than himself to organize and demand a decent cut of money.

Vaudeville entertainers frequently earned little money unless they were stars but they continued performing hoping for the big chance, often traveling across the country by train carrying their props and sheet music arrangements from town to town where small orchestras or combos would play for them. Without microphones in many venues, comic performers had to speak loudly and distinctly and emphasize their payoff lines, a style which is evident when one watches Eddie Cantor perform. His voice, which was naturally thin and high-pitched, is always strongly and clearly projected for all to hear, even when he is on film.

About the time that *Roman Scandals* was being made, Eddie Cantor, although playing a wide-eyed innocent in the film, was actually working behind the scenes to help motion picture actors obtain proper compensation. At the time, actors literally belonged to studios, which contracted them for many years whether they used them or not and frequently punished them for speaking out by giving them inferior work or not working them at all. They also meddled in their private lives, arranging dates and invented "romances" as well as hiding or preventing marriages. To combat this Eddie, along with a number of important performers such as Frank Morgan (The Wizard of Oz himself!), established the Screen Actors Guild or SAG. At first the

# SCREEN ACTORS FORM NEW GUILD

HOLLYWOOD, Oct. 9.—(Æ)—More than five hundred Hollywood film players were banded together today under the Screen Actors' Guild in an organization which severed their connections with the New York stage and film actors' groups.

Heretofore only a small organization, the old guild added 501 leading actors and actresses to its rolls at a mass meeting last night after speakers declared the players faced a crisis in the proposed salary control regulation in the NRA code now under consideration.

"We must have a Hollywood organization for Hollywood actors and actresses," said Eddie Cantor.

Ann Harding declared it was time that an active organization by Hollywood actors, representative of all players in the local industry, should be formed. She recalled the time when difficulties within the industry had been brought to the attention of the New York Actors' Equity with unsatisfactory results.

About eight hundred actors and actresses, many of them present or former members of the Academy of Motion Picture Arts and Sciences, were present and many of those who did not become members last night, said they would mail their membership contracts in today.

Eddie Cantor was elected president of the guild. Adolphe Menjou and Fredric March, both of whom resigned from the academy because they said they felt an independent organization of actors should be formed, were named first and second vice presidents respectively. Miss Harding was chosen third vice president with Groucho Marx treasurer and Lucille Gleason assistant treasurer.

group wanted only to help established actors, but Eddie, sensing the importance of the moment, urged a more egalitarian approach, seeking to help all actors. With Eddie's support and guidance, and his stint as the president of the Guild, plus his personal friendship with FDR, then president of the United States, the Screen Actors Guild became a key organization that weakened the power of the studio chiefs by 1937.

Eddie Cantor's support for "Everyman," echoing the character he portrayed in vaudeville and on screen, extended to extensive charity work as well. In the 1930s, movie theaters ran a newsreel series called *The March of Time*. Eddie came up with the idea to call a charity fighting against infantile paralysis or polio *The March*

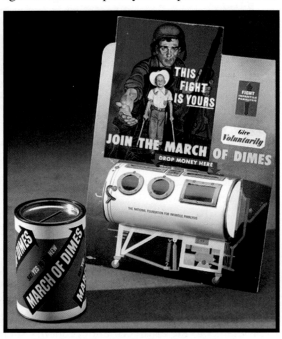

**March of Dimes collection tin and display**

*of Dimes*. This was the disease that his friend FDR suffered from and the charity that FDR had founded in 1938. The idea was that if everyone contributed a dime, the disease could be cured with research. Much of the money contributed was collected by school children in small containers, which they filled by going door to door in their neighborhoods. When Roosevelt died in office in 1945 his face was put on the dime, an appropriate action because it was the dime that played the critical role in combating the illness from which he suffered!

## ROMAN SCANDALS AND BURLESQUE

The term burlesque in 20th century America came to mean basically striptease acts such as Gypsy Rose Lee, Lili St. Cyr, Candy Barr and others interspersed with bawdy comedy performed by second-rate comedians. By the 1950s the comedians were largely out and the shows became extremely lurid with performers such as "Evelyn West and Her $50,000 Treasure Chest." But this is not what burlesque was originally.

Burlesques were originally parodies of a popular highbrow work of the theater or literature or both. In the 19th century, Shakespeare or Viennese operas or major theatrical works of the moment were fair game for lampooning with terrible puns, lowbrow characters and a general sending up of the pomposity or highbrow language of the original work. Of course these spoofs required at least some familiarization on the part of the audience with the original work and so the burlesques were usually limited to something major. The Marx Brothers grasped this idea very well and in 1930s films such as *A Night at the Opera*, the concept of taking a lofty opera and reducing it to a baseball game using violins as bats was just the sort of thing that made up the concept of a burlesque. Often these works were done as ethnic parodies with lowly Jews and Irish and other ethnic groups being substituted for the lofty characters of ancient Rome, France or Vienna.

Burlesques were particularly popular and innovative at a theater in New York City owned by Weber and Fields (Joe Weber and Lew Fields) who were known for their burlesques or travesties of current Broadway hits which they performed at the Weber and Fields Music Hall. Of course in the later 19th century works about ancient Rome would be all the rage with the huge influence of classical civilization on the art of the day and the popular teaching of Latin to help young people improve their English skills in the public schools. Students were taught that the Latin language was at the root of the English language and if one traced the roots of words to their origins one could become a better speaker and writer. In fact, this is actually true, and yet Latin is rarely taught anymore in public schools. As a result, one might add, people have lost the subtle meanings of words and end up misusing our language much more frequently than they used to do. In addition to the emphasis on classical language training in schools, the most popular book and play at the time was Lew Wallace's *Ben-Hur*, a story focused on ancient Rome and its interweaving with the story of Jesus' life. *Ben-Hur* was the best-selling novel of its entire decade!

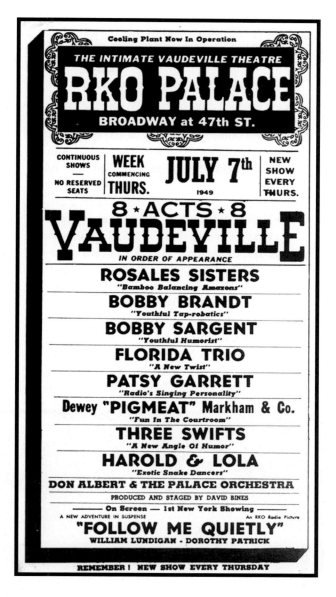

An example of a travesty or burlesque of ancient Rome as popularized by Weber and Fields is the 1900 *Quo Vass Iss? A Tragedy Upon "Quo Vadis,"* a parody of the widely read pro-Christian novel *Quo Vadis*, written by Henry Sienkiewicz in 1895. This was the novel that inspired *Ben-Hur*. The Weber and Fields production also made fun of Wilson Barrett's play *The Sign of the Cross* in which the famed London actor Barrett starred on Broadway to great success. If Christianity were parodied in a major play in like manner today there would be howls of protest but here the Christians are made out to be overzealous and wacky alcohol prohibitionists with the lead character Lythia's name being a comic reference to a healthful spring water which was in vogue at the time. In her book *Ancient Rome and Modern America*,

Margaret Malamud describes the crazy names and characters of the Weber and Fields burlesque compared to the original works:

> In another burlesque of the novel *Quo Vas Iss? A Travesty Upon "Quo Vadis"* by Edgar Smith, the characters were given comic variations of the names of characters in the novel *Quo Vadis* and Wilson Barrett's toga play *The Sign of the Cross*: Marcus Finishus (Marcus Superbus), Petrolius (Petronius), Zero (Nero), Popcornea (Poppaea), Fursus (Ursus), and Lythia (Lygia). In this burlesque of the toga genre, Lythia is a member of the Christian Temperance Union, which has closed the city's saloons. Marcus Finishus is in love with Lythia, who makes the sign of a lobster instead of the fish or a cross. Lythia is accused of having bewitched Fido, Popcornea's pet dog. Zero sends her to the arena for being a member of the Christian Temperance Movement and wanting to burn "Rum." Fursus fights the bull with Lythia tied on it, and both are pardoned by Zero. Slang is used to puncture the moral pretensions of the toga genre: 'Hail to Petrolius, the oily Roman gent, if he is not a cuckoo, we do not want a cent, though mighty Zero's reigning, it's Petrolius we hail; and the people love him better than they love a bargain sale. Hail Petrolius, hail!' ….The use of dialect and slang to mock the affectations of the white, Anglo-Saxon, Protestants appealed to Jewish and Catholic immigrants.

*Roman Scandals* continues the tradition of burlesques which Weber and Fields had made such a staple of American and particularly Jewish-American comedy with its parodies of the *Ben-Hur* chariot race, its deflation of the majesty of ancient Rome into a center of corruption and intrigue (which of course it really was), and its paralleling of the ancient world with the problems and foibles of the world of today. The film also embraces the sexier aspects of burlesque with its see-through tunics and pre-code production numbers and its hilarious seduction sequence with the empress attempting to bribe Eddie through sex to help her conspire to poison the emperor.

**Eddie gets the point of Ancient Rome in *Roman Scandals*. (Photofest)**

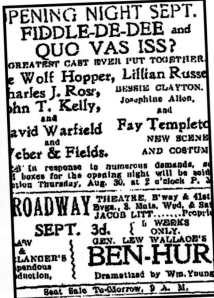

## ROMAN SCANDALS AND BLACKFACE

When Eddie inadvertently is given a mud treatment in the women's spa, he quickly realizes that he can disguise himself by posing as an Ethiopian doctor. Once he "blacks up" (a term I grew up with in show business), the blackface becomes an excuse for performing segments from minstrel shows, which Cantor starred in in his younger days. In a sequence that seems strange to the modern young viewer, Cantor in blackface suddenly begins to strut around the spa by sliding his feet and he starts to speak grammatically incorrectly and chuckle "yuk, yuk, yuk." To explain this curious sequence, we need to explain a few things about blackface entertainment.

Eddie Cantor dons blackface makeup when he poses as an Ethiopian doctor in *Roman Scandals*.

Minstrel shows were enormously popular in the early 1930s and white entertainers of all ages commonly blackened up even in colleges, high schools and elementary schools. In fact minstrel shows and blackface entertainment persisted in America into the early 1960s. I myself as a child entertainer regularly performed in blackface until 1957 when I was simply told by my employers at CBS that it was no longer "viable." A popular blackface female act, The Duncan Sisters, continued into the early 1960s doing their *Topsy and Eva* comedy routine derived from Harriet Beecher Stowe's pre-Civil War novel *Uncle Tom's Cabin*. By the middle 1950s however many citizens, black and white, were calling for

minstrel shows to cease, claiming they were racist and gradually a nation that became increasingly concerned about being politically incorrect not only stopped them but virtually erased them from our collective memory!

The famous Supreme Court Decision, Brown vs. the Board of Education made it illegal for state laws to insist that white and black students attend separate public schools since the idea of such laws was to deny blacks their equal opportunity for education. This ruling, made in 1954, provoked substantial racial tension all across America and particularly across the deep South where Governors Orville Faubus of Arkansas and George Wallace of Alabama physically blocked school integration. As this and other laws to stop discrimination were increasingly enforced, the non-politically correct entertainment of vaudeville, which mocked the major ethnic groups and religions in America openly, could not survive. Television required non-offensive family entertainment and the great ethnic insult comics of earlier days such as The Duncan Sisters or Benny Rubin found their fame slipping away quickly.

39

**Advertisement from 1833 features Thomas Rice as Jim Crow**

But in the 1930s these minstrel shows were popular all across America and comics were free to insult Italians as wops whose men liked their women ample in size, to mock the Irish, who were often described as drunken potato heads, and to go after Jews, who put up with horrible songs like "When Mose With His Nose Leads the Band." People generally didn't think twice about it and comedians such as Gus Van specialized in insult songs rendered in dialect. African-Americans had the worst of the insults to be sure, since they were depicted as lazy, violent sub-literates with grotesquely exaggerated facial features.

Whites performing in blackface can be traced back to at least the 1820s and Thomas "Daddy" Rice, supposedly the Father of Minstrelsy. He was said to have observed a stumbling, crippled black man hobbling along and mimicked his movement. The man had the name or was given the name Jim Crow. He was a slave whose butchered English was no doubt the result of a lack of educational opportunity. Thus the black stereotype of the shuffling black, fracturing English with a southern drawl, was born, a pathetic, slow-witted creature using plural subjects with singular verbs and vice-versa, and generally abusing the language he was given no chance to learn properly. Blacks were depicted as stereotypes: lazy, watermelon-eating, razor-wielding, gullible, untrustworthy, irresponsible, slow and dull, caring only to sleep and eat, but always happy to jump around, dance and sing in groups.

By the 1840s Daniel Christy toured with Christy's Minstrels featuring popular "negro" songs by Stephen Foster such as "De Camptown Races," "Old Folks at Home," "Old Black Joe" and "Oh Susannah." These tunes were normally performed at minstrel venues although they later were memorialized and memorized by all American school children and sung communally at elementary school assemblies. Daniel Christy made a great deal of money with his troupe and the songs initially reached a wide audience because they were reproduced and sent all over the country, helping to grow the American sheet music industry which, blossomed just before the turn of the last century.

However, Stephen Foster received no royalties and eventually fell onto hard times in New York City, even though much of America was singing his music. Destitute and abandoned by his wife (for whom he had written the hauntingly beautiful "I Dream of Jeannie with the Light Brown Hair") and his family, Stephen fell and struck his head in his small flat and lay dying for days before he was discovered. He was just 37 years old. After he died, heirs rummaging through his effects unearthed "Beautiful Dreamer," perhaps his most poignant and beautiful song, and sold it.

The minstrel show format varied from troupe to troupe but gradually emerged in three parts. In the first, comedy, dance and song occurred around a semicircle, at the end of which were two principal performers who assisted the interlocutor or master of ceremonies. The MC

40

sat at the center of the semicircle, sometimes in advance of it. The end men were called usually Mr. Tambo and Mr. Bones. They played the tambourine or clicked animal bones in the program traditionally and also cracked racist jokes with one another such as:

Tambo—Is you been born in Darkest Africa?
Bones—Yes I is born dere.
Tambo—It must have been in de darkest part!

The bones consisted of rib or lower leg bones of various animals such as a cow or smaller animals such as a dog. The bones were about six inches long and had a slight curve and could be knocked against each other with two hands. In my performing days with minstrel shows in the 1950s bones were not used but rather wooden or metal spoons and Mr. Bones would "play the spoons" to keep his rhythm and was called "Mr. Spoons." Sometimes if there was no spoon player, a washboard might be used to simulate the sound of the bones or spoon. The second part of the program featured acts performing in front of a curtain. These were usually individuals such as someone telling a monologue, a singer, or a tap dancer or it might be a small group of singers. During this second act, the most elaborate set in the show was brought in behind the scenes. It was usually a plantation setting and the last part of the show featured more specialty acts such as acrobats or eccentric dancers in front of the semicircle. Then there was usually a group finale. This is the way I remember minstrel shows being presented in my youth. But it could vary. Normally only men performed but even in the 1920s women could have their own minstrel shows or the shows could be mixed with men and women.

In a strange byproduct of the popularity of the minstrel show, blacks actually had their own minstrel shows, which featured blacks imitating whites, who were of course imitating caricatures of blacks. Many black entertainers such as the legendary Bert Williams wore blackface when they performed. Black comedians followed this tradition in some cases into the 1950s, an example being the comedian Pigmeat Markham who always blacked up before going out on stage. When I performed in blackface I had to carry a kit with me from which I could make up using burnt cork, while I would wear white gloves and a tux, and I would outline my lips with Noxzema skin cream which made them very white.

Even though discrimination against blacks after the Civil War continued, early black entertainers such as James A. Bland (1854-1911) made important contributions to American entertainment. A composer and performer, he wrote "Carry Me Back to Old Virginny" in 1878, which became the state song of Virginia until recently when some resented its seemingly racist lyrics and others felt that it had been written by a black man and should not be their state song, so there were arguments on both sides of the race issue with the result that it was deposed. Bland, for that matter, had been a much earlier victim of racism, ending up buried in an unmarked grave. Thus the first great African-American composer of popular music died in total obscurity. It wasn't until 1939 that his grave was found in the Philadelphia area and an honorific monument erected by ASCAP, the American Society of Composers, Authors and Publishers.

Bert Williams, who was a Jamaican, was another major black entertainer, in the early 1900s, first through his partnership with William Walker and later on his own as a comic monologist telling long stories and tall tales that put him in wild and dangerous situations and seemed to fill him with trepidation. The audience could usually see the punch lines coming but he would hold the final outcome of the story until the very end to build up humorous audience reaction. He was also a pantomimist, singer and composer and occasionally even appeared

SUNG BY LOTTA AND ED. MARBLE IN "MUSETTE" AND "ZIP."

1. Carry Me Back to Old Virginny. (Song & Chorus.)
2. In the Morning by the Bright Light. (Cal Song.)
3. Oh dem Golden Slippers. (Song & Chorus.)

Words and Music by JAMES BLAND, of Sprague's Georgia Minstrels.

BOSTON:
JOHN F. PERRY & Co., Music Publishers.
13 West Street.

**Bert Williams was the first great black star and became famous performing in the *Ziegfeld Follies*.**

in silent films. But it was as a star, the first great black star, with the *Ziegfeld Follies* that he became nationally famous. He performed in blackface with Eddie Cantor in a series of vaudeville routines in which black vs. white jokes often played a major part. It marked the first time that an interracial performance had been featured in a major Broadway production. Eddie Cantor eventually lived to regret his early career as a blackface performer as he became a supporter of equal rights for African-Americans and the N.A.A.C.P. or National Association for the Advancement of Colored People, a group still active today. But, much to his credit, he supported the career of Williams who, although he could perform at the New Amsterdam Theater for Florenz Ziegfeld, could not watch the show from out in front with the white audience.

The Golden Age of the minstrel show was 1860-1890 but even in the later 19th and early 20th century Primrose and West, Al G. Fields, Emmett Welch, and George "Honey Boy" Evans had enormously popular troupes. George Primrose and William "Billy" West were pioneers in the enlarging of the minstrel shows and making them entertainment on a grand scale with popular stars. Lew Dockstader (real name George Alfred Clapp [1856-1924]) became a household word in the 1910s as a vaudeville, comedy and blackface minstrel star. He had his own minstrel company and between 1906-1909 the very young Al Jolson (real name Asa Yoelson, from Lithuania) had his early training with Lew and went on to perform blackface and sing about the South and his "Mammy" for years to come. It may seem absurd today to imagine the immigrant Jew Jolson in full blackface singing about Dixie and cotton picking in the Southern fields but

people flocked to see Jolson do just that in shows like *Big Boy* 1930 and movies like *Mammy* 1930. In *Wonder Bar* (1934), Jolson teamed with choreographer and designer Busby Berkeley to make a vision of "darkie heaven" complete with pork chops growing on trees, tap dancers like the great Hal Leroy leaping out of a giant watermelon while in blackface, and Jolson himself in blackface singing about "Going to Heaven on a Missouri Mule."

In my youth and even from the beginning of minstrelsy black singers, and white singers who sounded like them, were called Coon Shouters. The term coon was intended derogatorily and seems to have derived from the black facial masking of a raccoon. In early minstrel shows dating back even to the 1820s white men impersonating blacks would portray particular stereotypes such as the Zip Coon, which meant a flashy dressing, fancy-stepping (later in the 19th century even cakewalking) black man all dolled up to impress the ladies. George Washington Dixon (ca. 1801-1861) was a pioneer in blackface entertainment and may have developed the Zip Coon character as an urban black man trying to appear sophisticated, strutting and sticking out his hip. The song" Zip Coon," for which very early sheet music survives, became his signature tune and he was the first major star associated with blackface

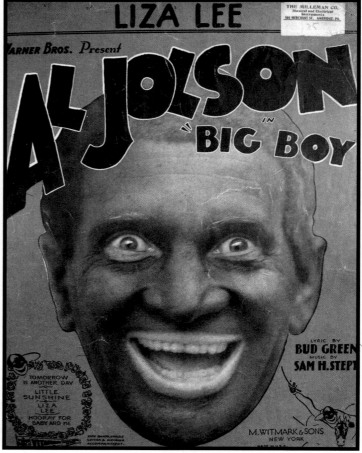

minstrelsy in America. It is that Zip Coon character that Eddie Cantor is recalling in *Roman Scandals* as he snorts, chortles and shuffle walks.

## ROMAN SCANDALS AND SIGMUND FREUD

*Roman Scandals*, like all the pre-code Eddie Cantor vehicles, has a generous helping of sexuality. In the 1920s and early 1930s people talked a lot about Freud and the notion that people had a more complex inner makeup than had previously been imagined. There was the *id, ego* and *superego*. Simply explained, the *id* represented raw primitive forces within you such as your *libido* with its desire for warmth, sex, food and sometimes aggression. The *ego* mediated between the *id* and the world around you so that you didn't lose control. The *superego* was rather like your conscience and was subject to outside influences such as your parents. The releasing of the *id* was something that young people thought about and older people complained about when they viewed young people as having no restraint. Such things as pre-code movies, automobiles, lighter clothes for women, smoking cigarettes, and Parisian women who were discovered during World War I were all viewed by the older generation as contributing factors to releasing the *id* of young people. So was the veiled sexuality of the "Living Tableaux" of women, nearly naked, in Florenz Ziegfeld's *Follies* beginning in 1907. Ziegfeld's shows were still considered suitable for families but they were followed up with more overtly sexual displays such as *Earl Carroll's Vanities* from 1922 and *George White's Scandals*, beginning in 1919 and featuring the famous "Scandal Walk" by scantily dressed chorus girls. So blatant in his displaying of showgirls was Earl Carroll that he became known as the "Troubadour of the Nude." In 1926 Earl was arrested and even imprisoned for six months in Atlanta for staging a private party in

which a showgirl bathed nude in illegal liquor! If Ziegfeld maintained the pretense of innocence, White and Carroll went unashamedly for the *id*!

Irene Bordoni, one of those Parisian bombshells who appeared after World War I, sang double entendre songs, which were very popular. Sexual innuendo was all over the music world, particularly in the flapper period and the early 1930s. Polish import Anna Held, the common law wife of Florenz Ziegfeld, had already been singing in the 1910s that "I Can't Make My Eyes Behave" and Irene Bordoni complained "Don't Look at Me That Way," because "my will is strong but my won't is weak." Bordoni featured naughty libido songs where she could see in the man's eyes the sexual, Freudian *id* waiting to emerge and she'd sing, "Jeepers, Creepers! Where'd you get those peepers?"

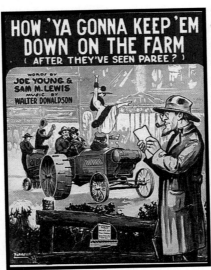

and "there's a hocus pocus about your focus that's nobody's business dear." She would complain about those "sudden flashes behind your lashes" and how "my pupils forget their scruples." Bordoni had lots to say about the secretself waiting to come out from every male, as she would sing, "When you arrive, I simply thrive, but if you want to get home alive, "Don't Look at Me That Way!" (1928). In songs such as these, Bordoni was even suggesting premarital sex initiated by the woman who, just like the man, couldn't control the passion within. For the older generation, this sort of thing was dynamite.

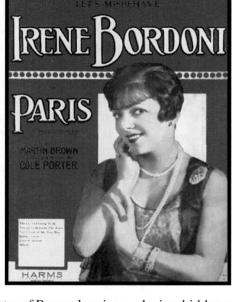

Fred Waring's collegiate orchestra of Pennsylvanians sang songs such as "Any Ice Today, Lady" and "Oh, Lady Be Good To Me," about ice delivery men having sexual trysts with housewives whose husbands were away and who were eager to have a good time during the afternoon in the days before electric refrigerators were common and the ice man wasn't needed anymore. Waring also sang things like "I've Never Seen a Straight Banana" (1927) with lyrics so naughty he had to leave some out for his recording of the song and let the hearer imagine them as he just hummed the rougher parts of the tune. Later, Waring in maturity would "go straight" and become a pillar of American society, emphasizing strong patriotism and Christian values, abandoning his sexy double-entendre hits and wild collegiate persona of the past at Penn State, but then the early 1950s, the age of Joseph McCarthy, were very different from the 1920s and Fred was an adapter. In his spare time, by the way, Waring backed the marketing of the first electric kitchen blender!

During the 1920s Freudian and psychological words entered the everyday language of Americans. Rich people would go into "analysis" and sometimes discuss their progress openly and shockingly at soirees. At such sessions they would discover that they had an "inferiority complex" or even an "Oedipus complex," which referred to the ancient Greek story memorialized by the playwright Sophocles about an heir to the throne of Thebes who was cast out by the king Laius when he was a child because an oracle from the priestess of Delphi said that the young man would kill his father. The abandoned Oedipus was left with his feet pierced, unable to walk. The name Oedipus actually means swollen foot in ancient Greek, which refers to the condition in which he was found. The

boy grew up and unknowingly killed his own father after a dispute and eventually he freed the city of Thebes from a monstrous sphinx. Oedipus then married his own mother. An Oedipus complex, in psychoanalytical theory, meant that the young child, while his *ego* and libido or *id* are developing (ages three to five), has unconscious desires to possess the parent of the opposite sex and eliminate the parent of the same sex.

The editors of *The Catholic Telegraph* newspaper worried a great deal about sex and constantly lobbied for reform but the young people who had faced the ravages of WWI and had a taste of French lifestyle ushered in a new era of increased frankness and enjoyed lacing hidden meanings into everything in order to slip something by traditional society and the older generation. There had scarcely been a bigger generation gap than that between the parents and young people in the 1920s, groups that embraced two vastly different worlds. Women were getting off of their Victorian pedestal and becoming more independent, now with the right to vote. The Christian traditional family man Fred Stone, one of the greatest comedic stars of the Broadway stage of the 1910s and a defender of traditional values, once ran into Earl Carroll, the entrepreneur of the new 1920s sexuality on Broadway. Normally a kind and modest man, Stone wanted to murder Carroll and came close to doing so at the encounter.

Eddie Cantor made a whole career of double-entendre songs such 1910s gems as "Would You Rather Be a General with an Eagle on Your Shoulder or a Private with a Chicken on your Knee?" and "Row, Row, Rosie, Rosie Row for the Shore" about an attempted seduction of a girl who had the misfortune to be with a man out in a rowboat. "Ma, He's Making Eyes at Me" was another big hit for Cantor. And such tunes as "When I See All the Loving They Waste on Babies," "Noah's Wife Had a Wonderful Life" and "Give Me the Sultan's Harem" are just a few of these typical Cantor "lay it between the lines" songs.

*Roman Scandals* is full of these wonderful double-entendre Eddie Cantorisms both in song and dialogue. In one the empress Agrippa (Verree Teasdale in a see-through *palla*) is trying to seduce him. He talks about not wanting to play cards with her because "she'll want to shuffle the whole deck." In a typical song from the film called "Put a Tax on Love" double entendres comprise almost the whole tune including such lines as:

**Eddie tries to stay innocent but the royal court has numerous temptations in *Roman Scandals*.**

> Break your Frigidaire and then,
> Let's go back when men were men
> Bring the iceman back again
> Put a tax on love
> Married couples have no fear
> Though at first you're taxed severe
> It grows less and less each year
> Put a tax on love.

Thus we can see that Eddie's persona, most especially in his early career, was principally based on double entendre songs that draw the viewer into a situation which seems innocent but which soon yields something naughty. Through all of this Eddie is nudging and winking to us and of course rolling those banjo eyes in awareness.

One great example in *Roman Scandals*, which is totally lost on contemporary audiences, has Eddie Cantor explaining the love life of Mickey and Minnie Mouse to his potential ancient Roman buyers when he is put up for auction as a slave. At one point, he tries to explain what has become of Minnie Mouse. Suddenly, he dances around in a Harlem shuffle and sings out, "There goes Minnie, kicking the gong around." This seemingly absurd display by the innocent Eddie is actually a nudge to more sophisticated members of the audience that he is referring to a song performed by African-American superstar Cab Calloway at New York's Cotton Club called "Minnie the Moocher." The idea is that since this is a family film the kids won't understand what's going on here, but as an adult YOU will. And audiences once did.

"Minnie the Moocher" was a huge hit for Cab Calloway when it was recorded in 1931. By 1932 it had been used in a popular cartoon featuring Betty Boop. In the song this Minnie (whom Eddie is deliberately confusing with Minnie Mouse) was a user of cocaine or a "cokey" although many people would not have understood this outside of New York. In Harlem street slang and in Chinatown particularly the term "kicking the gong around" meant that you were going down to get opium to smoke. Sophisticated viewers of the movie would have gotten this reference and Calloway had written a song in 1931 called "Kicking the Gong Around," which was also widely known. This is typical Eddie Cantor. While observing a seemingly innocent character we are able to be led by him into a situation with a subtext that might seem innocent on the one hand but which is full of double entendre. Minnie in Cab Calloway's song is ultimately not Minnie Mouse but a Minnie who is a red-hot kootch dancer or stripteaser who hung out with a guy named Smoky, who was a cokey:

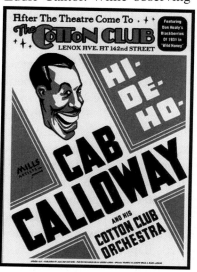

> Now, she messed around with a bloke named Smoky,
> She loved him though he was cokey,
> He took her down to Chinatown,
> He showed her how to kick the gong around.

The 1931 Calloway sequel song, "Kickin' the Gong Around" reads:

> If you don't know Minnie,
> She's tall and skinny,
> She gets her pleasure
> Kicking the gong around!

The term gong or gonger was New York and San Francisco street language for an opium pipe from as early as 1920, but the use of it as nudge-and-wink humor in a 1930s family film is typically Eddie Cantor. Today people use the term bong for a water pipe used to smoke opium and absorb the active ingredients of morphine, thebaine, codeine and papaverine and get high. But Eddie's reference to such things in a 1930s family film is nothing short of wild!

## RUTH ETTING
### (1896-1978)

In the slave market sequence scorching torch singer Ruth Etting belts out "No More Love." Originally intended to have more of a part in the film, which was to be her first principal feature-length starring appearance, Ruth suffered the cutting out of most of her footage as Olga, the Emperor's Favorite. The song remains however and reveals her powerful voice. Ruth Etting was nearing the down side of her career by the time of *Roman Scandals* but from the 1920s through the early 1930s she had over 60 hit tunes and became one of the first consistently popular American pop singers. In the flapper era she became known for tunes like "Shine On Harvest Moon," "Button Up Your Overcoat," "Shaking the Blues Away," "Exactly Like You" and "Mean to Me," which all became standards. But it is as a torch singer that she really made her mark and, along with Helen Morgan, became one of the great divas of her generation. Songs such as "Love Me or Leave Me" and the haunting "Ten Cents a Dance" leave a strong impression that Etting was a dramatic chanteuse and not just a 1920s flapper.

Just a simple unaffected young girl from David City, Nebraska, she set out to become a costume designer by

**Ruth Etting Comforts Wounded Husband**

Appearing tired and distressed, Ruth Etting (right), singer, and her step-daughter, Edith Snyder, watch over Myrl Alderman, who was wounded by gunshot in Miss Etting's home near Los Angeles. Miss Etting and Alderman, 30, a radio musician, were secretly married in July, 1938. Martin Snyder, 42, former husband of the vocalist, was held on suspicion of kidnaping and attempting to murder Alderman.

studying art in Chicago, but that town was a gangster haven in the 1920s and she soon fell under the domineering control of Martin "Moe the Gimp" Snyder, portrayed by James Cagney in the Ruth Etting biopic *Love Me or Leave Me*, starring Doris Day as a game but miscast Etting. Admired by Chicago gangsterdom and even by Al Capone himself, Etting's career prospered under the tutelage of Moe, himself a small-time gangster once described as a "floating voter," which meant that in Chicago at that time you might vote early and often in elections. He married Ruth in 1922. She was a sensation at the Marigold Gardens nightclub and soon Ruth became one of the biggest stars of Flo Ziegfeld's *Follies* of 1927.

From 1930 to 1933 America was caught in the throes of Etting Mania in which dolls, cosmetics and lots of movie short subjects were made featuring the popular hit maker. But 1933 was the beginning of a tapering off for Ruth that would eventually see her divorce Moe Snyder in 1937 and take up with her pianist Myrl Alderman. Soon the possessive Moe shot Myrl, who recovered slowly while Moe, who had friends in the mob, was released after only one year in prison for attempted murder! This scandal ended Ruth's popularity quickly but she seemed just as happy to live a quiet life out of the limelight with her husband, at least until the 1939 death of her young daughter from rheumatic fever and a plane crash in 1941, which seriously injured her husband yet again. By the time of *Roman Scandals* her whirlwind career had seen her record some 200 songs, guest on all major musical radio shows at the national level, be featured in six Broadway shows and make 35 film shorts. Her vocal stylings dif-

**Ruth Etting poses for a publicity shot for *Roman Scandals*.**

fered from the more operatic or light opera styles of many of her contemporaries and she helped to set a trend in torch singing and popular music that continued up to the advent of rock-and-roll and still continues on programs like *American Idol* to this day.

Because her voice was not so high, she recorded well and made huge numbers of records. Her voice timbre and clear diction also allowed for listeners to understand her words clearly so that great composers particularly wanted to write for her, also because she sold enormous quantities of sheet music. But by the time of *Roman Scandals* she was 37 years of age and was beginning to look more matronly and middle-aged. In her earlier heyday she had been a sex symbol as well as a chanteuse and had been photographed semi-nude by Alfred Cheney Johnston. *Roman Scandals* provides an important opportunity to hear a legendary vocalist powerfully sing a mediocre torch song just before her career began to fade away.

### ROMAN SCANDALS AND THE YEAR 1933

The end of 1933 was extremely difficult for Americans. Following the stock market's initial crash, brief rallies and deep plunges of October and November in 1929, the stock market lost 30 billion dollars and huge numbers of businesses failed, leaving streets with soaped-up store windows as a typical sign of the times. The Republican president Herbert Hoover appeared powerless to do anything about the free fall of the early 1930s, just hoping, as he said, that "prosperity is just around the corner." Comedians of the time changed this to "posterity is just around the corner" when things didn't get better. When many were forced to give up homes or apartments and live in their cars, folksy comedian and former *Ziegfeld Follies* star Will Rogers joked ironically that "we are the only nation to head to the poorhouse in an automobile." American males, feeling impotent and unable to be their family's breadwinners, were unimpressed with Hoover's exhortations to self-help or his belief that a policy of *laissez faire* (leave everything alone) in which "the business of the United States is business" would eventually bring back prosperity.

By September of 1931, 305 major banks had folded and by October the number was 522. By 1932 there were more than 13 million unemployed. Many people took advantage of the season's oversupply of apples to try and sell them on the street corners. Many young people left their homes to ride the rails as hoboes and look for better opportunities in other places. There they ran into hostile railroad workers and often were attacked and robbed. Mi-

*Building Provides Mooring Masts for Zeps*

NEW YORKERS may soon become accustomed to the sight of giant lighter-than-air liners moored to the tops of downtown skyscrapers, for the Empire State Building, now under construction at 34th Street and Fifth Avenue, when completed will be topped by a mooring mast of the latest type.

This new building, which will rise to a height of 1100 feet will top the Eiffel Tower of Paris by 174 feet and will be the tallest structure in the world. It is planned to make this building the western terminal of trans-Atlantic airships.

**Fast Burning Tear Gas Candle**

THE successful use of tear gas in quelling prison riots has resulted in great interest by prison authorities in this chemical agent which does its work without causing injury. The Chemical Warfare Service of the army, as a result of requests for a tear gas device that will produce a gas cloud immediately of high concentration, recently has shipped to Governors Island, New York, two dozen of the new universal fast burning tear gas candles for test there.

These candles were developed in order to meet the demand for a tear gas weapon that will produce an effective gas concentration so quickly that a rioter will be made helpless immediately. The fast burning candles are used in the same manner as a grenade but differ from the latter in that they have a larger capacity, and the tear gas is generated with almost explosive violence. Thus the gas gets into the air with no delay and in great volume.

The older grenades were somewhat slow in ignition and the gas was generated slowly. The fast burning candle ignites so rapidly after leaving the hand that by the time it hits the ground it is giving off its fumes in great quantities. The test of these candles will be watched with great interest not only by the army but by civil authorities, who agree that tear gas is a most effective and humane method of quelling disturbances.

This composite photograph shows how the Graf Zeppelin compares with Empire State building.

**Oval Auto Cylinders Cut Length**

AN automobile engine has been built in England with elliptical cylinders, the idea being to save length, the narrow way of the cylinders being placed in a fore and aft position. Thus a 3x4¾ cylinder would be equivalent to a 3¾ round cylinder but take no more length than one 3 inches in diameter.

**This page from Aug. 1930 *Modern Mechanics* illustrates the plan of mooring zeppelins at the Empire State Building.**

grant workers and transients suffered enormously as did farmers in dust bowl areas such as Oklahoma. These problems, which had already begun before 1929, were later chronicled by John Steinbeck in the 1939 novel *Grapes of Wrath* (filmed by John Ford in 1940), dealing with the plight of sharecroppers amid drought and depression in Oklahoma. The problems of the Depression poor were also chronicled in the music of activist and folksinger Woody Guthrie, known as the "Dust Bowl Troubadour."

What actually caused the Great Depression is better understood by economists than archaeologists although a preliminary survey exposes numerous possible culprits: over-investment, under-consumption, lack of regulation (the *laissez faire* policy of Hoover), panic and fear of investing. One huge problem was that due to financial arrangements involving the United States, England and the backing of issued money with gold, it became cheaper to borrow money for the purpose of investing in the stock market. This was called "buying on margin" and huge numbers of people poured their life savings in to try and get rich quickly. For example, someone could buy $10,000 worth of stock for only $1,000. Eventually the market was stretched too thin with investors who had nothing behind their 10% investments to back up their money, creating a bubble in the market. When this "bubble" burst in October of 1929 it caused widespread fear and panic and massive selling off of remaining assets.

Skyscrapers, which had promised a new age of prosperity in the 1910s and 1920s, went largely empty or well under capacity as businesses collapsed and could not fill them. It had been thought that these huge vertical towers would usher in a new era of prosperity in which partygoers would take elevators to the tops of the buildings and then head through a doorway onto giant pleasure dirigibles that would be moored to the tops of the buildings through tethering towers. In 1929-1930 this futuristic vision was particularly popular and was embodied in the movie *Madame Satan* (1930) in which revelers dressed up as cats climb a blimp-tethering tower while singing a song entitled "Doin' the Catwalk." In the film, they eventually enter the dirigible where an enormous party is in session celebrating the power of modern energy and featuring a dancing personification of supercharged electricity!

Most movies avoided the depressing aspects of the Depression and diverted viewers with stories about the rich and famous or featured total fantasy escapes such as *Roman Scandals*. 1933 was a year in which the public barely had money to even go to the movies. Broadway shows folded one after another, as evidenced in the 1933 movie *Golddiggers of 1933*. Old Man Depression was a common personification, as was the so-called

wolf at the door. Milk deliveries were hampered by people stealing the bottles from other people's front stoop and there were constant breadlines and bank crises. Estimates suggest that as much as one third of the people of New York City were unemployed in 1933 and those figures did not count another pressing problem, the underemployed.

Many women retained their low-paying jobs while their husbands might be unemployed. Some women became gold-diggers (women seeking a wealthy provider for short or long-term needs in exchange for companionship) or even prostitutes to make ends meet. The term gold-diggers had become popular to apply to women during the California gold rush of the 1840s but enjoyed particular popularity during the Great Depression. A popular approach for women who had the looks and inclination was to become a gold-digging showgirl who might attract a wealthy male who might be targeted to set her up with a penthouse in exchange for her services as an escort or as a mistress. That this occurred on a considerable scale is suggested by the extraordinary frequency of movies devoted to this subject at the time. Perhaps the most sensitive of them is *Blondie of the Follies*, featuring two fascinating portrayals by Marion Davies and Billie Dove as impoverished young ladies unable to bear the devastating effects of the Depression and forced to find a way to eat. Davies' father (James Gleason) loses his job while suffering from a heart condition and her lazy brother (Sidney Toler) is also unemployed, leaving it to her to find a way out through show business and gold-digging.

Remaining a "good girl" and still managing to succeed became the fulcrum which many young girls had to balance on at the time if they were good looking enough to get into the situation. Often, the lives of such women ended in tragedy. Some have attempted to underplay this women's dilemma but the fact is that after the Great Depression the percentage of U.S. women engaging in premarital intercourse rose sharply, much of it as a result of the soldiers returning from World War I, as the work of Margaret Sanger has shown. But the Depression became another trigger for this sexual revolution when rock bottom hit in 1933 and changed the mores of America.

## FRANKLIN DELANO ROOSEVELT

Into this scenario of Depression misery came the president FDR (Franklin Delano Roosevelt) and the escapism of the movies exemplified in a great part by Eddie Cantor, who had lost everything but survived. Roosevelt too had taken some hard knocks. He suffered from polio which had crippled and weakened his legs, so much so that he would not permit himself to be shown attempting to walk and there was a silent agreement with the media not to show him walking, being carried, or attempting to move about with his legs in any way. His more powerful upper torso could be shown and he was normally photographed in a seated position. This was not such a big issue in the days before television and FDR was able to use his theatrical and stentorian voice effectively on the radio as no other president ever had.

FDR, like Eddie Cantor, understood how to use media to mirror the demands of the time. He used simple catch phrases and sound bites that people remember to this day. The Japanese attack on Pearl Harbor in 1941 was "a day that will live in infamy." The Depression and the mammoth bank failure could be defeated because "the only thing we have to fear is fear itself," as FDR stated right away in his inaugural address in 1933. Roosevelt smiled and projected confidence with that same sort of inner peace and calm during the storm that many see in Barack Obama, a great admirer of FDR's "never let them see you sweat" philosophy. FDR also assembled a Brain Trust, a mix of young and older specialists largely from academia to battle the Depression with substantive programs and catch phrases.

Some of the principal players were the following all but forgotten men. Thirty eight-year-old whiz kid Adolph Burle from Harvard, Professor of Law at Columbia, helped to fashion the New Deal. Louis Howe, who was ever present at Roosevelt's side, functioned as White House Chief of Staff before the title existed. Raymond Moley was a pioneer New Dealer, who soon broke with FDR despite writing most of the inaugural address. He then became a Republican conservative who eventually supported and was honored by Richard Nixon. George Peek promoted agricultural reforms and supported rescue programs. Rexford Tugwell of the Wharton School of Finance at the University of Pennsylvania worked to help farmers survive devastating markets and drought and was also involved in providing rural housing for urban poor. Hugh S. Johnson became a dominant force for the National Recovery Administration before exhausting himself and burning out in 1934. F. Palmer Weber, who had an activist background, played a key role in examining the concentration of wealth into the hands of a few while seeking to find ways to make the New Deal more egalitarian and helpful to the poor. James Warburg of Harvard was a financial expert who helped Roosevelt cope with banking problems.

Although many Republicans have strongly criticized Roosevelt for producing government sponsored programs that were ineffectual, in fact statistics show that Roosevelt's New Deal as he called it actually helped considerably to offset Depression hysteria and economic disaster. It is true that the programs didn't end the Depression and a later attempt to scale back government stimulus packages actually caused the Depression to gain ground again. But there is no question that FDR had a major effect on keeping the country from going under right after the Hoover administration when his do-nothing administration had the country in growing panic and free fall. It is difficult to imagine what would have happened to America without the New Deal. FDR does not deserve all the credit. His wife, Eleanor Roosevelt, was a compassionate and well-received first lady, photographed for news shorts in movie

**Photograph of a WPA work project in Atchinson Kansas.**

theaters as she doled out the famous "7 Cent Lunches" in a soup kitchen for a breadline. It is clear that not every appointment that FDR made worked out nor every policy but he was willing to try various things to stimulate the country rather than sit back and watch it implode.

The NRA or National Recovery Administration was one of the first parts of Roosevelt's New Deal, created with the National Industrial Recovery Act of 1933. It was designed to look after workers by guaranteeing a minimum wage and stopping unfair business practices. By 1935 the Supreme Court ruled the NRA unconstitutional, stating that it violated the concept of separation of powers between the government and the business sector. But by then many of the stimuli devised by FDR had begun to help. There was the Works Progress Administration, which was designed to put people back to work improving the American infrastructure. In Tucson, at the University of Arizona, for example, it meant offering minimum wage to students who might be able to stay in school and get an education whereby they might improve themselves and get a better job once the Depression was over. The University of Arizona campus was rustic in the early 1930s as well as sandy and desert-like. The WPA helped to fill the campus area and surrounding blocks with sidewalks and the initials can still be seen today as the paving remains from this period over much of the campus. The result was that many students found work and could stay in school while others could send small amounts of survival money home to their families and the campus was beautified. This sort of stimulus package proved very helpful for the campus infrastructure and similar experiments occurred throughout the country. The WPA, as supervised by Harry Hopkins, another of the New Deal Brain Trust, became the largest employer in America. Many at the time and now described it as unconstitutional Socialism or Fascism but in this time of desperation in America it proved to help many people survive day to day.

The CCC or Civilian Conservation Corps began right away in March of 1933 under Robert Fechner and put people to work on rustic projects, often in national parks, and helped large numbers of city kids to not only go to a working camp, but to develop a sense of pride, for they were required to send a portion of their small income back home to help their families. The CWA or Civil Works Administration was a brainchild of brain truster Harry Hopkins, already mentioned above. It was designed to find gainful employment for 4,000,000 unemployed. Some of the jobs undertaken were criticized by Republicans as reflecting what was called a "boondoggle." The term seems to have derived from the Boy Scouts, who used to take rope and make a knot or ring that could be used to hold their scarves together. They were called boondoggles but the term was gradually expanded to refer to any useless task that someone was paid to do during the New Deal.

Another goal of FDR's early months was to stop corruption and problems like "Pork Barrel Spending," which meant that politicians would load up bills with local pet projects and unnecessary spending in order to have their support to make a bill pass. The term arose from the 19th century practice of farmers receiving gifts of barrels from politicians seeking their vote. These barrels were used for storing pork originally but the term was transferred to any kind of attempt by a politician to ingratiate himself to his constituency and to attract votes with questionable projects. In sum, FDR's policies were designed to get the country moving again. Opponents found the reforms went too far and insisted that the country was going to become socialist or totalitarian. My stepfather, for example, hated FDR and always referred to him as "that Communist." But my maternal grandfather insisted that without him America would have gone under and democracy ended. My stepfather however insisted that only WWII stimulated the economy again and the New Deal was a complete failure. Not even my own family can agree on FDR.

Movies such as *Roman Scandals* were designed to provide hope and escape, much like an FDR Fireside Chat. The chats, 30 in number, began in March of 1933 when FDR took over and hit the ground running for his

The CCC working on a federal project.

The silent *Ben-Hur* (1925) featured a major chariot race between stars Ramon Novarro and Francis X. Bushman.

first 100 days, and the chats continued into 1934. They dealt with topics that were causing fear for the American people and they began with the banking collapse crisis. Many of the early chats dealt with explanations of the New Deal and attempted to stabilize the currency. *Roman Scandals*, coming later in the year, had the same calming effect. It provided boundless optimism and offered escapism into another time and place. It provided scapegoats for the ills of society, in this case allowing audiences to identify with corrupt government officials at a time when corruption in the senate and congress was widely known about (for this, see the 1933 movie *Manhattan Melodrama* in which Lee Tracy as a new congressman attempts to rebel against the naked corruption all around him). Most importantly, it reinforced the American dream and myth of the mobile society where hard work and humanity lead to rewards and success. In *Roman Scandals*, one could go from rags to riches and there would be a happy ending and your troubles would melt away if you always looked on the bright side of things. And Eddie Cantor himself was proof of this.

## ROMAN SCANDALS AND BEN-HUR

*Roman Scandals* is intended as a spoof of the blockbuster epics of ancient Rome such as *Sign of the Cross* (1932) and *Cleopatra* (then filming). It particularly spoofs the great silent film *Ben-Hur* (1925), which built up to a major chariot race between Ramon Novarro (Ben-Hur, the Jewish prince) and Francis X. Bushman (Masala, the Roman centurion). This race was set in the circus at Antioch in Syria about A.D. 33. The film was based on a novel by Lew Wallace, *Ben-Hur*, which had become so popular that it was only outsold by the Bible and nearly everyone had read it or at least read some of it by the time the movie was made and many had seen the famous stage play. Lew Wallace had been the governor of Arizona territory, and wrote the book while he was supporting Sherriff Pat Garrett, who was tracking down Billy the Kid and attempting to end range wars and cattle rustling in the wild Southwest. Somehow, Lew, who was fascinated by the Bible and ancient Rome, found spare

Ben-Hur pulls ahead of his hated rival, Messala, in the spectacular chariot race.

from Metro-Goldwyn-Mayer William Wyler's Presentation "BEN-HUR" TECHNICOLOR® Camera 65

**The William Wyler-directed *Ben-Hur* remake in 1959 starring Charlton Heston won 11 Academy Awards and became an instant classic.**

time to pen the novel, which although at first unsuccessful, ultimately proved to be his only blockbuster hit.

In 1900, *Ben-Hur* was brought to Broadway and staged with the culminating chariot race being managed by using horses on tracks. The losing charioteers were ejected violently via a mechanical spring. Crowds could not get enough of the stage show, which ran well past the death of Lew Wallace in 1905. By 1925, *Ben-Hur*, having only recently completed its seemingly endless stage run, was brought to the screen. Of course the centerpiece of the film had to be the chariot race that everyone would compare to that in the book or the one in the stage show and so Yakima Canutt, the partly Native American early-Hollywood rodeo star from Washington state, and B. Reeves Eason, the director, were brought in to organize the remarkable chariot sequence which was filmed with 42 cameras. Pressure from Louis B. Mayer for more speed and realism led to some nasty spills and one major pile-

up, which is still visible in the film. Stories of at least one fatality also abound but remain unconfirmed.

The chariot sequence of *Ben-Hur* helped to give rise to the concept of what I call the "speed movie" which are 1930s films that feature a big finish that gets faster and faster and faster, often using speeded up footage, until the breathless climax. Such films abounded in the 1920s and 1930s and the serials of the time also helped to propagate and perpetuate this idea of the big, speeded up finish. Movies such as *Non Stop New York* (1936) featured a finale with an airplane that had a hero and villain fighting in and even on top of the plane as it flew out of control and threatened to crash. *Carnival Boat* (1932) featured a thrilling logjam gone wild that built up faster and faster for hero William Boyd. Train movies took advantage of the newly developed high-speed rail of the time to provide a thrill a minute ending, one of the best of these being *The Silver Streak* (1934) in which a high-speed

**Eddie Cantor explores the sillier aspects of a chariot race in *Roman Scandals*. (Photofest)**

train must transport an iron lung to Boulder Dam before a young child dies of polio. *The Silver Streak* was also the nickname for the Burlington Pioneer Zephyr which on May 26, 1934 set a speed record for travel between Denver and Chicago, making the more than 1,000 mile trip in just over 13 hours, with speeds up to 112-miles-per-hour. Such speed records for trains and planes frequently filled the news in the 1930s.

These speed movies, and there were lots of them in the early 1930s, including countless Westerns, featured dashing climaxes with sharply ascending crescendos of music, speeded up footage and a happy conclusion. *Roman Scandals* takes the concept of the speed film to the limit in the wild chariot race sequence at the end of the film.

If *Ben-Hur* is limited to the chariots and horses, *Roman Scandals* explores the more ridiculous aspects of chariots gone wild in the countryside: pedestrians who may get mowed down, a goose at first goosing Eddie Cantor from behind and then being used as a honking horn, a chariot that dissolves into something resembling

snow skis and a vehicle trying to advance with square wheels. The inter-chariot fight between Ben-Hur and Masala revealing Masala's dirty tricks was a centerpiece of the earlier film and is parodied in *Roman Scandals* as the emperor's charioteer wraps his whip around Eddie's neck and tries to pull him out of the chariot to which his feet have been nailed down!

## ROMAN SCANDALS AND ANCIENT ROME

The Rome that *Roman Scandals* creates parallels that of Cecil B. De Mille's Roman epics in that its buildings are all white. This is the result of the fact that Roman buildings that survived as ruins over the centuries normally lost their gaily painted exteriors and were reduced to gleaming white marbles, limestones, tufo and foundations. Although the ancient city of the imperial period would have been a symphony of bold colors including red, yellow and blue, the modern myth that Rome was a gleaming white city is perpetuated in the Cecil B. De Mille films and in *Roman Scandals*. The myth was also supported by the

The *Roman Scandals* sets made brilliant use of black-and-white design.

It is very difficult to know the precise time in which *Roman Scandals* was intended to be set. The Circus Maximus where the ancient Romans held their chariot races is present but it had a long life—from the Roman republican period or even before—down to late antiquity so it can be of little help in dating the film. The mention of the empress Agrippa is one clue. There was no empress Agrippa but the name Agrippa normally referred to the male best friend and military commander of the Roman emperor Augustus, namely Marcus Vipsanius Agrippa, which would place the film between 31 B.C.E. (when Augustus became the first emperor) and the end of his rule in A.D. 14. However, if the scriptwriters had really intended for the empress to be named Agrippina, the daughter of Agrippa, there would be two possibilities for the date of the film. The names Agrippa and Agrippina are usually found in the later first century B.C. and the first half of the first century A.D.

The first emperors of Rome were known as the Julio-Claudians because of their family tree which consists of intermarriages among two family groups (the Iulii and the Claudii). The early Julio-Claudian emperors were:

Augustus 31 B.C.E.—A.D. 14 (assisted by Marcus Agrippa)
Tiberius A.D. 14-37—Stepson of Augustus
Caligula A.D. 37-41—Elevated to power after Tiberius is killed
Claudius A.D. 41-54—Elevated after Caligula is killed
Nero A.D. 54-68—Elevated after Claudius is poisoned and forced to commit assisted suicide

fact that these were black-and-white films anyway, and adding color to the sets and models would have been of no benefit. In *Roman Scandals*, art director Richard Day enjoyed playing with the two colors—black and white, whether it be for Negro slaves contrasting with white Roman spa girls or contrasting black-and-white sets.

The notion that Rome was made of white buildings was given further credence by the large model of the city put on display in the E.U.R. district of modern Rome first in 1935 during Mussolini's period as dictator. It was built by the archaeologist Italo Gismondi and attempted to show all of Rome in the time of the emperor Constantine in the early 4th century A.D. The model was built on a 1:250 scale and has attracted enormous attention over the years, being added to by Gismondi up to 1971 as new ideas about the appearance of the ancient city came forth. Its principal drawback is having the city appear entirely white. It was used as the basis for the aerial view of Rome used in the modern movie *Gladiator* (2000) but with two unfortunate results. First, once again ancient Rome was shown as entirely white, which it wasn't, and secondly the panorama copies the Gismondi model so faithfully that *Gladiator* affords us a lovely overhead view of the Basilica of Constantine, built in the early 4th century. But since the film was set in approximately A.D. 180 this is completely inappropriate.

Josephus (David Manners), Eddie (Eddie Cantor) and Emperor Valerius (Edward Arnold) shoot craps in *Roman Scandals*.

Agrippina was the sister-in-law, stepdaughter and daughter-in-law to Tiberius, mother of Caligula and sister-in-law to Claudius as well as grandmother of Nero. Agrippina's daughter was Agrippina the Younger who was the great granddaughter of Augustus, adopted granddaughter of Tiberius, sister of Caligula, wife of Claudius and mother of Nero. So if the name Agrippa or Agrippina is supposed to indicate anything in the film, it may mean that we are most likely in the Roman empire of the early-to mid-first century A.D., a time of much political intrigue, danger of poisoning (as suggested in the film) and cruel imprisonments of conquered peoples.

**A disguised Eddie and the captured Briton princess Sylvia display the contrasting black-and-white art direction.**

The capturing of the Briton princess Sylvia is another strong indication of date for there were British queens and royal females who were leading their peoples at this time. One thinks immediately of Boudica of the Iceni and her revolt against the Romans in circa A.D. 60 under the emperor Nero. There was also Cartimandua, Queen of the Brigantes, who was loyal to Rome between A.D. 43 and 69 in her extensive power base in northern England.

The emperor, however, in *Roman Scandals* is not named Caligula or Claudius or Nero but rather Valerius which is a big problem. The Valerii were one of the oldest and most important family lines or *gentes* in Rome (one family line was called a *gens*) but there was no emperor named Valerius and emperors who used the name Valerius within their full names were associated primarily with the later third century A.D. and even the fourth century. There was however a Valeria Messalina, a member of the family, who was the third wife of the em-

**Gloria Stuart and David Manners pose in a chariot during filming of *Roman Scandals*.**

peror Claudius and there were various Valerii who became consuls under Augustus, Tiberius and Claudius but none of them was an emperor.

What can we conclude about the period of time within the Roman empire when *Roman Scandals* was alleged to take place. Most likely we are supposed to be somewhere around the mid-first century A.D. and the screenwriters have left it deliberately garbled figuring that most people going to see the film would have no clue as to who ruled at what time in ancient Rome and those Latin students who did would find the movie funny enough anyway so that they wouldn't care! After all, the slave market sequence is full of phony and senseless Latin inscriptions anyhow.

### ROMAN SCANDALS AND THE MUNICIPAL MUSEUM OF WEST ROME, OKLAHOMA

West Rome, Oklahoma is an unlikely place to have a great art museum but it is intended to show that Mr. Cooper and his cronies, really all crooks, are part of the highbrow members of this rural community. Of course it turns out that Cooper pretends to know all about ancient Rome and its art but it is actually Eddie who really understands the

The influence of Greek and Roman architecture such as the Parthenon can be seen in paintings, museums, buildings and even movies.

past in depth. Eddie is forced to sleep in the museum and hang his laundry on its statues and yet only he appreciates the ancient world more than the pretentious blowhards who attend the opening ceremonies.

In fact, the museum is not really a museum but a cast gallery where copies of great ancient works of art are displayed. Such cast galleries, often referred to as museums, were installed in smaller communities in order to provide inspiration to young artists as examples of good taste. Thus, in this "museum" are images of the Nike or Winged Victory of Samothrace, the Dying Gaul, the Venus de Milo, the Farnese Hercules and the Apollo Belvedere, or, in other words, the most famous examples of classical art that every schoolkid studied.

Artists copied the attitudes and proportions and idealism of these figures and produced their own allegories and variations on classical themes. The Chicago Exposition of 1893 was full of such images and the mid and later 19th century Neo-Classical Academic art of such European painters as Henri Gerome, William Adolphe Bouguereau and Sir Lawrence Alma-Tadema held sway over much of Europe and America and continued to be influential even into the early decades of the 20th century.

That this actually occurred across America may be seen from the example of John Pickard (1858-1937), who founded the Department of Art History and Archaeology at the University of Missouri in the small central Missouri town of Columbia. Pickard traveled through Europe in 1895 and 1902 visiting studios that made casts of ancient works of art and sold them. Most of these casts were of famous Greek and Roman works and he exhibited these at the university as a teaching tool for his classes and an inspiration to the younger generation of students learning about the classical world.

In 1933 academic art collections were a valued part of the university art curriculum but by 1940 such collections of casts were considered increasingly old-fashioned in an age that was turning increasingly to more modern styles and the classical tradition was beginning to lose its influence on the art world. At this time the University of Missouri pushed all the casts to one side and hid them behind a curtain where they stayed until they were brought out again in 1960!

The "museum" in *Roman Scandals* is basically constructed to show off the generosity and highbrow qualities of the corrupt bosses of the town, who are only interested in the effect of their construction on the community but know nothing about the subject matter. They are people driven by greed and lacking in souls and it is ironic that only the impoverished Eddie can truly appreciate the quality of the sculpture.

## ROMAN SCANDALS AND
## ROBERT E. SHERWOOD (1896-1955)

Co-author of the story behind *Roman Scandals* Robert Sherwood was a man for all seasons. Founder member of the famed Algonquin Literary Circle (1919-1929), he had also been a hero in WWI and a member of one of America's most distinguished families. The Harvard-educated giant (he was 6'8" tall) was noted for his satirical wit, and in 1926 he authored his own parody of the classical genre, *The Road to Rome*, a successful Broadway play which formed the basis for the 1953 M-G-M musical movie flop *Jupiter's Darling*.

*The Road to Rome* had been an allegorical play, which contained comparisons between America of the Calvin Coolidge Republican administration and Rome of the end of the 3rd century BCE. Despite his wartime heroics, he often used anti-war themes in his works, particularly in his earlier years before the development of Mussolini's Fascism and Hitler's Nazism turned him away from this stance. For the screenplay of *Roman Scandals*, he teamed with another anti-war writer, George S. Kaufman, who had been for years the drama editor of *The New York Times*, a fellow member of the Algonquins and a workaholic author of numerous successful plays and movies, including much work with the Marx Brothers. Kaufman was particularly known for his ability to come up with funny gags and humorous situations.

Sherwood had an intense dislike of over-inflated Cecil B. De Mille spectacles so that bringing great Roman epics down to earth was an enjoyable effort for him. He immediately saw through De Mille's formula of lavish sets, larger than life characters and blatant sex and was delighted to poke fun at it.

With two anti-war writers working on the story and a director, Frank Tuttle, who was a member of the Communist party, the film should have contained a stronger anti-war message. But Eddie Cantor was at his height in creative control at this point and was more interested in a box-office hit than in a political message film. He was also eager to support the New Deal and the ideas of Franklin Roosevelt. Thus, although the vaudeville gags suggest Kaufman and the overall thematic structure of corruption in high places suggests Sherwood, and the production numbers reflect the inventiveness and sexual fascination of Busby Berkeley, the focus was that Eddie Cantor wanted screenwriters who would deliver fun for the general depressed public. Therefore, Sherwood and Kaufmann left the project quickly as they found themselves losing creative control. *Roman Scandals* is therefore Eddie Cantor's production and he and his colleagues have created escapist fun for us all to enjoy!

RELATED READING FOR THIS SECTION:
Allen, Frederick Lewis, *Only Yesterday* ( Harper & Row, 1964)
Allen, Frederick Lewis, *Since Yesterday* (Harper & Row, 1968)
Arwas, Victor, *Art Deco* (Harold Abrams, 1992)
Badger, Anthony J. *The New Deal: The Depression Years 1933-1940* (Ivan Dee, 2002)
Barsacq, Leon, *Caligari's Cabinet and Other Grand Illusions* (New American Library, 1976)
Battersby, Martin, *The Decorative 1930s* (Collier, 1971)
Cullen, Frank, *Vaudeville Old & New*, Vols. 1 and 2 (Routledge, 2007)
Goldman, Herbert G., *Banjo Eyes* (Oxford, 1997)
Greif, Martin, *Depression Modern* (Universe, 1977)
Leuchtenberg, William E., *Franklin D. Roosevelt and the New Deal: 1932-1940* (Harper Perennial, 2009)
Terry, Jim and Tony Thomas, *The Busby Berkeley Book* (A & W, 1973)

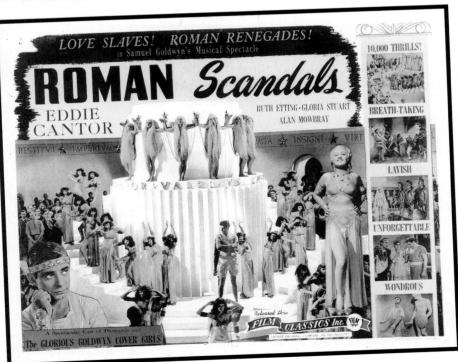

In 1998 I had the pleasure of privately dining with the famous film editor and Academy Award-winning director Robert Wise and his wife Millicent here at the University of Arizona. Wise had come to speak to my film class about his films including *The Day the Earth Stood Still* (1951) and *West Side Story* (1961) and to receive a Lifetime Achievement Award from the U of A. Valuing his opinion, I took advantage of the moment to ask him about one of my favorite directors: Dorothy Arzner. "What did you think of her work?" I asked, hopefully, "Because you edited one of her most important films, *Dance, Girl, Dance*." "She was a hack," he said, "who never did anything very interesting."

Consulting Professor Marjorie Rosen's book *Popcorn Venus*, a widely acclaimed 1973 study of women in the cinema, I was hoping for a better evaluation there. She had this to say about the early screen's most successful female director:

> Arzner, the total professional, perhaps rarely went out on an innovative limb, but she never botched a film, lost her

**Dorothy Arzner directs *Dance, Girl Dance*.**

Cast: Katharine Hepburn (Lady Cynthia Darrington); Colin Clive (Sir Christopher Strong); Billie Burke (Lady Elaine Strong); Helen Chandler (Monica Strong); Ralph Forbes (Harry Rawlinson); Irene Browne (Carrie Valentine); Jack La Rue (Carlo); Desmond Roberts (Bryce Mercer)

Credits: RKO Radio Pictures; Producer: David O. Selznick; Associate Producer: Pandro S. Berman; Screenplay: Zoe Akins; Based on a Novel by Gilbert Frankau; Directed by Dorothy Arzner; Music: Roy Webb; Musical Director: Max Steiner; Cinematography: Bert Glennon; Editor: Arthur Roberts; Set Decorators; Charles Kirk, Van Nest Polglase; Costumes: Howard Greer, Walter Plunkett; Black and White; Mono; 9 Reels; 78 Minutes; Filmed December 21, 1932-February 3, 1933; Premiere New York City, March 3, 1933; Wide U.S. Release March 31, 1933

temper with colleagues and could always be counted on a for a clever and sleekly competent package...If the body of Arzner's work reveals little of an avant-garde or elevated consciousness that might have helped divest the screen's mythology of its potency, perhaps it was because she was a product of American society and was also required to conform within the studio system.

Could it be that both these learned individuals are dead wrong? Even the great critic Andrew Sarris thought her to be of little consequence.

In the early 1970s Dorothy Arzner was rediscovered by the American feminist movement and became something of a *cause celebre*, largely on the basis of her best-remembered films *Dance, Girl, Dance* (1940),

*Christopher Strong* and *The Wild Party* (1929). A 1994 book by Judith Mayne re-evaluated her further and dealt with Arzner's lesbianism in her private life and how it may have come through in her films. Virtually all the serious literature written about her has focused on the feminist aspects of her films. The idea that Arzner's films are "different" because she was a woman and brought a unique perspective to male dominated Hollywood is unquestionably valid. Dorothy herself wrote in 1937:

> The story of life is a woman's story.... The men of course are participants in the action of this great stage, but, reduced to their fundamentals, the motivating forces of nearly every human act are feminine inspired.

Twenty-three years ago I met Sally Sumner, a documentary filmmaker in Tucson, Arizona whose family had been extremely close to Dorothy Arzner. "Aunt Dorothy" had been a major influence on her young life and Sally's mother "Bunny," grandmother Mildred ("Mimi") and Dorothy were all good friends. So influential were Dorothy's long talks with her that Sally became inspired to become a filmmaker herself, a profession which she accomplishes successfully to this day, running her own business known as Firehouse Productions. Sally was able to provide valuable insights about her "aunt" and, to my amazement, retained in her possession a remarkable document given to her by her mother—a rough draft of a previously unknown autobiography begun but never finished by Dorothy Arzner. It covers the years from her birth to her entry into the film business with William De Mille as one of his scenario typists.

The document was given by Dorothy in 1955 to Sally's mother to look over and comment upon. The document, used with Sally's permission here, tells us about Dorothy's early life and is appended to this article. This partial autobiography was not found at UCLA in the Dorothy Arzner archive with Dorothy's scrapbooks and collected memorabilia and therefore appears to be an important new piece of information in the Dorothy Arzner story. It seems that Dorothy began it soon after her move to the desert community of La Quinta and then abandoned it during that period of her life when there seemed to be little interest in her work.

But in 1973, as the feminist movement was becoming increasingly important in America, Dorothy Arzner was rediscovered, and in 1975 she was honored by the Directors Guild of America with a retrospective. She was deemed important because she was the only woman filmmaker generating a significant major studio output from the later 1920s to the early 1940s, spanning the entire 1930s. And film historians such as Claire Johnston found unique qualities in her film work:

> The central female protagonists react against and thus transgress the male discourse which entraps them....These women do not sweep aside the existing order and found a new female order of language. Rather, they assert their own discourse in the face of the male one, by breaking it up, subverting it, and in a sense, rewriting it.

Each person who approaches significant works tends to bring to them an understanding based on his or her own experiences and knowledge, and Ms. Johnston's arguments do indeed reveal much about her own perspective on a male dominated profession and the kindred spirit she felt with Dorothy. Certainly, there is much evidence of role reversal in Dorothy's films and her women dare to be real individuals and can outsmart men and do most jobs just as well or even better than their male counterparts. The early feminist essays on Dorothy raise important points about the women in her films. For example some of them over-identify with the male universe because that's the universe that is in charge and so they try to emulate it. It is also true that the men in Dorothy Arzner films are more often than not peripheral, marginalized or just plain loopy characters, who think more with their private parts than with their brains, while the women really run just about everything important that is going on.

Pam Cook, another important early critic and one of Arzner's rediscoverers, offers ways of "Approaching the Work of Dorothy Arzner" but feels that "we are looking at a body of work produced within the constraints of a studio system heavily determined by economic and ideological factors....Our object will be to define some strategies for a critique of patriarchal ideology in general." She adds that: "Patriarchal ideology refers to the patriarchal laws which govern our society and which produce contradictions...." Cook, it seems, dismisses Arzner as an *auteur* because of the constraints of the studio system and reduces her work to what it can reveal under scrutiny from a feminist perspective.

What concerns me about viewing her work through only a feminist prism, important as that is to do, is the fact that none of the articles or biographies written about

Arzner seems to recognize her as a cinematic *auteur* in the old-fashioned sense that film critic Andrew Sarris used to talk about. When I read the feminist discussions of Arzner's films, I wondered if she was intending to do only what the feminist critics had said she was doing in her films or if she had other ideas in mind. The assessment of *Christopher Strong* that I offer will attempt to make the *auteur* claim for Dorothy Arzner and to point out some elements that the reviewers and biographers seem, at least to me, to have overlooked in her work.

That Arzner performed her artistry within an imposed Hollywood studio system makes her accomplishments the more remarkable to me. Her little network of principally female conspirators, Zoe Akins principal among them, concocted complex, unique films that were not completely understood in their own time by the critics or general public and still are not today, but these films sold tickets at the box office, that most important fact which allowed Arzner to keep working fairly consistently at the top of a man's profession. Was Dorothy Arzner an early feminist and was she seeking only to make feminist movies or were there other influences in her life that drove her? What did she think about, admire, study and pursue? What was her view of life? Are we currently assigning too much of a role to the feminist-related aspects of her films and too little to other forces that inspired her? Shouldn't these "other" forces, if findable, be taken into consideration also as we try to find out who this mysterious, private and complex woman was and assess her motivations and her work? But let's not get ahead of ourselves.

**Zoe Akins**

### EARLY LIFE

Dorothy Arzner (born January 3, 1896 or 1897–died October 1, 1979) was born in San Francisco. Her birth date was said by her to be 1900 but has been disputed by film scholars and is usually placed at 1897. However, recently unearthed documents from one of her close friends suggests she may have been born as early as 1896 and confirms that the date was definitely either 1896 or 1897. Arzner's birth records were destroyed in the 1906 San Francisco earthquake, so she can be forgiven for making

herself appear younger in her own autobiography. As the innocent victim of a broken marriage, little Arzner coped bravely with a hard-working father, who both wanted her and yet shunted her about from place to place, and a stepmother who didn't want her around at all. She spent her pre-teen years largely on the move, hardly lasting any place long and eventually moving to Los Angeles where her father opened a café sometime after the 1906 San Francisco earthquake next to "The Grand Opera House," one of the oldest theatres in Los Angeles, located at First and Main Streets.

The theater, built by local developer Ozro W. Childs, was at one time the largest theater in Los Angeles and featured operas, plays and musical performances, even showcasing Edwin Booth in 1887. In 1894 it had become the Los Angeles home of the famous Orpheum Vaudeville Circuit and continued as such until 1903. The theater district began to shift to the south and west in Los Angeles but the theater continued successfully until 1910 by which time it was used primarily as a movie house even though on July 6, 1896, the Grand had been used experimentally for the first commercial exhibition of movies in Los Angeles. The projectionist of the Edison Studio films was Billy Porter, who later became pioneering director William S. Porter, who made *The Great Train Robbery*.

The restaurant connected to the theater provided ample employment for Arzner's father but kept him horribly busy. Her father took up with another woman, allegedly after infidelity by her real mother, and this broke up Arzner's home. Her parents divorced when Arzner was still a child, perhaps around the age of five or six, and she never saw her mother again, because her father, in the midst of the acrimonious breakup, left orders to bar the natural mother from access to her child because she was said to be a tramp. Despite repeated and near desperate attempts to find Arzner, her mother never succeeded and was blacklisted within the family as a woman of poor moral values but the truth or falsity of that accusation is still uncertain.

Arzner and her older brother grew up being sent from relative to relative while her busy father ran several successful restaurants and became fairly wealthy. Sent to live with her aunt and uncle, she was dominated by her older cousin, a girl who resented her moving in and competed with her for family attention. Forced to spend a great deal of time alone because of the acrimonious relationship with her stepmother, she became bookish, introverted and yet extraordinarily athletic, and developed a love of art history, architecture and ancient Greek and Roman civilization, which was later crystallized and developed in the Westlake School for young ladies in Los Angeles where she was able to take four semesters of Latin and study art history.

Westlake was to become a formative influence on young Dorothy Arzner. It was founded as a private, moneymaking enterprise in 1904 by two friends and Stanford graduates Frederica de Laguna and Jessica Smith Vance. It was unusual for ladies to invest and create a business enterprise and the small school they founded occupied just two buildings initially but soon caught on and expanded.

The Westlake School for Girls on Sixth Street and Alvarado Street, was named for its location near Westlake Park in Los Angeles, now known as MacArthur Park. Both founder women dreamed of providing opportunities for young ladies to advance themselves and gain a sophisticated education. More than a finishing school, Westlake was designed to help young women get the skills they needed to go to a fine college and even have careers of importance. Miss de Laguna had received an M.A. degree at Columbia University and had become a professor of English Literature at the University of Southern California, which was an unusual achievement for a woman in this period. Her friend Miss Vance had taken her own M.A. at Stanford, then taught at Mills College in Oakland and gone on to become an Assistant Professor in English at Stanford. Finally, Miss Vance, trained in Greek and Latin studies, became a Professor of Classical Greek and Roman Philology and Literature at U.S.C.; she was always eager to spread the joys of the Classics to a wider audience because she felt that Classics and the study of ancient

**Westlake School for Girls, 1928**

Greek and Latin was helpful for clarity of thought and understanding the origins of English language words. Miss Vance enjoyed teaching great works of literature including the Latin poetry of Virgil and Horace and, especially, the Greek tragedies of Aeschylus, Sophocles and Euripides, playwrights of the golden age of ancient Athens in the fifth century BCE.

The two women operated Westlake as a women's college preparatory school from its inception, with de Laguna as the principal, until their deaths: de Laguna in 1942 and Vance in 1939. During that time these two women remained devoted to the concept of educating young women to become a creative force in society. Wasting no time, the two applied immediately for accreditation for their prep school and young ladies were being readied for U.S.C. Soon after, Stanford accepted Westlake girls as well. This was followed by accreditation with all of the major East Coast schools and Westlake became a major force that helped young women of good families stand out when it came time to be admitted to a major college.

Starting with the two small buildings, Westlake quickly increased to six and suffered growing pains that eventually required major expansion and moving to a new location, but Misses de Laguna and Vance presided over all of this with a combination of calmness and determination, ever mindful of their objectives and always willing to give extra time to special students. When Arzner attended Westlake, she was a fish out of water. Despite her father's wealth, she had been raised largely on the wrong side of the tracks, suffering abuse, indifference and even attempted rape. A rebellious tomboy, who had learned to take care of herself, she was a combination of introvert and rebel. She had difficulty fitting in and lacked the social graces of the other girls such as which fork to use and when (she later expressed this awkwardness through Joan Crawford in her film *The Bride Wore Red*) and although her father had the money from his restaurant business to pay for her schooling, she was light years apart from the society girls she was expected to pay homage to when she arrived. The result was an explosion, which led to Arzner's ostracism from the Westlake group and even to such hostility that she was attacked by a gang of upper class girls there and forced to fight for her life.

Arzner managed to stick it out largely because she was befriended by Sally Sumner's great grandmother, who lived nearby and helped her to adjust to Westlake. In addition, the two founder ladies, who were also teachers, not only helped Arzner to adjust but also singled her out for special encouragement, often offering the enterprising young Arzner extra sessions with them whereby she did readings and tutorials in classical Greek and Roman literature and in the arts. Arzner became particularly sensitive to art and architecture. She began to think of living in a palace herself, but one which would combine modern architecture with the stately elegance of mansions she remembered as a child in San Francisco. This strong sense of visual environment and architecture, learned from Miss de Laguna, and the reverence for the ancient Greeks which came from Miss Vance, would remain major influences on Arzner's life and she would often speak of her mentors reverentially as they continued their efforts for the young women of California over many years.

Miss Vance and Miss de Laguna moved Westlake to a larger site on Westmoreland Avenue in 1917 and by 1927 the two ladies had realized so much money that they were able to buy land from real estate developer Harold Janss on North Faring Road and the school became a key inspiration for the development of the Holmby Hills area into a fashionable location with wealthy people in the area desirous of sending their daughters to this fine school. Arzner began to feel that she too could realize her dreams in life. Her escapist readings of the Horatio Alger stories while a child and her learning about art and the ancient world at Westlake fueled a desire for excitement and adventure while her mentors kept assuring her that all things were possible for special people, even if they were female. Surrounded by strong women as mentors, Arzner began to see her way out of her humble childhood life and began to set goals and focus herself although she was unsure whether to follow her love of the arts or medicine, for she had a long standing ambition "to help raise the dead as Jesus did with Lazarus" and becoming a doctor seemed the best route to accomplish that.

Throughout her life the Westlake connection would remain a strong influence on Arzner and particularly important were the lessons from Miss Vance about art and the classical ideal. In later years when Arzner was advising young people such as Sally Sumner interested in going into the film business she would remind them to look at the Classics:

> There are only a few basic stories and themes and the ancient Greeks knew about these and presented them so it is how these stories are told that is important, not that you are telling anything new. Ancient Greek ideas are very important. Pay attention to Greek tragedy and the classics.

Dorothy Arzner and Joan Crawford stop for a coffee break while filming *The Bride Wore Red*.

Now in her middle teens, Arzner coveted and appreciated her warm relationship with Sally Sumner's great grandmother Pearl, who all but adopted the young girl and made her a part of her family, creating a closeness Arzner would treasure until her dying day, especially because it contrasted with the meanness of the Westlake society clique that insisted that Arzner be a victim of their extensive hazing of new students. Grandma Pearl's daughter Mildred, known as Mimi, also went to Westlake but was about two years younger than Arzner, according to family records. Mildred and Arzner had much in common and became close friends as well, both being strongly adventurous and focused women who wanted everything out of life that they could get. Yet each had a quiet nature in public and both enjoyed the simple pleasures of gardening. When the automobile was developed and introduced commercially, Mimi was 12 years old and since there was no Department of Motor Vehicles, she was allowed to become the first woman to own and drive a car in Los Angeles! A photo of her standing proudly by it still exists.

Mildred Strong Rivers Atwood Demott, known as Mimi to her friends, was born on April 9, 1898 and the significantly older Arzner may actually have been born on January 3, 1896 since the family is insistent that Arzner was two years older than Mimi. Mimi's first of three marriages took place in 1916 with Dorothy Arzner as a bridesmaid so that she would have been 20 years old or possibly 19. The marriage did not last but Mimi and Grandma Pearl and Arzner remained friends over the years even through all of Mimi's marriages and divorces. Henry Rivers, the first husband, was an entrepreneur of a good family, which owned real estate and numerous business enterprises, at least until 1929, so that Mimi was able to enjoy the good life until it was learned that husband Henry's brother Frank had had $300,000 stolen by his office manager and Frank got cited for tax invasion. Frank and Henry were forced to pay taxes on income they no longer had, the stock market crashed, and they quickly lost their commercial real estate holdings in downtown Los Angeles and Van Nuys, and the family castle/mansion that Mimi delighted to live in was also taken. Mimi did not stick by her man but rather headed for a three month occupancy of Reno and divorced Henry right away. Mimi was a quietly forceful woman and part of that Westlake group that was not going to settle for an ordinary life or be content to be without substantial funds. As far as she was concerned her man had failed her and his obligation to give her a proper lifestyle to which she was entitled was not met. This was not the way women were traditionally taught to think in America at the time but Mimi did not intend to live her life as an ordinary woman.

It was while Arzner was in her teens in the later 1910s that she began to realize that she was "different" from many of the other girls not just in her uncommon intelligence but also in the fact that she was not interested in the romantic company of boys, and finally realized that she was a lesbian although, after her horrifying experiences as a child, she always remained quiet about her sexuality and did not talk about it often with family members who usually described her as a "celibate person." It was sometimes said however that Arzner was interested in the flamboyant film director James Cruze with whom she

was to work later on and whether she was bi-sexual or a lesbian may never be known.

Arzner never talked frankly about her sexuality but did discuss being attacked by a man when she was a child and being confused about the morals of her actual mother, who was branded as a tramp by the family. In her childhood she had always admired male literary heroes such as found in the Alger stories, acted as a tomboy, loved sports and preferred to dress as a boy so much that her family began to worry about her not being "normal" or what today we would say is dressing "butch," to use the terminology often present in lesbian literature. Rejected and treated callously and cruelly by her stepmother and physically restrained from seeing her natural mother, Arzner was also traumatized by her parental relationships. She adored her father but he refused to do more than provide money for her and see her occasionally, since he was influenced by his new wife, who felt Arzner was an inconvenience. And yet this stepmother was another of those powerful women who dominated their male partners and kept the principal control in their relationships, a theme which recurs in most Arzner films in which the men are weak or peripheral to the dominant females. Arzner told of one occasion when her stepmother forcibly dragged her along over a long extent of ground in order to deny her what she wanted to do. Family members have noted that Dorothy was:

> Crazy about her dad. Just adored him, although he actually abandoned her much of the time and kept her distant through her entire youth so he could live with her stepmother, who couldn't stand her.

Arzner did manage to spend a good deal of time around her father's restaurant but she was never able to stay in the presence of her stepmother for very long without trouble ensuing.

Winding up her Westlake years, Arzner needed to think about her profession. Having been deeply affected by the death of the baby of two of her older friends in her neighborhood, she decided to become a healer "like Jesus," entering a religious transformation which persisted throughout her life. This led her to begin a career in medicine at the USC Medical School. Hearing the dreadful accounts of World War I and the appeals from President Woodrow Wilson in March of 1917 to young people to help their country, she decided to serve during WWI as an ambulance driver in California with a corps similar to the Red Cross. Upon completion of her "military" duty

The cast and crew of *The Squaw Man*, including C.B. DeMille pose on the Paramount lot 1913. (Photofest)

which never saw her sent overseas to high adventure as she had hoped, she needed to find something to do with her life and used her service connections to get a job as a scenario typist for William De Mille (1878-1955), the older brother of the renowned movie director Cecil B. De Mille. In 1914 Cecil had made a hit with the silent movie *The Squaw Man* and had helped to create the southern California movie business. William's little daughter would become the famed choreographer Agnes De Mille.

With William and Cecil around her, Arzner was able to witness the growth of the Hollywood movie system from its infancy into a rapidly expanding empire that developed from the Lasky Picture Company to Famous Players Lasky when movie theater ownership and distribution was added into the mix. Ultimately this consortium led to Paramount Pictures.

William De Mille was the son of a lay Episcopal minister who had entered the entertainment field as a playwright and who had in 1915 followed his almost uncontrollable and adventurous younger brother Cecil out to California to become a screenwriter and director. It was a case of being in the right place at the right time for 19-year-old Arzner, who quickly became the most efficient assistant De Mille had at the Famous Players Lasky company, learning to be a script clerk (even though she couldn't type very well), then a cutter and finally an editor of 52 silent films. Having witnessed the arrogant young Cecil De Mille in all his pretentious and authoritarian glory, she quickly decided that being a director was what she wanted to do. That women rarely had achieved such status in the nascent movie business didn't deter her as she kept working her way up until she got her chance through her sheer brilliance, perseverance and competence.

By 1922 at age 25 she had learned a great deal about the fast growing business of movies from Mr. De Mille and went to work as an editor for Fred Niblo, considered one of the very best of the silent film directors. Her editing of the bullfight scene of *Blood and Sand* left audiences wondering if Rudolph Valentino really had braved the bullring as a matador or if they were watching clever editing. She then went on to work for James Cruze (1884-1942), another of Hollywood's early great directors, doing important work for his 1923 classic *The Covered Wagon*, an epic western filmed on location in Utah. Cruze claimed to be half or quarter Ute Indian and insisted that his maternal grandmother was burned at the stake for giving birth to twins. He also said he had 17 siblings but nobody could tell if half of what he said was true as he was as much con man as craftsman and much of the time 100% alcoholic which left Arzner forced to save the day periodically by filming some of his scenes while he was

AWOL. She also continued to work for him on another celebrated epic of the time known as *Old Ironsides*.

James Cruze lived life on the wild side. He fathered an out of wedlock child with beautiful silent film actress Marguerite Snow, then married her in 1913, but he had divorced in 1922 just before Arzner went to work for him. Despite his bad reputation, Dorothy Arzner spoke for years and years about how much she loved "Jimmy" as she called him, and some family members even felt that Arzner might have been willing to become Mrs. Cruze had the situation presented itself. He was certainly the male love of her life and he spent considerable time showing her how to behave (and not to behave!) as a director, how to write for the screen and how to edit. He also taught her to observe detail and atmosphere and, when he was focused and sober, he could direct epic pictures as well as De Mille. He was a man of unquestionable vision, a fascination with history and a flair for directing action that made him the highest paid director in Hollywood, rivaling and perhaps exceeding De Mille and D.W. Griffith for a time and making $6,000 per week. In 1926 he was named one of the 10 most important directors in Hollywood. Films such as *Old Ironsides, The Old Homestead, Merton of the Movies, Ruggles of Red Gap* and others kept him in high demand in the 1920s.

But he was also pursued by his own demons, particularly his fondness for the opposite sex and his love of the bottle. In 1925 he married silent film star Betty Compson but this reportedly only led to constant battling, infidelities and bouts of wild partying. Still, the Cruze association was a spur to Arzner's career that helped her reach the goals she had set for herself. Cruze guided her in dealing with the studio, sticking up for herself, and gaining self confidence about her own talent. Arzner also learned from him what not to do since he was always in trouble. Without her, Cruze went into a slow decline, making some strong films and some not very good films. On June 14, 1929,

Dorothy Arzner's editing of the bullfight scene in *Blood and Sand* convinced audiences that Rudolph Valentino was in the bullring.

he was forced to go to court to explain why during the filming of *Old Ironsides* one man was killed and several others were injured during a scene near Catalina Island involving the use of dynamite. In his quest for period authenticity and atmosphere, Cruze considered humans expendable. Although he escaped the law numerous times, debts piled up, accompanied by chronic alcoholism, and led to the demise of this talented Bohemian.

Meanwhile, by 1927 Arzner was gaining a reputation at Paramount as a knowledgeable and highly skilled editor who might be expected eventually to direct but who was limited by being a woman. She had hoped to get her chance, which came when Paramount was seeking someone to put across a series of women's pictures to attract a particular audience and Arzner had threatened to jump to Columbia which was a much inferior poverty row company known derogatorily as "Columbia, the germ of the ocean." Its president Harry Cohn was dead set on getting her to work for him. Paramount executives had to think about what to do with a woman of her talent, but at this time there were no other major women directors in Hollywood. In the early years of the century there had been the French woman Alice Guy who had successfully directed for the pre-Hollywood Solax Company in Flushing, New York.

In the earliest days of film, with the craft of filmmaking in its infancy and not yet big business, women had more opportunities to direct and produce. Lois Weber was a writer, actress and director who had her own production company and was the first woman to direct a feature, *The Merchant of Venice* (1914). Marion Leonard, actress and writer, appeared in over 190 silent shorts, Florence Turner was an actress and writer who formed her own production company and produced over 30 short films, and in 1915 was the top box-office star in America. Cleo Madison, actress, director and producer, was so successful that she worked herself into a nervous breakdown in 1922. The list of women creating silent films is surprisingly long. It included Ida May Park writer and director of over 50 silent films;, Ruth Ann Baldwin, writer and director at Universal; Florence Lawrence, an actress who appeared in over 290 silent films and started her own production company; Ruth Stonehouse, actress, director, writer, who made more than 179 silent films; Lule Warrenton, an actress, director and producer, who formed her own production company; and serial queen Grace Cunard, an actress, writer and director of over 180 films from 1910 through 1946, although by 1929 she was doing bit parts and little writing. These were just some of the women writing, starring in, editing, or directing movies. What happened to Hollywood equal opportunity when it started out so promising? After WWI movies became a global commodity, which caught the attention of Wall Street bankers and investors, who began to control the studios and the studios controlled the theaters. Independent production companies were forced out and big studios began to take over Hollywood. There was no room for women behind the camera in the new unequal opportunity Hollywood. Dorothy Arzner was the only major woman filmmaker left standing by the later 1920s.

In March 2010 Kathryn Bigelow became the first woman to win the Academy Award for Best Director for her film *The Hurt Locker*, which also took home the Oscar for Best Picture. Bigelow's achievement would not have been possible without all those women who paved the way for her.

Still, in 1926, Dorothy Arzner was a long shot to direct for a major studio. Eventually, it was thought that as a woman she might know best what would appeal to women and make them buy tickets to see fashions on parade along with a competent story. This led to her first directorial job on the silent *Fashions for Women* (1927)." The film was successful and a career was born.

## DOROTHY ARZNER AND MARION MORGAN

On the set of this picture Arzner found a woman who would become her partner for life and with whom she would share ownership in a beautiful home in the Hollywood hills—Marion Morgan. Morgan had been a professional dancer in vaudeville shows and was another one of the many strong entrepreneurial women who surrounded Arzner in her late teen and early adult years. Morgan was also motivated by ancient Greek and Roman classical themes. She had successfully organized and funded her own performance troupe and as early as 1916 was using dance to create high performance art which was, in the words of Judith Mayne, "based on themes from classical legend and antiquity."

Morgan was influenced by a strong movement of the time that had been developing simultaneously in America and Europe to get away from traditional dancing poses and to use dance in a more modern, free, interpretive and dramatic manner. Despite this modernity, a great inspiration for Morgan came from the world of ancient Greek myth. In this she was reflecting the influence of dance theorists such as Isadora Duncan, who donned Grecian tunics and staged programs inspired by Greek myth, attempt-

Arzner's silent *Fashions for Women* has unfortunately been lost.

**Classical Greek and Roman themes can be seen in this 1922 photo of the Marion Morgan Dancers.**

**Dorothy Arzner and Marion Morgan pose together in a 1927 photograph by Arnold Genthe.**

**Isadora Duncan**

ing to embrace nature-inspired movements rather than imposed traditional balletic steps. This school of thought became widespread by 1913 when the Theatre des Champs-Elysees in Paris was built and its sculptor Antoine Bourdelle carved the image of Isadora Duncan in relief over the entrance. She also appeared among images of the nine Greek muses painted by Maurice Denis inside the theatre.

Isadora herself was a San Franciscan, the same as Dorothy Arzner, and the dancer had followed her dreams and moved to France where she taught and spread her ideas. She was also a lesbian who was not afraid to "come out" and had numerous affairs which were gossiped about in artistic circles but seldom written about in mainstream American media or discussed in polite company. Isadora traveled the world and became a role model for Morgan and Arzner, and even moved to Russia at one point in the 1920s. She was hugely influential on American dance in the 1920s and Marion Morgan was a disciple who harbored her own classical inspirations and love of nature to explore as she developed her own dance troupe performing in vaudeville between 1916 and 1925.

For example, Morgan's *Attila the Hun* celebrated the barbarian invader who brought ancient Roman civilization to its knees just after the mid-fifth century A.D. Inspired by the marbled look of ancient Greek sculptures and Roman copies of them, as well as images of the famous marble Nike with clinging, nearly transparent carved drapery, who was shown adjusting her sandal from the

balustrade of the Temple of Athena and Nike on the acropolis (or high city) of ancient Athens, Morgan chose her dancers carefully and dressed them accordingly. One contemporary described the dancers in Morgan's troupes in this manner:

> The bared limbs of the dancers look as if modeled in marble, while the fluttering diaphanous draperies float gracefully around them.

Morgan presented Greek, Interpretive, Egyptian, Oriental and Dramatic dancing and soon became busy in Hollywood choreographing exotic movie dance sequences, which eventually led to her collaboration with Arzner. For the very successful silent film *Don Juan* in 1926, featuring John Barrymore and Mary Astor, Morgan created a "Bacchanalian Revel," celebrating the God of nature and wine in Greek antiquity, a divinity given over to ecstatic celebrations by his female followers, the maenads. In the same year Morgan did a follow-up Moorish Bacchanalian orgy for *A Night of Love*. Morgan then caused a sensation in 1928 by creating the sequence of women dancing in the sky for the Nancy Carroll vehicle *Manhattan Cocktail*. The film opened with a classical Greek prologue offering the tale of Theseus, the hero and king of Athens, and Ariadne his beloved. Theseus went from Athens to the island of Crete to rescue Athenian maidens, who were being held in a maze at the imperial palace and sacrificed to a bull-headed monster known as the Minotaur. Ariadne offered a thread on a spindle for Theseus to unravel to keep track of how to

get out of the maze after he killed the bull creature. The dance was intended as an allegory for Fred (played by Richard Arlen) and Babs (Nancy Carroll), who are trapped in the maze and Broadway stood for the Minotaur as it entrapped and ensnared the young hopefuls.

Morgan felt strongly that film was art and should be used to achieve a higher plane of consciousness, a second level of meaning that would inspire the viewer. Arzner found her stimulating, sophisticated and fascinating and they shared a love of art and the classical ideal. In a 1935 postcard from Vienna, just a few years after the release of *Christopher Strong* and before Arzner was preparing to make the highly classical *Craig's Wife*, Morgan sent Arzner a postcard from Vienna stating:

> Nothing matters to me now except a raising of consciousness, a gigantic task when one has the human mind to deal with, not only one's own but the onslaught of contacting minds… To give me peace keep up the mental work. It will somehow lead to harmony. We both have a path to travel. I still love you. Marion.

As is evident from the letter, Morgan, with her insistence on art to reveal a higher plain, which can be used for raising consciousness, became one of Arzner's principal consultants in the assembling of her films, so theirs was initially not only a romantic but a collaborative artistic relationship as Morgan had a strong sense of visuals that was particularly suited to cinema. They decided to move in together and build a dream home, which led Arzner to withdraw all of her money from the stock market just months before the crash. They set up house in 1930, staying together more than 40 years until the end of Morgan's life. The timing of Arzner's withdrawal saved her life

savings and left her well off for the rest of her life.

Dancer and creative consultant Marion Morgan surrounded herself with artistic friends and had a strong and many said arrogant and domineering personality. One of the reasons many of Arzner's friends stayed away from her after her film days was because she was so often at home with Morgan who, they said, was always shooshing Arzner and humiliating her in public. Morgan was accused by Arzner's friends of putting on airs and controlling and planning most aspects of Arzner's life. Speculation persists as to whether this relationship flourished because of love, or fear of loneliness on Arzner's part, or both. After Morgan died in 1971 Arzner became quite lonely and her rediscovery in 1973 helped to comfort her in her later years.

**Marion Morgan (c. 1920s)**

But the Dorothy Arzner of the later 1920s was a study in complexities. In public she was shy and introverted due in a large measure to her horrendous childhood and her feeling of being raised without social graces. Whenever there was a group of people, especially those she didn't know, she tended to be quiet and could depend on Morgan. She was very intelligent and dignified but never could spell or do punctuation so that she always felt inferior to those who could. She had strong ambition and belief in herself because of her training in the Westlake School and the strong women who had entered her life but she had been beaten down and made insecure by uncaring women, male predators and abandonment by her father. Quiet and lonely by herself, she came to life on the movie set where she could hide behind her role as THE director. She could become Cecil B. De Mille and attempt to mold everything to the meticulous vision of the film universe she was creating, a parallel world into which she could put her life experiences and exorcise them. When comfortable with what she knew, she could be dominant. When on her own in the real world of the everyday she was less secure and greatly dependent on Morgan.

Her complex personality would manifest itself when she would be part of a crowd. If people she did not know were involved she spoke little until she was comfortable. In a restaurant, because she had grown up in this environment, she was at home and would often send the food back with sharp criticism. Comfort and competence meant control.

In her first films Arzner struggled to find her style as she was following the basic guidelines laid out by her studio, but gradually her lifelong personal interests began to come through and this led to the production of some remarkable and unique films. Along the way, Arzner became one of the top-10 directors in Hollywood, someone considered so good that Harry Cohn, president of Columbia Pictures, is reported to have followed her home begging her to work for him. She is credited with inventing the concept of the movable microphone to enhance the movement and sound reproduction of the actors in talking pictures. She became the first woman to direct a major talking picture and the first to sustain a career in Hollywood as a director. She was the first woman admitted to the Director's Guild of America. She was the first major independent female director of talking pictures. She made Rosalind Russell popular, promoted the careers of Katharine Hepburn and Fredric March and gave Lucille Ball one of her first significant roles. She even became the first woman to be a scenarist and editor on a widescreen movie—*Old Ironsides* (1926).

Arzner's work was overlooked and marginalized for years and she has only recently been appreciated as a wonderful filmmaker and also as the teacher of Francis Ford Coppola. As we have seen, her work is primarily saluted by feminist critics but often apologized for by some of them because she was a part of the studio system. So is there an Arzner Dialectic? Can one take themes and apply them across the board to a series of Arzner films as one can with an Alfred Hitchcock or Howard Hawks or a Fritz Lang? I would submit that it is possible to lay out a number of basic tenets that went into most, if not all, of Arzner's mature period films. And one valuable hint comes from a remark that she made to her neighbor's little daughter Sally Sumner back in late 1950s Los Angeles:

All of my films are Greek tragedies.

A glance at Arzner's major works suggests there is more than just a little truth to the above, so digging up a little ancient history here will prove instructive for establishing my thesis.

# A LITTLE BIT ABOUT
# ANCIENT GREEK TRAGEDY

The Greek tragedy as a dramatic form grew up in ancient Athens during the sixth and early-fifth centuries B.C.E., reaching full development in the fifth century with the works of such playwrights as Aeschylus, Sophocles and Euripides. Sophocles' *Antigone*, written ca. 442 B.C.E., is a good example of a fully developed Greek tragedy. Oedipus is the king of Thebes in Boeotia, Greece and he has two sons named Eteocles and Polynices. Oedipus' family or "house" is cursed because his royal ancestor Laius was a kidnapper. A prophecy from the great oracle of Delphi said that Laius would produce a son who would kill his father and marry his own mother.

So Laius, not wanting this prophecy to come true, but not wanting to kill his son directly, pierced the boy's feet when he was three days old and exposed him on a mountaintop. A shepherd from the nearby town of Corinth discovered the boy and gave him his name Oedipus, which means "swollen foot." As the boy Oedipus grew to manhood he encountered a stranger on the road to Thebes, argued with him and killed him. And that man was his own father, Laius, the king of Thebes.

Along this same journey Oedipus encountered a terrible monster known as the sphinx, which was terrorizing the people of Thebes by blocking their roadway, forcing them to respond to unanswerable riddles, and then killing them: "What has four legs in the morning, two at noon and three in the evening?" Oedipus correctly answered that it was man, who crawled at birth, walked erect in middle life and used a cane at the end of life. The sphinx died and Oedipus was hailed as the new king of Thebes; the grateful citizens proposed him in marriage to Jocasta, wife of Laius, whom Oedipus has killed. Thus Oedipus married his own mother.

Eventually realizing what he had done, Oedipus blinded himself and wandered off, leaving his sons to dispute the throne and to battle for Thebes, with Polynices attempting to unseat his brother. As the curse on the House of Laius continued, both brothers were killed in hand-to-hand combat and a new king of Thebes was named: Creon, the brother of Jocasta. Since Eteocles was the current king of Thebes, he was allowed to be buried with appropriate royal honors. But it was decreed by Creon that Polynices, technically a usurper, could not be buried properly. And now the tale comes to a dramatic head which is of significance to us.

Antigone and Ismene were both sisters to Eteocles and Polynices. Ismene was an obedient, traditional young woman who respected the law of the state and didn't think beyond that. Antigone however was guided by a higher law, as she says in Sophocles' play, and must bury her brother Polynices. But the penalty for doing this is death. Nonetheless she buried the body and was caught.

Antigone was overcome with grief and ended her life by hanging herself, but King Creon's own son Haemon was in love with the girl and killed himself by falling on his own sword out of grief. Eurydice, wife of Creon, was horrified by the shame and scandal that resulted and killed herself too. Too late Creon realized that he has been tyrannical and not moderate or wise enough in his decisions. In trying to follow man's law he has been insensitive to a higher law and yet as a mortal he is trapped and has done wrong in a situation that he thought he had handled correctly, leading to his becoming overcome with shame and grief. He has eventually learned wisdom and moderation through suffering.

Such tragic stories were familiar to the ancient Greeks and were offered as morality plays, which were instructive and set standards for the young to be inspired by, and they were also filled with subtle artistic details, which could be admired by the public—the use of irony, symbolic content, the singing and dancing of the chorus of elders, the staging of the performances themselves. The high standard of acting on the Greek stage could be traced back to the first actor Thespis of Ikaria in Northeastern Attica, Greece, who not only produced, sang in and starred in choral plays, but gave his name to all future actors, to this day known as thespians. He was the first to stand out from the chorus and actually perform as an actor.

*Eironeia,* or as we call it irony, was one of the artistic details which occurs in Sophocles' plays. It means inadvertently expressing the OPPOSITE of what you are actually meaning to say. A good example would be when Oedipus unknowingly marries his own mother Jocasta and Jocasta exclaims, "Isn't he the perfect husband?" In fact, he really wasn't because he was her son, and the killer of her husband, who was his own father!

*Hubris* is another ingredient we can expect to find in Greek tragedies by Sophocles. The tyrant figure, in this case Creon of Thebes, thought that he knew everything about handling the situation of the burial of Polynices, but in reality he was being arrogant, and engaging in *hubris*, the sort of pride that goes before a fall. In ancient Greece, *hubris* meant unnecessarily humiliating the victim of your arrogance and was particularly associated with wealthy, powerful figures such as tyrants. It often resulted in major retribution by the gods, who would bring the tyrant down and force him to realize the error of his ways. There were many warnings given by blind seers such as Teiresias (an ironic situation because blind seers can "see" the truth) and especially by a chorus of elders of the town, whose wisdom and moderation went unheeded. The chorus was an essential part of a Greek tragedy or comedy, often representing the average person or the townspeople, who would express their concerns or give advice, which would be understood by the audience—but usually not heeded by the principal characters until it is too late.

Constant choral attempts to enlighten the tyrant comprised an essential element of Sophocles' works and provided important guidelines for the audience to use in patterning their ethical and moral behavior. Wisdom appeared to come from knowing how to handle the difficult situations in which one is put in life, being caught between the traditional and the progressive, the legal and the higher law, the conservative and the independent. Moderation and the ability to listen to advice were characteristics that people admired in achieving this right road and these ideas were often cited by the chorus.

In the *Antigone,* two kinds of Greek women were presented, the traditional and the independent. Ismene followed orders and listened to the decrees of King Creon and would not challenge authority because she felt that it was not her place to do so. But Antigone, out of love for her brother and also because of her own nature, was driven to appeal to a higher law, and believed that she had been put in an impossible situation. Her behavior seemed bold and unwarranted to the more traditional people in the society, but she felt she had to honor her brother no matter what the consequences to herself. In doing this act, Antigone was behaving like some wild animal, not a reserved woman. Women in Greece were often compared to animals that needed taming as Antigone and Ismene were said to need (women needed "bridling" in Sophocles' work and Antigone had shrill bird-like cries over the viewing of Polynices' body).

There was also a generation gap in ancient Athens, as brought out by Sophocles (and later Euripides). Ismene was the more traditional girl, while Antigone was a more modern woman, independent, questioning of authority and unyielding to the proclamations of the king. Did she not know her traditional place or was she following a higher law? But how could she obey a ruler whose rulings seem unjust? Was it her place to criticize? These are the dilemmas set in motion in Sophocles' story, which highlights women as complex individuals capable of a variety of intellectual opinions and a wide range of emotions. Even within an individual woman complex issues can trigger complex thought.

## CHRISTOPHER STRONG AND THE GREEK TRAGEDY

In 1933, Dorothy Arzner, with Sophocles firmly in mind, and with a Classical education fueled by four years of Latin and classical art studies at the highly reputed Los Angeles Westlake School for Girls, directed one of her most Hellenic of films, the sadly neglected *Christopher Strong*. At first glance this movie seems like just another creaky old "woman's picture," as critics often describe it. But upon closer inspection the film seems to have stepped right out of Sophocles' play and onto the screen, thanks to the collaboration of Arzner and screenwriter Zoe Akins. The story concerns an English Lord (Colin Clive as Christopher Strong) who falls head over heels in love with a dynamic young aviatrix or fly girl known as Lady Darrington (Katharine Hepburn). His burning passion leads to a torrid affair with his flashy beloved, forsaking his dull, traditional wife (Billie Burke as Lady Elaine Strong) and neglecting his daughter (Helen Chandler as the immature Monica Strong). Finally, the reckless Christopher impregnates his lover, thus setting up a moral dilemma which risks bringing scandal to his entire family and places the principals in an impossible situation. Critics have stated that this is a Hollywood film made within the star system for a female audience. As such, the ability of Arzner's collaborative team to make it something that rises above the ordinary must be viewed as all the more remarkable. That she only revealed to close friends what she was trying to do was typical of Arzner, who felt that her work should speak for itself.

In fact, Arzner's films such as *Christopher Strong* seem so strange and different from other films not only because Arzner brought female sensitivities to her work

about in my book *Unreal Reality*. His idea of the *femme fatale* or lustful female destroyer was embodied by Marlene Dietrich, who was personally well known by Arzner and Morgan and who had visited their home.

Von Sternberg only revealed to close friends what the secret of the uniqueness of his films was, and he would talk about "the beautiful cut by the strange." He felt that one's films should stand on their own merit and never be explained to "the unitiated." Within the studio system, Von Sternberg believed that one could aspire to make films on a higher plain, just as Erich Von Stroheim had done before him. Arzner, inspired by her Westlake training, also saw film as art and aspired to make each work into something unique that would stand on its own and not need to be explained in detail. She never talked about her work or her quest for a higher reality, a vision both she and Morgan shared. Von Sternberg's autobiography *Fun in a Chinese Laundry* is a cipher that never describes what he told intimates he was doing in his Symbolist films. Dorothy Arzner started an autobiography and discussed her years BEFORE she became a director, then abandoned the project. Rather than discuss her approach to her films, she left them to be discovered even after her death. Even in her classroom teaching she emphasized technique over personal interpretation.

In the history of the early sound film it was only Arzner, who consistently revived the Greek tragedy and put it onto the screen in modern setting while having to work within a studio system that never understood why her films appeared "different." And she only told her closest friends what she was doing. So she is not only dear to the feminist movement but is also important to teachers of the classics!

The film *Christopher Strong* has a potboiler plot. A member of British parliament is drawn into an affair with aviatrix Lady Darrington (Katharine Hepburn) and carries on a pretense of marital fidelity with his wife Lady Strong (Billie Burke). This causes complications for his wayward daughter Monica (Helen Chandler). When Lady Darrington becomes pregnant she must decide whether to continue to inflict harm on the Strong family or take her own life. Monica has also become pregnant but man-

but also because she was America's only filmmaker to take ancient Greek tragedies, adapt them and place them in contemporary settings. There were many who delighted in Roman and Biblical subjects such as Cecil B. De Mille, with whose family Arzner worked and whose technique she observed at the beginning of her career. There was also the mysterious imperious Josef Von Sternberg to observe working at Paramount from 1926 to 1935, borrowing heavily from classical mythology and the Symbolist artistic ideas of Antoine Wirtz, Josephin Peladan, Fernand Khnopff and Gustave Moreau, as I have already written

**Billie Burke, Helen Chandler, Ralph Forbes and Katharine Hepburn star in *Christopher Strong*.**

ages to reconcile with her former boyfriend, who must first divorce his wife (!) to marry her, despite the fact that another man has fathered the child. Monica's predicament ends hopefully but Lady Darrington's life ends in disaster. Lord and Lady Strong are left to carry on with their tattered lives and keep up appearances.

In the film there are many parallels to the *Antigone*—too many to be a coincidence. Creon the tyrant KING is replaced by Christopher Strong of the House of LORDS in London. Irony or *eironeia* is present throughout, principally in the fact that Strong seems strong but is actually weak and characters are repeatedly held up as examples of what they are not, Lord Strong is said to be faithful but isn't, Lady Darrington is said to not have had an affair but she is about to have one, and Lady Strong is said to be the most fortunate of women when she is the least.

As in the *Antigone*, the characters are quickly put into a situation where a curse is put onto their house going down through generations from father to daughter as a result of hubristic actions. Just as Christopher Strong, a lawmaker, has difficulty in obeying the law and refusing to obey his own avowed morality and sense of decency, so his daughter is caught in her own web of passion versus true love, when she has an affair with a married man and a baby from European gigolo Carlo (Jack La Rue). Lady Darrington (Hepburn) is clearly the Independent Sophoclean Woman who will not obey any traditional laws that she doesn't find just. She is often daring (hence her name) and even reckless. She lives outside the traditional world of women, being a world-renowned distance and altitude flyer in dangerous planes across huge expanses of the sea. She dresses as a man, drives men off the road by racing her car against them and is willing to have an affair with a married man. She may be considered a free spirit—or a reckless one—but she is a complex character and Arzner invites both the traditional and the modern female view-

**Lady Darrington's (Hepburn) love affair with Christopher Strong (Colin Clive) can only lead to tragedy. (Photofest)**

points to be considered, much as a Greek tragedy presents two sides of a moral dilemma or a character.

Lady Strong (Billie Burke) is a traditional woman, who stays home and looks after her husband's material needs while he is out philandering with Darrington. She suffers alone while her daughter, with purely Sophoclean irony, describes her as having the perfect marriage, in a sequence practically lifted from the *Antigone*. Monica Strong, her daughter, is trapped between the traditional woman (Lady Strong) and the Independent Woman (Lady Darrington). Monica is young and easily attracted to the daring aviatrix, which leads to her carousing and having affairs and ultimately getting pregnant and planning to kill herself. The freedom and modernity inspired by Lady Darrington has led to a life of recklessness, a pregnancy and family shame. But Lady Strong's super conservative lifestyle has contributed to the same problem!

In another touch of Greek tragedy, there is a chorus of people on the street shaking their heads in disapproval at these wild young people who, amid a world in Depres-

sion and turmoil for many, go about frolicking at all-night scavenger hunts and pay no attention to the important values of life. This imitation Greek chorus is represented by a policeman on his beat and an organ grinder who is playing "Nearer My God to Thee," a reminder that these young wild ones are lacking in good Christian values and are heading for a disaster, for the older members of the audience knew that this was the song being played when the *Titanic* went down back in 1912—21 years before! The Greek chorus is a device occasionally used in other films to move their narrative along as in *Cat Ballou* (1965), *Little Shoppe of Horrors* (1986) and *Mighty Aphrodite* (1995). Some have even noted that in *Star Wars* (1973-2005) the robots CP30 and R2D2 are a Greek chorus reacting as the audience would.

*Christopher Strong* has other strong overtones of Greek tragedy. The *hubris* engaged in by Christopher, who speaks about devotion to family but lives outside of his own moral code, is destined to lead to a literal "fall" from grace and he will gain painful wisdom through suffering, all of these actions typical of Greek tragedy. Similarly, Lady Darrington will feel the effects of her folly, and the curse, like that on the House of Laius described previously, will extend to the next generation and the next, from Lord Strong to Monica to her already tainted out of wedlock unborn baby.

As in Greek tragedy, animal imagery abounds in the film and no one who has seen it will forget Hepburn dressed as a gigantic moth (what antennae preparing to go to a masquerade ball. Of course the idea of a moth being attracted to a flame that will then burn her is obvious, but there are subtler animal touches too. At a country hideaway where Lady Strong is expecting to be alone with her husband and daughter, Lady Darrington intrudes. The Strongs have beautiful dogs which are kept so by the discipline that the family imposes, but Lady Darrington insists on giving the dogs table scraps. She represents the wild and undisciplined nature, which will corrupt the dogs. It is just one quiet scene but the tensions of the real-life conflict between the traditional and the independent woman are at odds. The message expressed through the animals is that lack of restraint and discipline produces a world of *chaos*. But so can being too traditional and over-disciplining. Moderation is the key.

Greek *eironeia* or irony is found throughout the film. For example, when Lady Strong exclaims to Christopher "what have I ever done to deserve the best husband in the world," she does not know that she is about to discover his infidelity. In the scavenger hunt party at the opening of the film, Lady Darrington is brought in as a girl over 20 who has never had a lover and Lord Strong is brought in as a married man still faithful to his wife, and yet that very night their statements will be proven ironic. Even more ironic is the fact that Billie Burke, the actress who plays the role of the wife, who refuses to believe in her husband's infidelity until she must, played that role in real life as the wife of the notorious womanizer Florenz Ziegfeld, who had died the year before, leaving her forced to work on this picture to pay off the enormous debts he left her! She was also the mother of Ziegfeld's daughter Patricia, who was approximately the same age as Monica Strong in the movie! How difficult must it have been for Billie Burke to play on film what she was going through in real life at the time (and yet Arzner

Animals are an important part of *Christopher Strong* and Greek tragedy as can be seen in this photo of Lady Strong (Billie Burke) and her beloved dog [Top] and Lady Darrington in costume as a moth [Below]. (Photofest)

and Billie were close friends)? In another of the film's complex ironies, Christopher's irresponsible daughter Monica, who is pregnant out of wedlock, and her worthless married boyfriend Harry Rawlinson (Ralph Forbes), who is not the father of the child, turn out to be the most responsible people in the film and those most willing to face the vicissitudes of life squarely and honestly! They

"Courage conquers death." (Photofest)

can even boast that they don't pretend to be anything else but what they are. Yet according to traditional society both have behaved outrageously.

Another borrowing from Greek tragedy is the strong sense of the inevitability of fate and the sense of impending doom. In the *Antigone,* most of the audience knew the story and could appreciate the sense of impending disaster and watch the playwright's presentation of the slow glide toward destruction of the family. Fate, destiny and chance play significant roles causing misunderstandings that escalate into disaster. In *Christopher Strong*, there are chance meetings that drive the story to its grim conclusion. Christopher and Lady Darrington meet by chance at a party and ruin their lives, Monica and Harry discover the lovers by chance at their secret rendezvous, while they themselves, ironically, are at the same secret rendezvous also trying to hide from the limelight. In an opening sequence at the scavenger hunt party, Christopher is arrogant and boastful about his fidelity and asserts that

he does not wish to be a prig, but in fact that is exactly what he will become, as well as a hypocrite because of this chance meeting. Lady Darrington, by chance, runs Harry off the road with her roadster and is obliged to allow herself to be drawn into his corrupt world because of it. In the beginning of the film, a tower clock resembling Big Ben ominously chimes as a reminder that time is running out and contrasts the stately chorus of working-class elders with the wild partying scavenger hunters, who have "nothing better to do" with their free time while the world burns up around them. For they are the idle rich cavorting in the very depths of the Depression, and although the film is set in England this wasteful and callous behavior would not have been lost on American viewers mired in a world that was approaching rock bottom.

The generation gap so deftly portrayed in the original *Antigone* is also strongly present in *Christopher Strong*. Lady Strong is stuffy and old fashioned and lacks perception about the changing world around her. The much younger Lady Darrington by contrast is alive with excitement and enthusiasm for life. She wears pants, engages in drag races, is obsessed with speed and airplanes. But Christopher is a prig who wants his women young, beautiful and full of excitement, when he wants them that way. The rest of the time he wants them "shackled" to him and at his beck and call. This is the view of most of the men in Arzner movies. It is the long suffering female characters, as is often the case in Sophocles and Euripides, who are the most interesting and have the most depth of character.

Of course, just as in a Greek tragedy, there is a moral at the end and most of Arzner's films are morality plays that end in instruction. In fact Arzner's little remembered radio show in the 1940s offered playlets that ended with a moral that was intended to offer guidance to the public. "Courage conquers death" is the moral of *Christopher Strong* as Lady Darrington finds the courage to kill herself rather than bring disgrace to the House of Strong and the House of Lords. Much criticized today by young student viewers because of the self destruction of Lady Darrington and the allowing of the male to "get away with it," the film was made in the early 1930s which was governed by different values from what we accept routinely today. In our own society Paris Hilton cannot only avoid having her life ruined by having her sexuality publicly displayed but can see this "outing" of her private life lead to a successful career in bad horror movies and TV reality shows!

## CHRISTOPHER STRONG AND CHRISTIAN SCIENCE

But *Christopher Strong* is also more than a filmed Greek tragedy. It also contains a great deal of Arzner's personal life philosophy. She was a Christian Scientist who followed the teachings of Mary Baker Eddy (1821-1910). Eddy, a sickly girl who was born in New Hampshire, married a rural dentist and as her marriage fell apart in Lynn, Massachusetts and her unhappiness grew, she began to think about the power of prayer to heal and the effect of positive thinking and healthy living, since she could not stand the sight of blood and had developed a dislike of doctors. Upon reflection, she decided that individuals should seek to be more like Jesus and Peter and focus on healing the sick without surgery and pills, even talking about the power of spiritually raising the dead or the gravely ill based on studying and devoting oneself to the Bible and biblical miracles. In 1866 she founded Christian Science and developed her idea at her mother church in Boston, adding a journal in 1883 that became widely influential. Her motto was "Courage Conquers Death" and in her teachings she stressed the importance of putting courage first in one's priorities so one could find the inner strength to heal.

In Arzner's personal life, this phrase "Courage Conquers Death" was very important and in *Christopher Strong* it is inscribed on the bracelet given to Lady Darrington, the daring woman, by Christopher, the great love of her life. It is also the phrase that Darrington remembers at the end of the film as she sets out to embrace her fate. The film begins with the organ grinder playing "Nearer My God to Thee" with the "chorus" forming a religious core that is going unheeded. It ends with similar music and the phrase "Courage Conquers Death," this time on Lady Darrington's tombstone. All of this makes *Christopher Strong* a very personal film indeed. As her last feature film directorial effort, Arzner began directing a film entitled *First Comes Courage*.

Early in her life, Arzner had wanted to be a doctor. This resulted from a strong desire to heal the sick and raise the dead, which had come from her Bible reading and her encounter with a neighbor family that had suffered a terrible tragedy. Shunted about from home to home, Arzner had difficulty finding lasting friends and a young couple, who lived near her in Los Angeles, befriended her and made her feel as if she were a part of their family. The wife was pregnant and looked forward to having her child but she miscarried and she and her husband were never quite the same, having become overcome with grief. This devastating experience led Arzner to seek a medical career at UCLA medical school, but her dislike of the program eventually led her to drop out quickly. Still enamored of helping the sick, she became an ambulance driver during WWI. This longtime passion for religious core values to sustain one's life and her desire to make herself like Jesus or Peter along with her basic need to help the few people in her life that gave her affection all led to her embracing Christian Science as a religious philosophy.

## CHRISTOPHER STRONG AND FEMINISM

Dorothy Arzner was rediscovered in 1973 by feminist critics such as Nancy Dowd and Francine Parker and further celebrated in a special commemorative issue of *Action*, the publication of the Directors Guild of America, and articles by Claire Johnston and Pam Cook in the mid 1970s. A tribute by the Directors Guild of America produced a gala evening with Arzner physically present, along with numerous notables such as Robert Wise (famed film director and director of the Guild and editor of Arzner's 1940 film *Dance, Girl, Dance*), Claire McCall (screenwriter on her *Craig's Wife*), feminist critics such as Molly Haskell (author of *From Reverence to Rape: the Treatment of Women in the Movies*), plus some of Arzner's friends including the Sumner family, who have participated in the preparation of this book.

The feminist critics noted that Arzner's major films have a different feel from the average male-produced and directed film of the time. In her films, the men are usually made to look like fools, governed entirely by their *membrum virilis* as opposed to their brains. This is certainly true of Christopher Strong in the film, who spouts wonderful words about loyalty and family, but is attracted to hot sex and an exciting and dynamic woman. Women in Arzner's films are always more complex than the men, often either exemplifying the traditional or the independent women portrayed in the *Antigone* or wavering between the two viewpoints. Lady Darrington wants to be more traditional but will not allow herself to be, as she puts it, "shackled." Lady Strong wants to be more independent but hasn't been raised that way and needs to be protected by a man; she just wouldn't know how to go about becoming a "modern" woman. Monica Strong, influenced by both women, constantly waivers between both extremes. Christopher himself waivers between his "duty" and his passion but, being a man in a Dorothy Arzner film, he cannot definitively make up his mind about anything important (so of course he's a prominent male politician)! The women in Arzner's films are nuanced creatures, who are never one dimensional either as go-getters or traditional figures, and this reflects the position of a woman such as Arzner herself. She was not taken seriously by her male counterparts until her genius and expertise were required, often to save them from embarrassment and rescue the film project.

As a subset of the feminist criticism, gay and lesbian critics have pointed out that Arzner was demonstrably a lesbian in real life who frequently dressed mannishly or, as they put it, "butch," but it was not something that Arzner was eager to discuss in public or even with friends. She was from an older generation where it was shocking and damaging to be outed in such a blatant way and she had seen how it had affected her friends David Manners and William Haines. Therefore, she was reluctant to speak much about her personal life, didn't appear on television giving interviews and didn't want to talk about her collaboration within what was called the "Sewing Circle," a group of dynamic lesbian women (often with ties to gay men) in Hollywood, who frequently collaborated on films and included her screenwriter for *Christopher Strong*

Zoe Akins, even though many members of the circle had marriages to cover up their private lives.

Arzner told friends that she did not feel a close bond with the feminist movement. She appreciated their consideration and interest and was delighted, after the death of her life companion Marion Morgan, to be rescued from loneliness and obscurity, but she felt that she came from a different world with different inspirations. Her inner struggle was to find a sense of belonging, to obtain knowledge and wisdom and to become a creative person of significance in a world where she had been made from birth to feel insignificant. In fact, these are often expressed feminist ambitions as well, but Arzner's struggle was private and personal and she didn't feel part of any "movement." She felt that her life was blessed with people who had helped her at critical times to achieve the success that she enjoyed, as if she was guided mystically by fate and destiny, like a hero or heroine from Greek mythology, a sort of Greek-myth version of Horatio Alger. Her inspiration came from the classical world and from Christian Science and from the help of a number of strong, independent women such as the founders of Westlake along with a few males as well such as William De Mille and James Cruze.

The feminist critics were asserting themselves in the middle 1970s. Arzner was the only female filmmaker to have amassed a significant body of work in talking pictures and, once her films were revived, certain aspects of them appeared to embody a different aesthetic from that of male films of the time. Her films seemed to take the traditional male approach to life and make it "strange," showing it up for the sheer idiocy and discriminatory and repressive practices that it embodied. Arzner's films seemed to mix up the genders, giving the women the strong parts and making the men mere appendages to them. She was credited with altering or questioning the traditional conventions of Hollywood to showcase the female point of view.

In 1994 Judith Mayne published her book, *Directed by Dorothy Arzner*, a combination feminist and gay/lesbian appraisal of Arzner's work. In the book she emphasized Dorothy Arzner as what she termed "a performative director," a description with a peculiar invented adjective not too easy to fathom but which, as I understand it, refers to the fact that Arzner mixed up genres and presented women as learning to wear masks and put on an act in order to get by in man's society. The women are therefore giving a performance and as we witness what they must do from their own viewpoint, with the males presented

**Dorothy Arzner on the set, c. 1930s (Photofest)**

as satellite figures, we note that Arzner is changing the conventions of Hollywood. These performances require costumes and it is Arzner's emphasis on different kinds of women's clothing that reveals the performance they must give to survive.

Mayne asserts that Arzner is concerned about the complexities of women's relationships, particularly noting that Arzner creates groups of women that are often pitted against one another or simply interacting with different points of view. Arzner is seen as sensitive to the complexities of women and as such can produce star-making performances for female actresses, while de-emphasizing the male roles and producing what Andrew Sarris once called "the spectacular spinelessness of her men." Arzner is also interested in emphasizing class differences, the rich versus the poor, with the poor often forming itself into women's communities for survival, because women's self preservation is an essential force in Arzner's films, according to Dr. Mayne.

Mayne is also aware of the frequent occurrence of ironic dialogue but doesn't attribute it to any particular source. She also details how males treat women as objects in most Hollywood films and give them what she calls "the look," which asserts their power and dominance, but Arzner's films treat women as more complex individuals, who manage through their "performative" displays to wield real power or present themselves for "objectification" by males. Thus, for example, a slinky dress can give a woman power over a man and also allow her to become viewed as a sex object by the male. In the man's world, the woman can take advantage of the male's primitive behavior patterns and manipulate him to her own advantage.

In her gay and lesbian critique, Mayne praises Arzner for frequent gender reversal and for repeatedly giving traditional male characteristics to the so-called "butch" woman, often creating androgynous or male-female figures. Lady Darrington for example dresses as a man and engages in traditional male athletic activities and all at-

Dorothy Arzner's female characters frequently have male characteristics, such as Katharine Hepburn in *Christopher Strong.*

tempts by Christopher to feminize her do not work and lead to her considering to be shackled.

The flaw with the feminism criticism, however valid, is that it is not interested in what ELSE Arzner is doing in the creation of her films apart from the feminist elements. This is understandable because in the early 1970s American women began to "wise up" and become increasingly aware of discrimination in the workplace, and the fact that in a number of other countries female babies could be legally murdered just for being a female, or that unfaithful wives or even wives who appeared in public without being properly covered might be put to death with impunity for the males

Arzner's films had been years ahead of their time in dealing with the plight of females in a man's world and it was a body of work that consistently maintained its viewpoint. Rediscovering Arzner was so refreshing to members of the feminist community that looking for other thematic structures in her work was not only unimportant for their own objectives; it was off message. Apart from a few films like the deeply moving and surprisingly unappreciated *Girls of the Road* (1940), written and directed by men but starring a real-life neglected heroine and WWII ambulance driver named Ann Dvorak, cinema dealing with the sometimes desperate plight of women in a man's world was extremely rare.

## CHRISTOPHER STRONG AND AMELIA EARHART

Another wonderful aspect about *Christopher Strong* is that it is also a portrait of famed aviatrix Amelia Earhart (now the subject of a new movie with Hilary Swank) as well as other fly girls who were "Darringtons" of their own, setting altitude and long-distance records with their dynamic flying. These unique women are celebrated in Arzner's film and Zoe Akins' screenplay as the unique individuals that they were in this age when there were aerodromes but not yet many airports and flying in experimental planes was daring and death-defying. Amelia Earhart was much in the news as a popular figure but she was not the only dynamic female in the air.

Amy Johnson was the daughter of a fish seller of Hull, England and she was able to purchase a secondhand plane, revamp it and fly in 1930 from England to Australia. She even did her own mechanical work and during the flight encountered one 2,000-foot drop that nearly killed her. She flew through a sandstorm in Iraq, broke her propeller in Burma and barely managed to get through her perils alive. A daredevil from childhood, Amy was proficient at *ju jitsu* and normally carried a loaded pistol in case any guys got any ideas.

But the aviatrix who most comes to mind as the role model for Lady Darrington in the film is Amelia Earhart (1897-1937). The Kansas born tomboy had already broken the women's altitude record by 1922 and by 1928 had become the first woman to cross the Atlantic, a fact that was much publicized, even though most accounts failed to state that she went only as a passenger. Like Lady Darrington, she loved to drive fast cars and to out-drive males and force them off the road. Inspired by macho former president Theodore Roosevelt, she also fancied herself a big-game hunter.

In the later 1920s Earhart hooked up with publisher George Palmer Putnam, who ballyhooed her 1928 crossing as a publicity stunt. At the time he was also publicity manager for Charles Lindbergh and had a reputation for knowing how to turn adventurous people into American icons through the press. Promoting her nationwide with a series of cross-country flights, the married Putnam also fell in love with her and they had an affair just as Lady Darrington and Christopher Strong did in the movie. Eventually he divorced his wife and accompanied Earhart on numerous flying and speaking tours, all the time pressing her to marry him.

The strongly independent Earhart differed enormously from Putnam's own wife and he was enormously attracted to her dynamic personality. With his help Earhart became a household word with her special flying suit featuring trousers and zipper top, up to then not normally worn by women. She also had a successful line of Modernaire luggage for the rich, modern woman and her fashions sold to the middle class at stores such as Macy's. They finally married in 1931, but her agreement written

**Amelia Earhart**

to Putnam still survives and shows the Lady Darrington-like quality of her character:

> I offer no Medieval code of faithfulness. I'll wed you for one year to try it out. I cannot agree to endure at all times the confinement of even an attractive cage.

It isn't much of a stretch to view all of Earhart's personality in the persona of Lady Darrington in the film and her complaint about being shackled to Christopher. The most remarkable thing is that the film ends in a fiery plane crash which takes the life of its pilot and apparently Earhart suffered a similar demise just four years later on her round-the-middle-of-the-world flight. Earhart's affair with the married Putnam and her independent attitudes were widely reported in her time and she was much discussed and admired in the Sewing Circle. Arzner denied at the time that the film was modeled on Earhart but this was just an act of prudence to avoid a lawsuit!

## CHRISTOPHER STRONG
## AND KATHARINE HEPBURN

Katharine Hepburn was not yet a major star when Arzner chose her to portray Lady Darrington, but she had a history of independence and, already, a reputation for being difficult to work with that had followed her from the stage. Arzner and Katharine Hepburn did not get on well during the making of the film, yet her performance is a strong one and well suited for the Earhart-like superwoman she had to portray. She was an appropriate choice to create this nuanced part of the independent versus the traditional woman and when Amelia Earhart smiled she looked so much like Katharine Hepburn that it was almost eerie.

Katharine's father, Thomas Hepburn, was a noted urologist who became controversial by advocating more public awareness of the dangers of venereal disease. Such an action was considered radical at the time, and Hepburn's mother Katharine Houghton campaigned for an equal rights amendment for women long before the hunger strikes, demonstrations and petitions of members of the feminist movement did the same thing between 1972 and 1982. Furthermore, Katharine Houghton's close friend was Margaret Sanger, advocate of birth control and a woman's right to choose with regard to reproduction and her own baby. Sanger was the founder of Planned Parenthood in 1916 at a time before women in most states lacked even the right to vote, and the Catholic Church leaders were campaigning vigorously against the organization and her. In fact at this time disseminating information about women's reproductive rights was considered radical and even sacreligious. Hepburn's family was well-off financially, but was snubbed by the prestigious families of Connecticut because of their political and social views and they were constantly in trouble with the church. They didn't ever back down an inch.

Raised to set goals in her life and to question authority and also raised with considerable wealth, Katharine was blessed with athletic prowess in a variety of sports despite her thin build. The family believed in the ancient classical tradition of "a sound mind in a sound body" (*Sit mens sana in corpore sano*), based on the writing of the Roman satirist Juvenal and her father encouraged participation in tennis, swimming, horseback riding and golf. She also won a bronze medal in a Madison Square Garden skating competition and was a golf semi-finalist in a state of Connecticut championship. Testing her mettle in freezing temperatures, she even became a polar bear club swimmer.

Her gifted, independent and seemingly indestructible family was dealt a sudden and devastating blow with the death of Katharine's brother, who hanged himself. But she gradually recovered and attended Bryn Mawr College where she was surrounded by many other free-thinking young ladies of means. These were generally the sort of well-heeled ladies whom Dorothy Arzner had encountered at Westlake, not always with the best of results. In fact, Arzner disliked arrogance in anybody and was quietly focused on making a place for herself. Katharine was unlike Arzner in many way and, while Katharine was at Bryn Mawr, it was not long until she got herself suspended for curfew violations and smoking, although her biggest vice may have been the nude bathing in the school fountain during the dark of night.

Her marriage to Main Line businessman Ludlow Ogden Smith, later to be a pioneer in proto-computer business design, ended when she tried to get him to change his name to hers! Later, after he suffered ostracism due to their quick divorce and he was removed from the Philadelphia Social Register, he changed his own name to Ogden Smith

**Katharine Hepburn in 1932 as the Amazon Antiope in the play** *The Warrior's Husband.* **(Photofest)**

Ludlow to try to obtain some social anonymity and return to society's graces! Hepburn had made the demand of him to change his name because she had no intention of giving up her then fledgling career as an actress by having the real name of Kate Smith. Kate Smith was the name of a famous radio star who was enormously hefty and rather ungainly. Hepburn didn't want the comparison and kept her maiden name. Nonetheless, "Luddy," like a male character in one of Arzner's films, somehow remained her friend for life, despite her nearly ruining his career.

Katharine's theater work was steady in the late 1920s and was helped by her Bryn Mawr and social connections, which led to her earning $80 per week. In 1932 she played a breakthrough role as an Amazon known as Antiope in *The Warrior's Husband,* based on an ancient Greek play known as the *Lysistrata* by the comic poet Aristophanes in 411 B.C.E. The original work centered on women withholding sex from their male consorts in an effort to bring about an end to war. This action also caused severe troubles between the men and the women. In the play her lack of clothing, her sports ability and her uncommon physical prowess made her seem to be a superwoman and she quickly made a huge reputation for herself as a sort of living ancient Amazon. RKO agent Leland Hayward, a noted talent scout and a notorious womanizer with a taste for actresses and debutantes, was instantly attracted to Katharine, and is said to have become romantically involved with her. She made screen tests for RKO and, acting as her own agent, demanded a salary of $1,500 a week for her work, an outrageous sum at the time. To her amazement they accepted upon Hayward's recommendation to do so and her film career began.

Katharine had a particular look that fit well with the early 1930s when the Art Deco movement, heavily influenced by the hard-edged art of Pablo Picasso and Georges Braque, was in vogue. Katharine commented: "I have an angular face, an angular body and I suppose an angular personality which jabs into people." Eventually, when the Deco movement gave way to an emphasis on the blonde and curvilinear look in Hollywood and stars like Jean Harlow, Mae West and Alice Faye won great fame, Hepburn fell out of vogue. By 1936 she was becoming increasingly known as box-office poison and exhibitors refused to show her films. She was finally demoted at RKO and assigned to appear in the low-budget *Mother Carey's Chickens*, which seemed to be intended as a cut-rate version of *Little Women*. This led to her buying out the rest of her contract so she could try for a comeback elsewhere. But in the early 1930s she had the right look at the right time.

**Hepburn poses on the set of *The Philadelphia Story* (1940).**

Tall (5'7"), lovely and slender in 1932, she was immediately cast with John Barrymore in *A Bill of Divorcement* and he wasted no time in making passes at her as well but Katharine was able to take care of herself and became more determined to retain her independence. At a time when other stars were cowering in fear of their studios, Katharine refused to kowtow to directors or established stars, wouldn't sign autographs, told off the greatly feared gossip columnist Hedda Hopper and quarreled with would-be interviewers. Katharine had already attracted the attention of the Sewing Circle, most particularly with her role in *The Warrior's Husband* in New York, so it seemed a fortuitous combination when David O. Selznick brought together Dorothy Arzner, Katharine Hepburn and playwright/screenwriter/script fixer Zoe Akins, three dynamic women. However, the mix proved volatile.

The unpretentious Arzner had grown up without the finer things and was faced with what she considered to be the spoiled young wild woman in Katharine. Arzner expressed her views through her work, quietly but definitely, and had a clear sense of how to direct a film, which had an overall viewpoint and look. Katharine was loud and frank and demanding and interfered with the direction, undercutting the subtle thematic and symbolic efforts that Arzner was attempting to achieve. Katharine was hoping to make enough of a fuss to get Arzner replaced with George Cukor, who would have paid more attention to the actress than the quieter Arzner, who was attempting to fit the actress into the overall concept. At this point in her career Katharine didn't have quite enough clout to get

Arzner fired although she tried, leading to her nickname "Katharine of Arrogance," a word play on Catherine of Aragon, the 16th century queen of England and first wife of the notorious Henry VIII.

The Arzner-Hepburn collaboration/confrontation was compounded by the presence of Zoe Akins (1886-1958), who was as pretentious and arrogant a person as could be. The daughter of a wealthy St. Louis Republican businessman, she lived in an ostentatious mansion on an estate called Green Fountains at 2401 Brigden Road in Pasadena with multiple servants and spoke with a ridiculously affected British accent that showed little trace of her Midwest origins. She married Captain Hugo Rumbold in 1932, son of the eighth baronet of Woodhall, a member of the British upper class from one of the country's finest families. Rumbold graduated from Eton and was a celebrated war hero, having received Belgium's Order of the Crown and been gravely wounded. He was also a well-known stage designer.

Akins had a growing reputation in Hollywood and had had hit plays and films recently. She enjoyed writing this screenplay about a British lord, even though her own husband was dying at the time from wounds he received in World War I.  Akins insisted on staying home and having the meetings for planning the film at her estate, no doubt also in part to show off her own wealth most conspicuously to everyone. Her husband died before the film was completed. The combination of situations and personalities created a deadly chemistry and the film did only modest business when finally completed so that all the tension and hard work were not seen at the time as making it all worthwhile. Katharine and Arzner never became friends and in 1975 when Arzner was being honored by the Directors' Guild of America, Hepburn sent this telegram:

> Isn't it wonderful that you've had such
> a great career, when you had no right to
> have a career at all.

Yet when the film *Christopher Strong* is viewed today it appears to show for the first time the Katharine Hepburn persona which would be a fixture in her later films: the flashy, fast-moving, fast-talking athletic superwoman, who can do all that a man can do and do it better. While Arzner cannot fully be credited with discovering Katharine, she can be acknowledged for developing her image, which is present from the first seconds we see her on screen running a hapless male off the road, wearing pants and rushing about at top speed.

In the curious mixing of these three great women, Akins, Arzner and Hepburn, one is left also to wonder about what plays within plays within plays were devilishly concocted as the film progressed. The film was a tongue-in-cheek reference to the private life of Amelia Earhart. It also cast actress Billie Burke, then in horrible debt, in a role she was forced to take to get money but which paralleled her own private life, married to a philandering husband who left her home while he carried on with chorus girls and she pretended to ignore what was going on. The film also paralleled Hepburn's private life at the time. First of all, she was actually the independent superwoman she portrayed in the film. She was also apparently having an affair with Leland Hayward, who was also married at the time to Texas socialite and renowned beauty Lola Gibbs. Hayward was attracted to dynamic women and had already been married to and divorced from Lola once, then had remarried her and now was actively pursuing Katharine during the remarriage, so much so that when Lola sued for divorce in Juarez, Mexico, Katharine was reported in *Time Magazine* as the cause and was described as "the future Mrs. Hayward." Furthermore, Lola was a noted pioneer woman aviatrix (!), a part played by Katharine in the movie! There are so many overlaps of the personal and the theatrical in *Christopher Strong* that one can understand that the tension during shooting must have been nearly unbearable as art was imitating life and perhaps also vice-versa as real-life and film-life intertwined and played itself out on a day to day basis

The environment with Zoe and Katharine disliking each other fueled tensions further, complicated by Zoe's dying husband and Katharine's long bout with the flu, and Katharine was concerned that her sister alpha dog Arzner was "too bossy" and autocratic. Everyone was delighted when this shoot was over.

And yet *Christopher Strong* is an important film. As we have seen it is the ideal film in which to witness the Katharine Hepburn screen persona as it was being created, molded by Arzner and Zoe. She already had an image as a Greek goddess and Amazon superwoman. This fit well with the original novel of *Christopher Strong* by Gilbert Frankau in 1932. In the novel Katharine's character was named Felicity and had the physical appearance of a Tanagra figurine. Tanagra was an area of ancient Greece north of Athens and famous for its enormous production of mold-made terra cotta figurines, many of them of lovely elongated female figures wearing small sombrero-like hats, a *chiton* or light cloak of wool or linen with an overfold at the waist and an *himation* or elaborate wraparound cloak. The author conceived her as a boyish figure, tan and athletic, with brilliant hair, living her life much as a man would. Katharine seemed ideal for Arzner to use in the fashioning of her Greek tragedy in modern British guise.

Through her use of the elements of Greek tragedy (the conflict of the individual with society, *hubris,* ironic speech, objects reflecting the characters, traditional and non-traditional women in conflict, chorus, final moral, etc.), Arzner fashioned a subtle masterpiece, which also gives insight into women's attitudes in the 1930s. Lady Darrington is the self-confident wealthy aviatrix able to dominate male counterparts with her creativity, skill and beauty, but whose unconventional life leads to confusion and suicide. Lady Strong is the traditional lady suffering quietly in the background and trying to apply traditional morality and values to a world that is quickly changing around her. The confused Monica Strong, who indulges in a lover of the month and harbors a desire to be a flapper and have all kinds of fun before she settles down, also admires the stability and traditional values of her own parents, a stability which helps to hold her own life together. While using her own family as an anchor,

Monica (Helen Chandler) and Lady Darrington both toy with danger, which leads them both to the brink of suicide in *Christopher Strong*. (Photofest)

she toys with danger, then succumbs to it, then flounders, as the safety valve represented by her family disintegrates. As Monica witnesses the deterioration of her own family, she gets caught in a frightening whirlwind, which leads her too to the brink of suicide

The finale, featuring the dramatic and deliberately tragic suicide of the pregnant Lady Darrington, differs from the finale of the novel, which left Felicity/Cynthia trying for the altitude record and possibly becoming dizzy from the increasing height and then crashing. But Arzner insisted:

> No, there was no other ending. Cynthia killed herself because she was about to have an illegitimate child....Suicide was a definite decision.

In producing a Modern Greek tragedy there would have been no other choice possible. for pride goes before a fall.

The nuanced characters of *Christopher Strong* may be seen as reflections of people Arzner encountered during her pre-film life experiences. Arzner's youth may only be described as tragic. She was surrounded by complex women and these nuances creep into her films and make them different from male-directed films. Lady Elaine Strong is long suffering and reminds one of Arzner's own aunt who was pushed to the breaking point by a husband, who suffered a midlife crisis and ran off to Scotland, leaving her to cope with the children. In Lady Cynthia one can be tempted to see something of the strong-willed young ladies that attended the Westlake School and made Arzner feel she was an outsider trying to be forced to their wills. And Cynthia was also much like her friend Mimi.

85

Arzner related to women who felt themselves superior and special, while at the same time understood women who were simply obedient and even suffering abuse in order to survive. That early life became the training ground for the mature director.

## DOROTHY ARZNER'S OTHER FILMS

### CRAIG'S WIFE
### 1936

If it is possible to note the influence of ancient Greece on *Christopher Strong*, what about the other films that Dorothy Arzner directed? While it is beyond the scope of this book to analyze every available film that she directed, it is possible to examine several of them here to demonstrate the role that classical culture plays in her art.

*Craig's Wife* is often described as a star vehicle for Rosalind Russell, who plays Harriet Craig, a lovely young woman whose successful husband dotes on her, but who really loves her palatial home more and treats it as if it is a living organism that she cannot bear for anyone to disturb in any way. She is manipulative and self-absorbed and eventually alienates everyone around her and is left horribly alone within her gargantuan living room.

This appears to be a simple cautionary tale that probably would have been in the hands of a lesser director but for Dorothy Arzner, the entire scenario is transformed into a Greek tragedy in modern guise, a morality play which shows the influence of such Greek tragedies as Euripides' *The Bacchae*.

In order to make her film conform more to the world of ancient Greece, Arzner decided to lock horns with Harry Cohn and Columbia Pictures over the set design. The supervising art director and designer was Stephen Gooson, one of the greatest designers in the history of Hollywood. But Arzner wanted a particular look for Harriet Craig's home, and particularly for the interior living room area. To this end she drew clandestinely on the services of William Haines, that one-time box-office champion whose insistence on being openly gay had forced him into a second career as a designer. Haines rushed in, using some objects from Arzner's home as well as replicas of ancient Greek statuettes and red-figured pottery and created the "temple" living room set for the film, infusing it with a strong whiteness that suggested the fine Pentelic marble of Greek antiquity. This white look was equated in the artistic mind with ancient Greece and Rome because when ancient ruins were discovered and visited in Greece and Rome, the buildings had almost always lost their painting, leaving only their gleaming white marble to show through. Neo-Classical artists of the 18th and 19th century were fond of erecting sham white ruins and garden temples to evoke the art of antiquity and books of engravings of ancient monuments, such as those by Stuart and Revett, were widely circulated and became the canon of perfection to emulate. Harriet Craig's home was designed to put her in a world of modern conveniences and ancient Greek art and inspiration.

The film opens with views of the Greek vases and statuettes and offers an eerie shot of the oversized living room with its Greek temple pediment for a backdrop, suggesting that we are in the presence of a royal hall worthy of an ancient Greek tragedy. The living room is even described mockingly by a servant as the "Holy of Holies" as we view the temple façade within it. The focal point of the room is the fireplace and mantle, which features a valuable Athenian Greek red-figured vase of the 5th century B.C.E.

Harriet Craig is concerned about protecting her possessions and her house. Once again the common people, including particularly the servants, and the relatives such as her aunt, find her actions bizarre but cannot communicate with her, so they are forced to lament to each other about her behavior and its possible bad consequences for everyone. In short, they function exactly like a chorus in an ancient Greek tragedy. Walter's Aunt Ethel (Alma Kruger) in a prescient comment says the rooms have died and are laid out.

Harriet is not only obsessed with protecting the purity of her home but she is also determined to keep out anything relating to nature from her home. She even disdains the trees outside her picture window and wants them dusted by the servants! In her rejection of the joys of nature and her concern about her husband and his friends going out to party and enjoy themselves, she is reminiscent of Pentheus, the royal figure of Euripides' *The Bacchae*, but with Harriet Craig in the male role, a role reversal which Arzner frequently employed. In Euripides' play, produced in Athens ca. 405 B.C.E., the tyrant Pentheus of Thebes refuses to honor nature and accept the frenzied rites of the god Dionysus. Because of this failure, female members of Pentheus' family are driven to dance and hunt and celebrate in an ecstatic frenzy the rites of the God and ultimately they must accept the power of nature. Pentheus does not believe in the power of nature and decides to dress up as a woman (!) and find out about the secret rites which include drinking heavily, ripping wild animals apart and shouting on top of a mountain. Too late he realizes that he must accept the power of the god and see the error of his ways. Eventually the power of nature razes Pentheus' palace to the ground through earthquake and fire.

If we view Harriet Craig as a Pentheus-type figure, isolated in her Greek royal hall and rejecting nature, the whole film begins to work on another level, as a Greek tragedy in modern guise. Harriet is filled with hubris and disdains nature. The film is a morality play, just as *Christopher Strong* was, with the moral repeated at the end: "People who live to themselves are generally left to themselves." There is an effective "chorus" of women including the two maids and Aunt Ellen, who correctly assess the problems with Harriet, but who are not heeded. Mazie the maid observes that "you can go crazy over a house the same way you can for anything else."

A sense of impending doom hangs over the head of Walter Craig (John Boles) and his obsessed wife Harriet (Rosalind Russell) in *Craig's Wife*. Note the statue on the table. (Photofest)

Billie Burke, friend of Dorothy Arzner, and her interpreter in several of her films, is Mrs. Frazier, the personification of nature who gardens all day long from morning until night and who is a gentle yet powerful force who engenders love, sweetness and hope, personified by her little innocent child and the beautiful flowers she produces and repeatedly attempts to bring into the Craig mansion. In real life Arzner had a great reverence for the power of nature and an enormous love of gardening, which was a characteristic of many of her close female friends. Gardening was seen as a restorative pursuit that brought one into a more spiritual plain and allowed clarity of thought. This view was shared by such high-powered individuals as Arzner's close friend Mimi, by Marion Morgan and even by Katharine Hepburn, who wrote about how much gardening meant to her.

By contrast Harriet is presented as a tyrant figure, refusing nature, barring Mrs. Frazier from her home. She is insulting and cruel and is described as a shrill bird. Her husband Walter Craig, by contrast, lacks perception about her true character. Nature has not influenced her, and Mrs. Frazier and her two year old grandson are kept out of the palace for fear the child will scratch something in it with his toys, which he eventually does. Harriet's husband Walter (John Boles) is aware of Harriet's physical beauty but has not yet been able to look at her soul and he fails to heed the warnings of the "chorus." Like most males in Arzner's films and even in this film, he is useless. In animal terms he is compared to "a dog on a leash" and a silly "pup," "like all men" or "three monkeys who hear, see and speak no evil." He is compared to "wife-ridden sheep." Harriet, the shrill bird, says that she could "build a nest in his ear and he'd never know." As the film progresses and "queen" Harriet puts on her finery, she wears a dress which is designed to resemble a linen Greek *chiton* which was favored by aristocratic women in ancient Greece. It features laurel leaves and gilding on the sleeves and is completely white.

There is a strong sense of impending fate and doom about the Craig mansion as the "chorus" continually warns of it but Harriet feels that she controls her own destiny so long as the house is protected and nature shut out. When a servant tries to get her trunk, he scratches the marble floors and Harriet behaves as if the house is a wounded lover. Her pride and joy is her collection of Greek art, which particularly includes calyx craters used in ancient Athens for wine mixing and celebrating at symposia and banquets, particularly in honor of the god Dionysus, lord of nature. At one point, when Harriet is complaining about the reveling of her husband's friends she complains to him as he is drinking and sitting near a lamp in the form of a *kantharos* (a Greek drinking and one

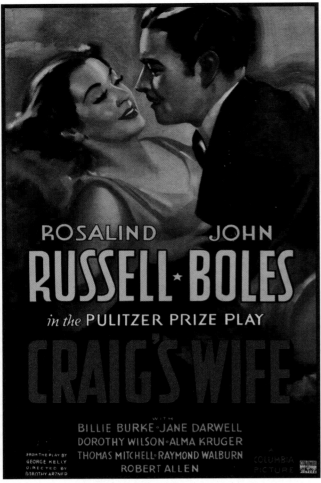

For Harriet as for Pentheus, nature is the enemy and her palace is a symbol of stability, security, order and respect in the community. When Harriet's world crumbles, nature intrudes into the house in the form of Mrs. Frazier and her roses and rose petals, and her world collapses. Pentheus is eventually attacked by his own mother, whereas Harriet is eventually attacked by her husband and aunt. Pentheus is beheaded and his palace destroyed by fire. The destruction of Harriet's palace is symbolized by the deliberate shattering of her prize Athenian Greek vase on her mantle by her "Dionysiac" husband and she exclaims: "It sounded as if the whole house fell down!" The burning of her palace is symbolized by the jarring pile of ashes and cigarette butts next to the shattered vase, deliberate disorder brought into the home and causing Harriet to reel at the end of her marriage and the sabotaging of her precious image in the community. When her world crumbles and the Greek vase centerpiece is broken, Harriet rearranges the remaining objects to fill out the mantle, trying to carry on as if nothing has happened, but the intrusion of nature personified by Mrs. Frazier and her flowers is the final blow.

Arzner is also fond of little ironies, the *eironeia* I have talked about with regard to the Greek tragedy earlier. *Craig's Wife* is full of them and they are often so subtle as to be easily overlooked. Early in the film she criticizes her maid for leaving the front door half open and at the end of the film when her life is destroyed she leaves the door half open and pays no attention. At the end of the film she is left holding a bouquet of roses and she had strictly forbidden roses and their petal droppings from being permitted into the house.

Arzner was also a great master of dual emotion, which is another factor often present in ancient Greek tragedy. Female characters are not good or evil but have nuance. Thus at the finale of the film many viewers feel sympathy for the isolated, weeping Harriet Craig while at the same time hating her. We feel that she is as ill as she is evil and needs professional care. We are told briefly that her childhood home was a broken one and that she had felt terrible loneliness and abandonment then along with her mother when her father left, and now her husband is leaving her too. Ambiguous feelings are the norm at the culmination of an Arzner film as the protagonist has gained *sofia* or wisdom through suffering too late to make amends and yet we can feel sorry for her. In *Christopher Strong*, Lady Darrington had learned too late that she could not live at the expense of the happiness of Lady Strong and she weeps as she gains this wisdom too late to change her fate. In another of Arzner's films we shall discuss, *Dance, Girl, Dance*, Maureen O'Hara in her final

of the symbols of Dionysus) that all he needs to complete his debauchery is "to twine leaves in his hair," which is a reference to Dionysus, the god noted for his drinking and twined-crown of ivy leaves.

Statuettes of Greek gods and goddesses frequent the room including one recognizable one of the so-called Artemis of Gabii, based on a lost original by the fourth century B.C.E. Greek sculptor Praxiteles of Athens. On the mantle appears to be a *lebes gamikos* with looping handles, which was an ancient Greek wedding vase that may be intended to symbolize the union of Harriet and Walter. In the hall is a bizarre herm (a bust on a pillar) of a female figure with large exposed breasts. It is most unusual and, since we are to assume that it must have been selected by Harriet, it startles us as we notice it in the hallway upstairs. Such blatant displays of female anatomy are not typically Greek and yet the form of the herm is in fact ancient classical Greek. It is bizarre in its garishness and may be intended to express repressed sexuality in that Harriet would be attracted to such a gross and not typically ancient Greek object.

scene both laughs and cries at the same time!

Apart from the now I hope obvious connection with Greek tragedy, *Craig's Wife* is an extraordinary film. Arzner did not have a reputation as a maker of female stars for nothing. Rosalind Russell, who never credited Arzner for helping her achieve stardom with this performance, is given the star buildup. Her final crying sequence is exquisitely framed with a disorienting diagonal formed from the shadow of the upstairs staircase to suggest her mental imbalance and to highlight her. Harriet's ruination is carefully led up to in order to catch in extreme close-up her precisely dropped tear. The camera pulls back to show the vast empty house as she receives the telegram announcing that Walter is leaving her.

**Walter's sister (Alma Kruger) can see the hardness beneath the beauty of Harriet Craig. (Photofest)**

Throughout the film Harriet is given numerous bits of business which reflect her character. She tidies up obsessively when things go wrong, and she flicks at dust which seems to be invisibly taunting her. She constantly averts looking people in the eye, especially when she cannot face her own lies. When criticized, she laughs almost hysterically as if to dismiss the critic but also as a defense mechanism preventing her from facing her mental illness. I am particularly fond of a strange head jerk that Harriet does when reacting to the invasive yet miniscule sound of Walter tap tap tapping his cigarette tobacco into place.

The architecture is also an actor in the film with the large and precious Greek vase on the mantle the symbol of the mad stability of the house. The temple backdrop turns the house into a shrine of a tyrant. The chairs are stiff and formal and Walter's aunt comments that, "I don't know how I'd sit in one of these chairs."

The feminist writers, particularly Judith Mayne, have correctly identified how Arzner tends to create groups of women who bond and who oppose other women and there is often a strong sense of class divisions between women as well. Arzner, having been part of both the have not and have classes, was well equipped to deal with women from both sides of the tracks. She had a particular love for the working girl and, working at close proximity on the set with her screenwriter (usually also a woman), she was most sensitive to the range of emotion of women. With the class tension and the tension between women, everyone in the mansion is just a second away from a confrontation, everyone is walking on eggs, and it keeps the viewer on edge throughout.

The other women briefly glimpsed in *Craig's Wife* are also nuanced nicely although we barely know them. They are loving, suffering, ambitious, manipulative, abusive and full of secret longings. Adelaide for example, played by beautiful Kathleen Burke, is a trophy wife, hitched to the homely, but well off, Fergus Passmore (Thomas Mitchell). She cheats on her husband and yet we see that he is overly paranoid, alcoholic and weak. She enjoys blatantly carrying on and Harriet accuses her own husband of being part of the revelry. Adelaide's behavior and Fergus' frustration lead to her murder by Fergus and Fergus' suicide. Marriage was for her a way to be independent just as it was for Harriet but with even more disastrous results. Adelaide is a complex figure. Do we excuse her because her husband is so weak or did she marry him only to exploit him and cause him sorrow? In a man's world a woman has to learn to make her way and to put on the costumes that she needs to survive. But this behavior was excused at the time in a man (the idea of boys will be boys) and yet seen as not proper for a woman.

Another aspect of Arzner's work has also been pointed out by the feminist critics: the demeaning treatment of men and the insistence on the helplessness and uselessness of the male. The presentation of John Boles,

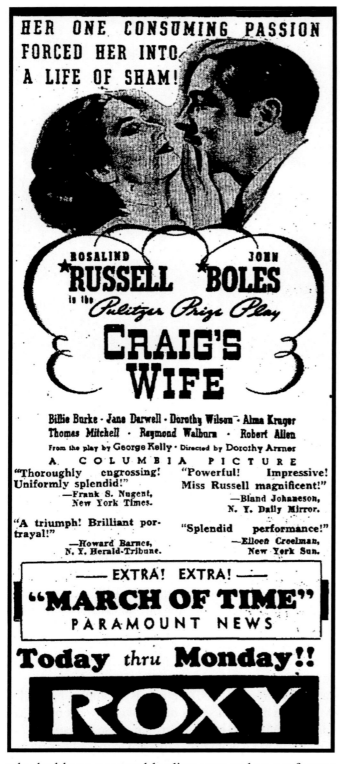

mentally ill. Her references to him as little boy, a romantic fool, and an inferior are like a constant drumbeat in the film and he finally can take no more for fear that Harriet will "reduce me to a wife-ridden sheep that's afraid to buy a necktie for fear his wife may not like it." Boles is treated "as if I were some sort of mental incompetent" and even his own sister tells him that he needs to become "the man of the house." Harriet keeps him jumping through hoops and openly boasts of the control she has over her husband and how she is arrogantly superior to him:

> If I don't like what he does, why he doesn't do it anymore….Better the destiny of your home be in your hands than that of your husband….A husband is necessary for the upkeep of the house….I married a romantic fool….

In one sequence, Harriet calmly and indifferently frames Walter for murder, then forbids and physically intimidates him from phoning the police to save himself. She then denies that it was her phone call checking up on the whereabouts of her husband that led him to be incriminated:

> The man isn't born I'd bother checking up on.

This last statement shows she is capable of telling lies against her own husband and even denies to herself that she is a possessive control freak.

Walter is not the only male to become a target. All of the men in the film are peripheral to the actions of the women. The men come and go but it is the women who actually control the household and manipulate the men. Even the young maid Mazie (Nydia Westman) has her own beau Tom, who drops by briefly to see her. He enters through the service entrance and in no time she manipulates him into peeling potatoes and he laments that Mazie is "training me for the next war." Shortly after, Harriet appears in time to call him "a stray tramp" who is also "a dumb potato peeling would-be mechanic." Not observed by Harriet is the fact that it is Mazie who got Tom to peel those potatoes in the first place. No wonder Tom takes off as quickly as he can.

We finally work up a degree of sympathy for Harriet at the finale when we see her crying and powerless to understand why everyone has left her. She realizes that she has done wrong, it seems, but doesn't understand how to cope with what has happened. Her only attempt to find

who had been a rugged leading man and was a former military counter-intelligence expert in real life, as a clueless wimp in this film is quite a surprise. He is humiliated throughout as a gutless puppy needing to be led around. Apparently blinded by Harriet's physical attractions, he does not see the real woman nor understand that she is

resolution is her feeble effort to rearrange the classical antiquities on her mantle to hide the fact that her precious Greek vase has been deliberately smashed by her husband. We also begin to realize just how ill she really is.

I have discussed Harriet's "condition" with a psychologist who informed me that this is a classic example of OCPD, which is "Obsessive-Compulsive Personality Disorder," an obsession with perfection, rules and organization and bizarre anxiety reactions when someone gets outside of his comfort zone. Realistically depicted are her insane desire for cleanliness even of the trees outside, her wild grimaces, hysterical laughter and odd twitching, her desire to keep tabs on her husband for fear he is outside the home enjoying himself, her willingness to protect herself by nearly framing him for the murder of a friend, her inability to consider any delegating of responsibility as successful. The condition is too accurately portrayed to be accidental and reflects either someone whom either Arzner or screenwriter Mary McCall knew personally or detailed observation of a significant study of the disorder first recognized by Freud in 1908.

*Craig's Wife* fits well as a companion film with *Christopher Strong*. Both films are most heavily influenced from ancient Greek tragedy, the latter owing more of a debt to Euripides and the former to Sophocles. Both films are morality plays. Both films have an unheeded chorus of citizens. Both films reveal nuanced characterizations of women. Both films feature a star performance from a woman. Both films give special prominence to women and portray men as ineffectual fools, who can easily be manipulated by women. All of these characteristics are part of the Dorothy Arzner cinematic dialectic, which can be seen to varying degrees in most of her other films.

## DANCE, GIRL, DANCE
### 1940

The story of *Dance, Girl, Dance* is a simple one. A group of young girls at a dancing school in New York are trying to become successful dancers. Since most men are slobs and don't appreciate highbrow dancing, the girls survive by taking burlesque gigs and showing off their bodies. Those who are the best-trained serious dancers such as Judy (Maureen O'Hara) don't have the bump-and-grind sex appeal of a poor dancer such as Bubbles (Lucille Ball) and so the male entrepreneurs hire Bubbles, who is the lowest common denominator for their leering patrons. Judy is attracted to spoiled and mixed-up rich boy Jimmy Harris (Louis Hayward) and doesn't know that she is being sought by Steve Adams (Ralph Bel-

lamy), who is a great dance impresario who both loves her and wishes to train her to become the artistic dancer she wants to be. Judy believes he is another male goon after her for sex, but eventually realizes his intentions are sincere and honorable and she sets out to become a great dancer with Steve.

Maureen O'Hara, Louis Hayward and Lucille Ball star in *Dance, Girl, Dance.*

Once one understands the unique dialectic of Arzner's films one can apply it to her other films. A few minutes viewing of the initial sequence of *Dance, Girl, Dance* (1940) is therefore instructive as an example and one can see the similarities in theme and construction to *Christopher Strong* and *Craig's Wife*. We are once again in the realm of Greek tragedy, but transported to the modern day, set not in a lofty idealized acropolis or high city of ancient Athens, Greece but in Akron, Ohio, as far away from Athens as one can get, in rubber town, the tire center of the universe. Curiously, Akron derives from the Greek word *acros* (used in the Greek word acropolis) and means high, referring in this case to the series of elevated or stepped locks along the Ohio and Erie Canals where Akron was located.

So, Akron has an ancient Greek name and is a Greek word used originally in connection with the sacred center of ancient Athens, the seat of veneration of the most important Athenian gods—Athena and Poseidon. Knowing Arzner's fondness for everything Greek, I find it hard to imagine the choice is a coincidence and more likely is just the sort of inside joke that she would have enjoyed (and used in other films such as *The Bride Wore Red*). It is very much the sort of thing that Josef Von Sternberg loved doing in his films—jokes that only a few members of the audience would actually understand but which would give each film a slightly strange, seemingly indefinable feel.

Once again we witness the beautiful lighting and composition that are hallmarks of Arzner's films, this time emulating the so-called *kammerspiele* or intimate German theater lighting that was developed by Max Reinhardt in Germany in 1906 for his special Berlin theatre, taking advantage of the newly disseminated use of electricity. In American cinema of the early 1930s such lighting was widely used by directors such as Wilhelm

Dieterle, Josef Von Sternberg and Robert Florey, to name a few. Von Sternberg was particularly noted for his cabaret sequences, full of visual clutter and reflecting spangles, which is exactly what Dorothy Arzner is evoking in the opening sequence. Furthermore, the film's producer was Erich Pommer, the once prominent UFA German film producer in Berlin, who supervised the making of *The Cabinet of Dr. Caligari,* and to whom Max Reinhardt was very well known. There is dramatic lighting with the foreground of the Akron nightclub in shadow and the background strongly lit in chiaroscuro or light and shade effects that were popular in German silent films of the 1920s and spread with the German, Hungarian and Austrian influx into Hollywood films of the later 1920s and early 1930s with Von Sternberg and his compatriots.

Again, as has been repeatedly demonstrated in the feminist literature about Arzner, the women in the film are the individuals of complexity and importance. The men sit lecherously in the audience admiring the girly show, among them Louis Hayward, playing a manic depressive, flighty goofball of a man who is alternately motivated by high idealism and his strong sexual drive. The women have great power over the men as in the *Lysistrata* and literally dazzle them with the sparkling reflections from their costumes, so that the men are blinded by their sexual power. The men appear as libido-driven, arrogant, insensitive, dangerous jackasses. The women are powerful goddesses or muses, who appear in front of the bandstand along with symbols of the Greek god Apollo, leader of the nine muses who are the patrons of the arts and literature. In the troupe we quickly focus on two women. One named Bubbles is completely independent and aggressive and not concerned with the rules (Lucille Ball) and one is the traditional woman, concerned about doing the right thing in society (Maureen O'Hara). Once again we are in territory of Sophocles' *Antigone*. But this time the traditional woman Judy O'Brien is compared immediately to the goddess Venus, who is not only the paradigm of idealized perfect beauty but also the Morning Star, appearing just before sunrise and the embodiment of pure love. The key song of the film is entitled "Morning Star" and Louis Hayward upon first gazing at her exclaims:

> You look like a star, you know, the morn-
> ing star.

As the image of perfect true love on Earth, Judy is made to speak in a completely calm, idealized voice almost as if she is a Stepford wife. She seems to wander through the film in a daze, and as the embodiment of perfect love, she can only be gentle and kind and mild, much as Mrs. Frazier (Billie Burke) in *Craig's Wife*. Maureen O'Hara was a strong personality as those who have seen her in *Only the Lonely* and *McClintock* might infer and in her earlier years she was quite a tomboy and physical athlete. In this film she is toned down to a breathy blandness that oozes mystically divine sweetness, until her incredible fiery speech attacking males in the burlesque hall. Her long-suffering quiet and calm demeanor throughout the film makes that explosion all the more dramatic at the finale and is another of Arzner's star-making performances. Judy has learned to be a modern girl and has gained wisdom through her suffering. It is significant that she wishes on the morning star Venus not for a husband as a traditional young lady would but rather for a successful career in dance! In the end her prayers to the classical goddess are answered for she gets both a husband and an impresario who can make her dreams of being a serious dancer a reality.

*Dance, Girl, Dance* has the feel of a fantasy as two struggling girls each find success in the Depression. It borrows heavily from the notion of fate and destiny and ironic dialogue found in the Greek tragedy. Judy in the depths of her desperation ironically tears up the card of the very dance impresario who wants to help her. In a sequence particularly worthy of Greek tragedy, her dance teacher, Madame Lidia Basilova (Maria Ouspenskaya), has prepared Judy to make her great audition to the gods of dance high up in their tower and states:

> We are but a few short steps from destiny.
> Never let it be said that the great Basilova
> did not make the last sacrifice for us.

Scant seconds later she is struck down by a car and killed! The world of the gods is inscrutable to mortals, so much so that at the end of the film Judy just sits down and laughs and cries at the same time when she realizes the games that fate and destiny have played at her expense.

Ironic sequences abound. In front of a burlesque house the girls inside are billed as "36 little ladies whose only wish is to entertain you," when in fact that would be the last wish they would have at this place. In another sequence the loopy and oversexed Mr. Humpenwinger, who sells artificial limbs, is obsessed with women's legs and seeks to be a patron of sleazy dance shows. Bubbles ironically succeeds as a dancer because of her lack of any real talent or, particularly, class. In fact she has to assure her male patron that "I ain't got an ounce of class, sugar, honest."

And through all of this, in case one forgets that the Greek gods are watching all the action of the Earthlings below, we get to glimpse the address book of Madame Basilova as she is preparing Judy for the great dance audition. In a listing just above the place she is going to call for an audition is a group labeled "The Athenian Club," another of Arzner's little jokes to remind us of the inscrutability of the gods to mortals functioning in a Sophoclean universe governed by fate and destiny. Arzner did the same thing at the beginning of *The Bride Wore Black* where the upper class bistro is called "The Cosmos Club."

As stated earlier, Arzner and Marion Morgan were both influenced by the approach to life and dance of Isadora Duncan. The idea that one should aspire to a higher reality by seeking the wisdom of ancient Greece and Rome was fundamental to Isadora's break from the traditional way of dancing to something more modern and less staid. The Greek and Roman world was her inspiration. Even in the main dancing sequence of the film, featuring the great Vivian Fay and members of her own troupe, the emphasis is on the contrast between the traditional or old school type of dance and the modern dance, which is more dramatic and emotional, more the sort of dance that Isadora had sought to create using Greek influence. So Judy needs to incorporate her traditional or more classical dance knowledge into something more modern just as she needs to combine her traditional lifestyle with something more modern and street smart. The term "classical" here refers to the traditional way of dancing with its rigid postures and attitudes rather than to anything Greek or Roman. Inspiration from ancient Greece and Rome will lead to an understanding of the best way to become a great dancer. To remind us of this, the

**Bubbles (Lucille Ball) Judy (Maureen O'Hara) and Sally (Mary Carlisle) are hard-working burlesque dancers in *Dance, Girl, Dance*.**

background includes a lovely ancient Greek key design. When Fay finishes, she is told that "your classical influence is a little strong," meaning that she has not yet fully integrated the new Greek influence and is still dancing in too stiff and formal a manner.

Completing the Greek and Roman references, the principal male Jimmy (Louis Hayward) is compared throughout to a bull, traditional and ancient symbol of male fertility and raging power. Bulls appear constantly in the form of little Ferdinand, the stuffed toy symbol of Jimmy. In one cabaret sequence a gigantic bull appears as a backdrop as Louis Hayward mouths the words to the band's song, which is *Morning Star*. The enormity of the bull suggests the maximum influence that Jimmy has over Judy at this moment.

**Maureen O'Hara**

Once again we see women presented as the principal figures of interest. Arzner even changed the part of the dance instructor from a male to a female. Males have the illusion of dominance but are either lecherous and evil or unfocused and generally worthless with the exception— and it's a rare one in a Dorothy Arzner film—of Steve Adams, the dance impresario (Ralph Bellamy). This is more than made up for, however, by the nastiness by which the female would-be dancers are treated. Jimmy calls them "the little ladies dancing their feet off before a jaded public, innocent victims of a man's avarice" and "the little ladies." Men are described by women as having "more arms than an octopus." In their hypocrisy the men seek lurid sex and the illusion of virgins at the same time and so the worldly Bubbles is ironically renamed Tiger Lily White!

In her speech in the burlesque hall, Judy delivers a great soliloquy, which has become memorialized by the feminist critics. It is a scathing indictment of the male world and its exploitation of women and openly mocks men, who "play at being the stronger sex" but "we see through you." One can look far and wide through the films of the 1930s, '40s, '50s and even '60s and not find anything quite like this declaration, rendered all the more telling by the strongly emphasized meekness of Judy in the film up to now. It is also a star-making moment for Maureen O'Hara as she shows her extraordinary range from the wide eyed innocent to the maturing modern girl. When she makes her speech we see she is both the traditional and modern girl at once and the explosive speech is triggered by her constant humiliation. It is also caused by the fact that Judy is like a goddess of the purest love and truth. She must speak honestly and her speech is the more effective because of her integrity. Once she erupts she returns to the shy woman she was and seems almost bewildered by the force of her own declaration. At the end of the film, when she is thrown into court and threatened with prison, her truthful response is so surprising and refreshing to the judge that he believes her!

Humiliation is a strong part of Arzner's work. Often it is the male who is humiliated by a *femme fatale* or else working girls humiliated by men. In *Dance, Girl, Dance*,

**Lucille Ball bumps-and-grinds her way to stardom in *Dance, Girl, Dance*.**

the immediate trigger for Judy's speech is her humiliation by another woman, namely Bubbles, who tricks her, forces her to play a stooge, makes her wait on her and powder her back and steals her beau just because she cannot stand to have anyone get something she couldn't get whether she wants that something or not. Jimmy had rejected her once and she didn't want to let Judy get away with it.

The humiliation of Madame Lydia Basilova is one of the reasons the part was recast for a woman. She was once a member of the famed Russian imperial ballet of Diaghilev, but now is forced to book strippers for lecherous men in Hoboken. She has become "a flesh peddler and a jellyfish salesman." She tries to delude herself that she is teaching the hula as a sacred dance when in fact it is a kooch dance to be done with "oomph." The lecherous Armenian booker Mr. Kajoulian observes that when the hula is properly done it is "too classy."

Initially, only Bubbles sees through this male dominated world by picking up men, taking them for all she can (Pomeranian dogs, furs, etc.) and then quickly dumping them before she gets too involved. She uses her wiles to manipulate and make her way. But she is a typically nuanced Dorothy Arzner woman. She cannot stand for anyone else to have success that she didn't have, she has a colossal ego and no shame and a desire to outwit, humiliate and control others and yet she secretly pays the rent for her two starving dancer pals because she doesn't want anyone to know that she has a good side to her personality that she tries to keep hidden!

*Dance, Girl, Dance* has survived as the most popular of Dorothy Arzner's films because it features Lucille Ball, a popular television actress for her *I Love Lucy* show, which still runs today after more than 50 years. Arzner gave Lucille Ball her greatest movie role here and the listless list of RKO films she decorated clearly reveals that. Both Maureen O'Hara and Lucille Ball are given star-making treatment here. The script deftly explores these complicated women and their differing approaches to surviving in the world of dance. One is a traditional woman and one is modern, one is Ismene and one is Antigone cast into a modern situation of survival that updates the Sophocles play and also infuses it with new ideas and sensibilities. It deserves its place as one of the great Dorothy Arzner films.

My only criticism of it would be the dance sequences involving Maureen O'Hara. Although a great female athlete, she lacks the grace of a true dancer and frequently is replaced with a double who has more muscular and defined body form. Because I was a former dancer, I am intensely aware of body conditioning and tone and there should have been more attention to this in the doubling for Maureen O'Hara, especially since Arzner had both Vivian Fay and Marion Morgan available for consultation. But this is a small criticism and one that many viewers may not be concerned with. Otherwise *Dance, Girl, Dance* can stake a claim to be an artistic masterpiece.

## THE BRIDE WORE RED
## 1937

By now I am optimistic that I have convinced the reader that Dorothy Arzner liked to draw on her personal life and interests, particularly within the sphere of ancient Greece, when making her films. But what of a movie such as *The Bride Wore Red*, which would at first glance appear to be as distant from the classical world in inspiration as could be?

The film is set in and around Trieste in Northeastern Italy, a kind of crossroads of German, Italian and Slavic influences between the Adriatic Sea and Slovenia. A certain Count Armalia (the ever devilish George Zucco) is enjoying an evening out with rich friend Rudi Pal (Robert Young) and they get into a debate wherein Rudi believes that good birth and breeding make the man and woman and the Count believes that it is just fate and the luck of good birth that sets people apart in society. He therefore

**Rudi (Robert Young) and Count Armalia (Franchot Tone) are like Greek gods playing with mortals—in this case Anni (Joan Crawford) in *The Bride Wore Red*.**

star vehicle for Joan Crawford. The movie was an absolute bomb and Joan Crawford reportedly fought tooth-and-nail over the concept of it and refused to cooperate with Arzner. The result is that Crawford gives a performance that seems too histrionic and scenery chewing for the part, too concerned with draining all the *sturm* and *drang* out of every opportunity, and Arzner's attempts to tone her down so that she would fit the more light-hearted scenario better did not work in this case. In short, Joan never did understand that her role needed to fit the piece because Arzner directed to fit pieces into an overall concept. The final result surrounds Crawford with an atmosphere of wit and light comedy while she seems to think she is starring in *Harriet Craig*.

But how could this film have anything to do with the ancient Greek civilization? I would submit that Count Armalia and Rudi Pal are like Greek gods whose discussions and feelings affect the mortals of the world below. They sit in their elegant palaces on high and spin the wheel of fate for humans. This concept is a staple of Greek tragedy and also Greek epic literature such as Homer's *Iliad* and *Odyssey*.

Now you may say that I have gone too far and that this is pure speculation on my part. And yet, we are informed at the beginning of the film that the meeting of the Count and Rudi takes place at the COSMOS CLUB, a place where the elite have the power (the term "omnipotence" is used) to change the destiny of mere common folks from misery to gold. With the help of these "gods" any man or woman can be made superior. Cosmos is a Greek word which suggests a divine order or harmony as opposed to the chaos that is found in the dive of Trieste where Anni works, described as the very lowest place on earth. Anni is sent off to test her ability to function as a privileged Earthling, as the gods' favorite. She is sent to Terrano, a name which actually means Earth but which also happens to be a rich wine-growing and resort area near Trieste.

And what exactly is the Count doing in sending Anni off on this great adventure? He says, "I'm fixing the Great Wheel. I'm fixing it so that you can win for a while." Images of wheels abound in the film, including the gambling wheels of the Terrano casino. But the wheel that the Count is referring to is the *Rota Fortunae* or the Wheel of Fortune, a concept well known to ancient Greeks and Romans and which reflects the capricious nature of Fate. The wheel can be spun by the gods and controlled by the Roman goddess Fortuna and the wheel can lead to happy

resolves to go to what is described as "the worst dive in Trieste" and find someone to send to a fashionable resort for just two weeks in order to see if she might fool the people there into thinking she is really a member of high society.

He selects a singer named Anni (Joan Crawford) at a wretched cabaret and offers her a two-week vacation in Terrana, a trendy but quite rural and distant community not far from Trieste. Rudi goes there too but doesn't realize that she is the girl that the Count has chosen to pretend to be a society girl and he falls in love with her. Anni's life in Terrana is complicated by the fact that she is attracted to a happy-go-lucky local postman named Giulio (Franchot Tone). With time running out on her stay, she must decide if she should encourage Rudi to leave his own fiancée Maddelena Monti (Lynne Carver) and then marry him or if she should marry the happy peasant Giulio. Will she choose true love or great wealth? The whole affair was originally written by the Hungarian playwright Ferenc Molnar as *The Girl from Trieste* and was a romantic Cinderella fantasy about the meaning of happiness and true love, but it was adapted here as a

or unhappy lives for mortals. Throughout the film the wheel is mentioned and viewed as we learn that "life is the great roulette wheel." Humans are told to mind that they "don't get too dizzy on that great wheel of life," and "a human is a little ball, helpless in himself, bouncing helplesslessly from slot to slot" in the great wheel.

As in the case of *Dance, Girl, Dance*, themes of Venus and nature are strongly present. The lovers Anni and Giulio gaze out on Venus the morning star, the symbol of true love. Giulio personifies the natural life, the peasant who knows the true joy of the beauty of the natural world, which is unknown to the wealthy, who shut it out. The great palaces of the rich can shut out nature's beauty and isolate the inhabitants from even its sounds, just as in *Craig's Wife* or in Euripides' *The Bacchae*. Giulio informs us, "I know Venus intimately." Also cited is the relationship of Venus and Mars, with Venus reported as being seen by Giulio winking at Mars. Venus and Mars are love and war, true contentment and strife, and they struggle together. In Roman mythology, Venus has an ungainly lover, Hephaestus, who is her husband and who makes a love triangle of the three divinities just as Giulio, Rudi and Anni make among the mortals. If she surrenders to her heart and to nature and to true love, Anni will find her happiness with Mars/Giulio, but if she goes through with the planned wedding to Rudi it will become an ungainly thing and she will always be thinking about Giulio.

Dorothy Arzner directs Joan Crawford on the set of *The Bride Wore Red.*

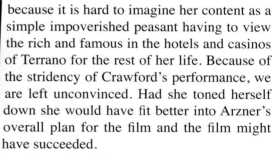

As is the case in the other Arzner films, we meet the traditional woman versus the modern woman. Maddelena is powerless to do anything but wait and see what will transpire. She is the Ismene of the *Antigone* in modern guise. Anni is an Antigone-type woman, not bound at all by convention and thoroughly modern, but in this case she is motivated by self-preservation, until she hears the beautiful call of nature. Anni is a nuanced character, as are virtually all of Arzner's women, in this case torn between the pull of nature and the lure of great wealth. By the end of the film we are not sure which side of her has won

because it is hard to imagine her content as a simple impoverished peasant having to view the rich and famous in the hotels and casinos of Terrano for the rest of her life. Because of the stridency of Crawford's performance, we are left unconvinced. Had she toned herself down she would have fit better into Arzner's overall plan for the film and the film might have succeeded.

The animal imagery so abundant in the other films we have examined is of course abundant here too. In fact when the god-like Count visits the lowest place on earth, Anni asks, "Did you come to stare at the animals in the zoo?" The peasants of Terrano are compare to bullfrogs and when Anni washes her face in the water, Rudi observes that she seems so wild and at home in nature:

You're like an animal, all instinct and emotion.

Nature and the simple life vs. the rich in their stately halls is a main theme of the film. Nature is also the place where one finds God through the purity of a simple life. To emphasize this, Arzner brings in Saint Lucy and has the peasants, functioning as a Greek chorus, sing "Santa Lucia" at her feast day on December 13, which in the ancient Roman Julian calendar is the longest night of the year. Lucy was allegedly a Christianized ancient Roman venerated as a saint because of her refusal to marry a rich pagan in ancient Syracusa (Sicily) during the Christian persecutions of the Roman pagan emperor Diocletian (A. D. 284-305). Embracing her worship helps those who are blind see the truth as she is the embodiment of *lux* or light. As the song "Santa Lucia" is sung in the film, it is a calling to Anni to see the true spirit of nature and marry Giulio and devote her life to the poor, just as Lucy gave all her possessions to them. Once consecrating herself to nature, Lucy could not be burned alive and received her divine reward despite having her eyes taken out with a fork!

In Arzner's curious mix of the Christian and the classical (which also governed much of her personal life), nature is seen as having mystical healing powers that the corrupt rich cannot see, the same message we have seen in *Craig's Wife*. Once again Venus can be our guide, as in *Dance, Girl, Dance*. Nature is represented by beautiful sounds which are shut out from the palaces of the rich. The tyrants cannot hear the voices in the wind, or see the beautiful grass and pines, or feel the healing power of a fresh spring. Anni is a person of the earth, of Terrana, if she would but realize it.

There is also a strong Greek-type chorus present in the film, in the form of the peasants of the town, every one of whom knows and supports Giulio and every one of whom tries to make Anni realize that she is one of them. The Feast Day of Santa Lucia provides an opportunity for them to convey their message as they parade by her.

*The Bride Wore Red* has much the look of a Josef Von Sternberg Paramount film. In this case Anni is played by Joan Crawford, but the film opens in a manner reminiscent of Lola Lola (Marlene Dietrich) in *The Blue Angel*. The cabaret is a bottom-of-the-barrel dive full of dramatic *kammerspiele* lighting and there is a song done by Anni, the ultra low-class female singing star of the place amid all sorts of visual clutter. After she sings "Who Wants Love," she is literally pawed by a drunken slob of a man as she attempts to leave the stage.

All of this is deeded Josef Von Sternberg/Marlene Dietrich territory. So are the little tensions set up in the film, which give the film a peculiar look and feel when viewed today. For example, we watch Anni struggle to eat at the fancy restaurant in Terrano. She is desperate not to be discovered and yet has no idea what silverware goes with what dish or what she should order. While she is in this terrible fix, the waiter recognizes instantly that she is really one of the common people and needs help. This waiter is determined to help her maintain her dignity, even after she is found out to be a fraud later in the film

and dismissed from the premises. He is the only one to open the door for her.

The interplay between rich and poor is deftly handled. When Anni arrives at the hotel and casino in Terrano, she is immediately recognized by the hotel maid Maria (Mary Philips). Anni wants to wear a flamboyant red dress and Maria, who knows what is appropriate, talks her out of it. The red dress symbolizes the modern flamboyant woman to Anni, but it is too showy and flashy and really only suggests her lack of proper breeding. When Anni and Maria are in public they are rich woman and servant, but when they are alone in Anni's beautiful room, Maria, in one sequence, literally PUSHES Anni off the divan to make room for HERSELF, something a real maid would never do to a rich person. But Maria knows that at heart Anni is really one of the common people. Still, the image of a maid in full servant's costume pushing her matron off of her settee gives the film a different look from most 1930s fare. In another sequence, the maid casually lights up a cigarette in Anni's presence with the same jarring effect on the viewer. There is also a stream of double-entendre, ironic dialogue here as well, much of it supplied by Billie Burke, who plays Maddelena's wary mother, the Contessa di Maina.

As in the case of Greek tragedies, the principal figure, in this case Anni, boxes herself into an impossible situation. Exposed as a fraud and disgraced in the eyes of her fiancée Rudi, she prepares to kill herself, much as Lady Darrington had done in *Christopher Strong*, who believed that "Courage conquers death" and killed herself to stop the cycle of heartbreak on the Strong house. Maria the maid, part of the peasant chorus of Terrana, can no longer play the game with Annie and berates her, "You are like a fire, with no heart, and you destroy everything around you." And Anni almost does kill herself, but barely decides against it for she says that that would require "courage greater than mine."

Annie is the core of this film and the men revolve around her. Giulio is simply a personification of nature while the other principal men, the Count and Rudi, are arrogant and abusive. Rudi is a prig who resents humans lacking a proper pedigree and the Count is not truly interested in the welfare of the poor as is clearly seen by his rude treatment of the waiter in the opening scene. Rather, he is just making a wager and testing an hypothesis because he has nothing better to do.

*The Bride Wore Red*, although a box-office failure, has all the ingredients of a typical Dorothy Arzner film and deserves to be revived despite the flawed performance of its star.

Dorothy Arzner's custom built home at 2249 Mountain Oak Dr. in Los Angeles.

## DOROTHY ARZNER AT HOME

Arzner's fascination with the classical world of the Romans and particularly the Greeks continued into her private life with the home she built at 2249 Mountain Oak Drive in Los Angeles where she lived from 1930 to 1951 when she and Morgan moved to La Quinta in the Southern California desert.

The Mountain Oak Drive home was her dream house where Morgan particularly enjoyed entertaining guests such as Marlene Dietrich. The house, which was often described as her "Roman villa," was a combination of the ultra-modern and the classical, just like the contrasting women in her films. The overall look featured total whiteness in the manner of a Hollywood version of an ancient Roman building designed for Cecil B. De Mille. Real Roman palaces and temples had painted exteriors but were never so in De Mille films and only became white after becoming ruins and losing their paint. The house had broad areas of white that ended in sharp edges and a simplified, lightly streamlined look. The front gate that led up to the porch was intended to be a stylized Ro-

man triumphal arch complete with an attic story, which, instead of containing a dedicatory inscription to a Roman emperor, could contain the street address or name of the home. The front porch was fronted by Doric columns featuring capitals that were attenuated versions of those of the Parthenon on the Acropolis or high city of Athens. These columns were also fluted in the classical Doric Greek style. Above the columns was a Greek architrave but with a simplified and streamlined overhanging double cornice above which came a clear and simple upper story with Mondrian-esque windows. It was a neat combination of the most contemporary design of the International Style, blended with De Mille-type white ancient Roman movie set, mixed with echoes of classical Greece.

## DOROTHY ARZNER AFTER HOLLYWOOD

Arzner left Hollywood feature filmmaking after falling ill with pneumonia during the making of her movie *First Comes Courage* in 1943. Although she would state that she had become weary of the system, friends said that she "was forced out of the movies by the chauvinistic

99

**Dorothy Arzner and Joan Crawford, on the set of _The Bride Wore Red_, would work together again in the 1950s on Pepsi commericals. (Photofest)**

treatment by the powerful men of the movie industry." This meant people such as Louis B. Mayer and Harry Cohn, who found her difficult to work with because of her insistence on achieving a certain look to her productions and because she was not only a woman but a known lesbian, who had not been publicly outed but who was known about within the film community.

Mimi's daughter Bunny reported:

> When Dorothy retired from the movies she wouldn't even go to see any of them. There was talk she had been forced out by men but she was never regretful and didn't talk about herself or her work much. For her work, she preferred to let it stand on its own merits. She was a quiet but strong personality. She taught Coppola but wouldn't go see his films or any others very often.

One reason for her desire to leave the business and lead a more private life may have been the growing dissatisfaction and more open bias against homosexuality in Hollywood. In the early 1940s attacks against transvestite entertainers and laws against such once dominantly popular entertainers such as Julian Eltinge had forced them out of business or underground. Arzner's semi-open lifestyle with Morgan was not to be tolerated in the Hollywood of the early 1940s. Joan Crawford had come dangerously close to destroying the life of David Manners and reportedly wrecked his Hollywood career with her quotes on his lifestyle. About Arzner she could be careless or vindictive in her remarks, and once reportedly said, "I think all my directors fell in love with me. I know Dorothy Arzner did." Arzner's lesbianism was a thinly kept secret and fear of being outed in these anti-gay times by a disgruntled actress or even technician may have played a significant role in her decision to quietly leave. After _First Comes Courage_, however, it was said that Arzner was ill and

**Dorothy Arzner's invention of the boom mike forever changed sound and filmmaking in Hollywood. (Photofest)**

suffering from pneumonia and that that was the reason for her leaving the profession, despite the fact that she made a full recovery.

During WWII Arzner produced two training films for the WACs and began her radio show *You Were Meant to Be a Star* which featured scenes from films or other sources which were acted out and followed by a moral and advice, which helped women to improve their lives and become stars in their own world. It was viewed as an "index to better living." Arzner created the show and hosted it. Biographer Judith Mayne reports:

> There may be something hokey about the constant attempt to draw moral lessons from the world of performance but there is something quite touching about these little essays as well.

Dr. Mayne adds that these programs featured women learning to perform in order to survive in the man's world and she notes that for Arzner, "to be female is to act a part." Like Greek tragedies, each program was treated as a morality play with Arzner herself acting as the advising Greek chorus.

In 1951 Arzner taught a film production course at the Pasadena Playhouse and made the move with Morgan to La Quinta, a lovely and then rather remote but trendy Southern California desert community not far from Palm Springs. There entrepreneur Walter Morgan had established the lovely La Quinta Resort as a no-tell getaway for many Hollywood stars and socialites including members of the so-called "Sewing Circle." During this period Arzner spent a lot of time in her garden and in retreat from the rat race, giving her time to think about writing her autobiography, which she began but never finished.

In 1955, much-married Joan Crawford married Alfred Steele who was President of Pepsi Cola, and Joan used her film connections to promote the product much to the annoyance of many co-stars in her films. She would give out Pepsi Cola pens incessantly to co-workers, who didn't want them and in 1958 enlisted Arzner, once her nemesis on the set of the film *The Bride Wore Red*, to make 50 different television spots for her new company. 1959 to 1963 was spent happily teaching film at UCLA, and visiting with friends such as Billie Burke.

In 1961 she was named director of The Religion in Science Foundation and continued her and Morgan's longtime interest in Christian Science by visiting the home of Mary Baker Eddy which both Morgan and Arzner did with great interest. By the early 1970s, Arzner had been all but forgotten but the nascent feminist movement led to a rediscovery and reappraisal of her films. This both pleased and displeased Arzner. Her close friend's grand-daughter Sally Sumner stated that:

> Dorothy turned a cold shoulder to the feminist movement. Dorothy had been around powerful, dynamic, pioneering women all her life and didn't think that the independent woman had been discovered in the 1960s and 1970s. She went along with their interest in her because it brought back respect for her films and a new appreciation of them, but she never saw herself as someone related directly to this movement and she didn't want to participate in it more than she agreed to do with regard to her own work.

Arzner could have become more of a *cause celebre* for the feminist movement than she did become and this was by her own volition, according to her friends. She did not wish to explain her films to anyone but felt that being known only as feminist filmmaker was not what she was completely about. Her films were very personal to her. Despite being made within the studio system, she always tried to imbue them with a higher reality, a love of the Greek classical tradition, a reverence for nature and a focus inspired by ancient Greek tragedy and Greco-Roman culture and myth. She was also inspired by Isadora Duncan through Marion Morgan and fascinated by male directors such as Cecil B. De Mille, James Cruze and Josef Von Sternberg (she once reported that Cruze treated me "as if I were his son).

Being remembered as a unique early director of women was nice but it was a view of her work she considered myopic. Instead of expressing what she DID do in her films, she, like Von Sternberg, refused to discuss her intentions. Today Dorothy Arzner is considered the

On the set of *Judge Priest* (1934), film director John Ford poses with Will Rogers, Dorothy Arzner and Irvin S. Cobb. (Photofest)

property of feminist and gay/lesbian critics. To them we owe her resurrection from the trash heap of forgotten directors of the cinema and to them we owe the realization that her work was different and important and offered a particularly female point of view that in her films turned Hollywood conventional cinema on its ear. But there was, as I hope I have shown here, even more to the Dorothy Arzner Dialectic than these critics and authors have recorded. Their view is sincere, honest and important but it was in Arzner's view focused on a particular agenda and was not concerned with what else she was trying to do with her cinema. The fact that she did it her way WITHIN the commercial studio straitjacket is extraordinary. And she sustained her position for 15 years in a male-driven system that was intolerant of mistakes from a female director (let alone a well-known lesbian). Dorothy Arzner's films still invite viewers to discover more and more layers of meaning and complicated interrelationships of character and environment. To this viewer, she was a woman of considerable depth and ability, whose full intellectual glow has yet to be fully appreciated. In a sense her films are so rich that it is in one sense unimportant whether she was male or female. She was an *auteur* filmmaker whose work, considered apart from her sex, can stand up to the works of the great directors of the cinema.

## FURTHER READING FOR THIS SECTION:

Biers, William, *The Archaeology of Greece* (Cornell, 1996)

Easterling, P.E., *The Cambridge Companion to Greek Tragedy* (Cambridge, 1997)

Goldhill, Simon, *Reading Greek Tragedy* (Cambridge, 1986)

Johnston, Claire, *The Work of Dorothy Arzner: Towards a Feminist Cinema* (British Film Institute, 1975)

Mann, William J., *Wisecracker: The Life and Times of William Haines, Hollywood's First Openly Gay Star* (Viking, 1998)

Mayne, Judith, *Directed by Dorothy Arzner* (Indiana University, 1994)

Morley, Sheridan, *Katharine Hepburn* (Pavilion, 1989)

Nestle, Joan, A Restricted Country (Firebrand, 1987)

Rosen, Marjorie, *Popcorn Venus* (Avon, 1974)

Stenn, David, *Clara Bow Runnin' Wild* (Penguin, 1988)

## INTRODUCTION TO A PARTIAL AUTOBIOGRAPHY

In 1988, I had just finished working on a documentary film project for PBS and the American Museum of Natural History in New York City entitled *Carthage: A Mosaic of Ancient Tunisia*. The film was shot by KUAT-TV of Tucson, Arizona and shot on location in Tunisia and particularly in the foothills of the Sahara desert among Bedouin tribes and archaeological sites of the Roman period.

During this "shoot" I had time to consult with the director, Sally Sumner, about anything and everything as we passed the time on long road trips. There weren't many female directors back then and, despite my having worked in the documentary film business for some time, I had never worked with a woman director. I was not of that older generation such as my stepfather, who felt that a woman's place was in the home or in a menial job, and so I was delighted to work with Sally, who directed a beautiful and moving documentary and was a joy to work with in every way, and who had twice the stamina that I had as we headed out towards the Sahara desert. But I couldn't help wonder what had gotten Sally interested in filmmaking.

I had been lecturing for several years back then about the classical influences I had discovered in the films of Dorothy Arzner and how Arzner was so underappreciated as an *auteur* filmmaker. Sally astonished me by saying that the big influence on her life and decision to become a movie director had been her grandmother Mimi's dear friend... Dorothy Arzner. Sally told me that Arzner had been a great admirer of classical civilization and in particular the ancient Greeks, a thesis I had long been proposing in my university classes but could never confirm.

She further noted that her own great-grandmother Pearl had helped to look after the young Arzner dur-

**Gwennie, Billy and Catherine Boynton (Photo Victor Valley College)**

ing her stay at the Westlake School near which Pearl lived. Sally's grandmother, Mildred Rivers aka Mimi, was an enterprising Westlake girl, who also befriended Arzner at a time when Arzner was feeling lonesome and down. Arzner also got to know another Westlake student and superwoman named Gwen Boynton whose mother was a prominent psychiatrist named Catherine Boynton. These ladies might all be considered early feminists by today's standards but at the time they were a group of wealthy, adventurous young ladies, who had been inspired by their Westlake teachers and the role models they had in their own family. Sally Sumner described this group as "tough, pioneer-type women who were very strong and were just not willing to take any back seat to anyone."

Dr. Catherine Boynton had come up with the idea in 1917 of establishing a getaway clinic in a beautiful natural desert environment away from the stress of life in the city. Her patients began to go to the high Mojave Desert where they relaxed and enjoyed the dry climate and the natural wildlife and exotic vegetation. By the 1920s the guest ranch, known as Rancho Yucca Loma, had grown to 1,000 acres, scattered with private cottages and unified by delightful restful evenings shared by the guests and hosted by Catherine and her daughter Gwendolyn, fresh out of Westlake. Rancho Yucca Loma was an instant success and became no longer the getaway place for the mentally depressed but rather a secret resort for who was who in Hollywood. Free from the prying eyes of the press, Hollywoodians could relax in a special community of friends and acquaintances sharing the rule "don't ask, don't tell." Thus many of Hollywood's homosexual community could come here in a tranquility they could not share in Los Angeles. William Haines, friend and collaborator of Dorothy Arzner especially on *Craig's Wife*, had tried to live in an openly gay lifestyle and was the number-one box-office star in Hollywood but his film career came to an immediate halt in 1931. Had he chosen not to come out of the closet, he could have survived in getaways such as Rancho Yucca Loma.

After 1929, Gwendolyn Boynton now Gwen Boynton Baker had brought out Sally's grandmother Mimi, fresh from her divorce, to help out at the ranch so that there, despite being nearly impoverished, Mimi might continue in the grand lifestyle to which she had become accustomed before the Depression. Dorothy Arzner was also part of this Westlake alumnae circle and was another of the dynamic young girls inspired by Westlake founders Vance and de Laguna as well as by Gwen's dynamic mom Catherine.

**Native art greeted visitors looking for a safe getaway at Rancho Yucca Loma. (Photo Victor Valley College)**

Rancho Yucca Loma was a getaway place for stars such as Clark Gable and Loretta Young, who produced a secret child named Judy, who was not known about during the glory years of the two stars but was one of the well kept secrets of this resort (Loretta later adopted her and the two had a love/hate relationship for years). Loretta often delighted in playing ping-pong with Sally's mother while relaxing there. No one loved the Rancho more than David Manners, who became a part owner of the place, helped to build cabins and hosted many guests. When David was threatened with being outed in 1936 on the set of *Love on the Run* by Joan Crawford, who had had a longtime dislike for her co-star, the refined David was thoroughly shocked and turned to his business investments to survive, deciding to leave Hollywood's venom and pressures. He spent much of his time at the Rancho Yucca Loma where he loved having guests gather around to listen to radio broadcasts of classical music and opera and he could paint and write. Manners had been one of Hollywood's most refined and competent leading men, having contributed so wonderfully to movies such as *Dracula*, *The Black Cat*, *The Death Kiss* and *Roman Scandals* and having been known as an actor who could make female co-stars look terrific as he fed them their lines. He was kind, encouraging and supportive of such stars as Katharine Hepburn and Barbara Stanwyck in their early days on film.

Rancho was also the place where Clark Gable grieved for Carole Lombard after her death by plane crash during a fundraising tour in World War II. Here William Holden struggled unsuccessfully to get along with longtime wife Brenda Marshall. Gossip columnist Hedda Hopper came too and everyone was on their toes around her! In 1937 part of Frank Capra's classic epic about a fabulous place called Shangri-La was filmed there. It was called *Lost Horizon*.

After Arzner left the film business in 1943, had a brief fling at radio and eventually moved from her dream house, Mimi and Arzner always remained very close and there was a deep friendship also for Mimi's daughter whom everyone called Bunny. Bunny is Sally Sumner's mother. When Arzner's life companion Marion Morgan died in 1971, Arzner stayed in touch with Bunny and daughter Sally because they were almost the only "family" that Arzner had left. The "family" believed that Arzner had stayed together with Morgan, whom almost no one liked, in order to avoid loneliness. When Arzner died in 1979, it was Bunny and Sally Sumner who inherited many of Arzner's personal items, including her prized collection of small ancient Athenian Greek vases of the fourth century B.C.E. and many of her home furnishings, which Sally now uses to adorn her own lovely home in Tucson, Arizona.

All of this provides a background to why Arzner decided in 1955 to attempt an autobiography but was hesitant to let it be widely known and ultimately decided not to

**Two vases from Dorothy Arzner's prized collection. (Courtesy Sally Sumner)**

**Arzner's home displays Greek and Roman influences.**

traordinary drive to make something of her life, to model herself after male prototypes such as Horatio Alger and even Cecil B. De Mille, with her overall goal being to become the boss, the director, and to "blaze a trail!" Her abusive upbringing made her extremely sensitive to everything in her environment, a useful element for a director. Abused children (I was one) often become adept at calming people down and picking up on the moods of people, particularly dangerous people. Thus when Arzner is dealing with the emotional states of women, her life experience observing women from all levels of society in the "home" environment and in the workplace made her a natural for directing films in which the emotional states of women were primary. Nowhere in the autobiography is there any mention of lesbianism. Women of her generation did not confide such things even in their autobiographies.

Arzner films are noted for their observation of backgrounds, costumes and lighting. These backgrounds reflect the lives of the characters, particularly focusing on the stately halls for the rich in the manor of an ancient Greek tragedy. Arzner admired the beautiful classical architecture of the great families when she was a child in San Francisco before the great earthquake. In her early life she was surrounded by the repulsive, the dirty and the vulgar and she developed a lifelong desire for the white, clean purity of ancient Greece and a need to keep all dust out of her home environment. She also developed a reverence for nature and particularly for gardening. Therefore it is not surprising that her autobiography is more fascinated with the visual environment and sounds of her various homes than it is with her own life. She is writing a narrative as if she were a Greek or Roman god looking down and directing the story of her life, which, like an Arzner film, is full of chance occurrences that seem driven by divine fate, most notably her quest to find her mother, which is resolved too late but which is strangely resolved through a chance meeting with, of all things, a fortune teller who pretends to tell her about herself mystically, but who turns out almost magically to be a close friend of her lost mother.

Her lack of interest in joining the feminist movement may be traced back to her experiences with groups of women with whom she had mixed experiences. True, she went to Westlake where she got to know some superwomen, but she was also initially reminded by her peers there that she didn't fit in and was from the other side of the tracks. She grew up with few girlfriends and found that she was different not only in her sexual orientation but in the way she related to privileged girls. When the upper-class young ladies of Westlake demanded that she bow

complete it. She trusted Mimi's family and so Bunny was given Arzner's secret manuscript. After 55 years, Sally has decided to allow the manuscript to be published in order to help better illuminate the life of this important woman director. The work only covers the period from Arzner's birth to her first work as a scenario typist for William De Mille at Famous Players Lasky. But the autobiography contains a number of important elements and insights about Arzner's nature and opinions even if it lies about her birth date. Arzner liked to think of herself as a modern woman and so she claimed she was born with the turn of the century even though she was not.

The diary reveals her love for classical culture and even proclaims that her birth occurred under the watch of the two-headed god Janus, Roman divinity of beginnings. One can see her appreciation for traditional architecture and her dislike of the ultra-modern and of course her own home was noted at the time for being a modern echo of classical Greece and Rome, with some of her own furnishings being used in the Rosalind Russell vehicle *Craig's Wife* in 1936.

In the autobiography, Arzner emerges as the traditional girl, kept in her place and seeking to be obedient in order to obtain affection, as she is shunted about from home to home while her father all but abandons her and keeps her long-suffering mother away from her. At the same time she learns to be a modern woman in her ex-

down and worship them and not only threatened her but physically attacked her in a mob, she developed a strong resentment to women pushing her around and became particularly sensitive to the organization of women into disparate and often conflicting groups. No wonder she found Katharine Hepburn so difficult to adjust to when *Christopher Strong* was being made. While Hepburn was enjoying money and upper-class privileges and enjoying being a rebellious student, Arzner had been virtually homeless, trapped with a brother, who was threatening to kill people with a gun, victimized by a pedophile, physically held back from her real mother, who was searching for her, and deprived of the security of the one foster home she liked by the great San Francisco earthquake.

Finally, after one reads the autobiography, it will likely seem surprising that her biographers up to now have hesitated to call her an *auteur* filmmaker, who like Hitchcock drew on life experiences and fears to develop a coherent pattern that runs through most of her films. Even from this small autobiography it is plain to see that Arzner's unbelievable life experiences molded her into making a certain kind of film with a certain viewpoint. And as she states there:

**Dorothy Arzner was a pioneer filmmaker worthy of the label *auteur*. (Photofest)**

> I have the thought that all we can ever do
> in our work is write our own biography.

I should also note that Dorothy Arzner, because of being skipped about in one grade and forced to attend many different schools, never learned to spell well and found punctuation to be a horrible challenge to her. She could always think cinematically because of her innate genius and her upbringing but grammar was never easy for her. In order to make her autobiography more coherent to the general reader I have taken the liberty to correct what she has put down and make it grammatical and easier to read. In a few cases where I have no idea what she was trying to say I have left things alone and invited the reader to puzzle it out for himself. This was an attempt at an auto-

biography and was dashed off as a rough draft, some of it jotted down stream of consciousness style. She never took the time to polish it for publication and that must be borne in mind when reading it. It is essentially a first draft.

I have combed through the various books and articles I could get on Dorothy Arzner but have not found this attempt at an autobiography listed anywhere, even among her papers left to UCLA where she taught for many years. It was given to me to help my research 22 years ago by the Sumner family. Because of having to write other books in the meantime and because I didn't realize that this may be the only surviving account of Arzner's life in her own hand, I left off getting this into print until right now. After viewing *Dance, Girl, Dance* recently, I came to realize again what an important and underappreciated filmmaker Dorothy Arzner was and I decided to sit down over several months and put these essays together along with the first publication of her autobiography draft.

107

# AUTOBIOGRAPHY

**By Dorothy Arzner**
**2701 Wilshire Blvd.**
**DU. 9 3141**

## Part I

It was San Francisco, the first year of the 20th century. That, in itself, has a certain significance. Whether it is dramatists who have dramatized San Francisco or San Francisco that dramatizes lives, I do not know; but many of the people in my world who have been born there have a particular individuality that dramatizes itself one way or another. Most of them have a deep love for that city, particularly the ones who were there before the 1930s. It holds rich memories and an excitement. Even young people, while sitting at the cocktail tables on the top of the Mark Hopkins Hotel, will comment on the beauty that surrounds them. The cocktails become secondary to the beauty of the two heroic bridges that span the bay—the Twin Peaks, with their heads in the mist—and the Golden Gate, truly golden as the great gold disc of the sun seems to splash its way down into the sea. Perhaps in one's blood there is an electronic connective with the place of one's birth. Perhaps it's the big city of the gold mining days that stirs us with a desire to blaze trails. Perhaps it's the realization of a dream—the dream of a man named Fair, who had a vision. He saw one of the most beautiful cities in the world—San Francisco.

There was a hill overlooking the waterfront town; they called it Knob Hill. Fair, the Virginia City gold-miner, built his home on top of that hill and three other associates did the same. His home is now replaced by the famous Fairmont Hotel. Across the street, the Mark Hopkins Hotel

**Fairmont Hotel, 1907**

replaces the home that was there. On the third corner one of the great mansions remains. This is no structure of useless Victorian cupolas. It is a solid classical structure built of dark-red terra cotta blocks of stone with the finest plate glass shining from large square windows, letting in the sun and light and giving a wide view of the sky and sea about. A graceful green bronze fence rail surrounds the grounds possibly designed and wrought by an Italian artist. A covered entrance lends dignity to a beautiful door and just inside are marble halls and a grand staircase. This is not structure to be replaced by so called modern architecture—this is as fine as one could wish for today. It has nobility. There is an excitement in the realization that a piece of architecture still stands that holds, in its form, the life and culture of the nineties in the West.

Snatches of stories have been told to me of flamboyant women and aristocratic sons, too warm-blooded for the conventions of the East. A hotel was named The Palace Hotel. I saw victories drive in to the courtyard of that hotel. The courtyard now is a large dining room—still beautiful—and has an air about it of a palace courtyard. The ladies riding in the victories wore large hats—tipped just a bit with a large tied ostrich plume falling across the crown and down on one side of their face. The men wore frock coats and derby or top hats. It seemed that every man wore a mustache—it was a sign that he was no longer a boy, I guess. The living moving pictures did seem gay. Beautiful horses pranced as they turned into the court. Within were red velvet and crystal chandeliers flickering a lovely yellow light. Even electricity was not so steady then. The wealthy of the gold rush were having their day. Virginia City—the Yukon—and from the East—all kinds of people poured into San Francisco. Trade started to boom with the Far East. Meetings and separations to seek more life and more and more life. Life clanked with the horse and cable car bells; it twinkled with theater and café marquees. It moaned with the steamboat whistles and laughed a little too loud with the ladies of the "Gay Nineties" now grown older. It crept in with the fog and roared in with the January storms off the Pacific.

In the midst of this melee and the beginning of a new century, the god Janus put into the records the birth of Dorothy Emma Arzner, born in San Francisco, California, U.S.A.

Father—born in Karlsruhe, Wurttemberg, Germany. Mother—born in Glasgow, Scotland.

In 1942 when all Americans had to prove their birthright as American citizens there was no proof that I had been born. The record had been destroyed in the devastating fire and earthquake of April 18th, 1906. My pride of birthplace was now being tested by questions. My last name, originally Artzner, was German. I had earlier responded when I heard the phrase, "a citizen of the world" that I liked the phrase. I liked the idea of belonging to the whole instead of being a limited person. However, school records and a bank record satisfied the inquirers that I had been in America for more than twenty years and all was well. I was not a German enemy. But I cherished the idea that I was a citizen of the world.

My father was an immigrant boy of 14 when he came to this country, alone, without relatives or friends. "Fabulous America" had reached across the world to become a boy's goal. To get to America was his ambition. There he could make money and be independent—make his own way. It took him thirty days to cross the Atlantic. He arrived in America with $20.00.

My mother was one of eight orphaned children born in Glasgow, Scotland. Her older brother John had come to America and as he earned the money dressing tools working in the shipyards, he brought them one by one to this country.

My brother David was four years older than I.

This was the small family pattern into which I was born, a kind of "behind the scene" reality of life related to the show that was going on out front. No red velvet or crystal chandelier—just a simple wooden cottage halfway up one of the hills, very similar to many others that stood in a row. These were small examples of Victorian architecture. Bay windows bulging from the parlor and wooden balls on dowel sticks for the decorative arches, colored glass around the door windows, and a fancy hand-turning bell. A long flight of wooden steps led up to the first-floor entrance door, above a basement. These houses are still standing in San Francisco. Only the basements have been converted to garages.

What is left of my first five years of personal experience are bits and pieces. No recollection of having a body—just a mind recording brief snatches of moving pictures that later took on significance and within one a depth of feeling toward them. I dramatized them. I tied them to later events. I saw them as beginnings of later crises.

When I was born my brother did not like having a little sister. He wanted a brother. He must have made it quite evident since I was told of it many times. I've won-

**The courtyard of the Palace Hotel, 1904**

dered to what extent this had a bearing on my becoming a tomboy because that was what I became in action as I stood at the end of a long hall and a baseball came flying at me. I either caught it or it went through me. Later my brother was so very proud of his little sister's superior ability that he would show me off by having older boys take turns at hurling their swiftest pitches at me and I can recall the sound of that solid thud as the ball came to a dead stop in my catcher's mitt, too big for my little hand, but somehow one can learn to handle inadequate situations.

There was something about my mother that was always exciting. I think it was the natural love of a child for its mother personified by being left alone a lot without her. She was small and had dark curly hair. Not at all the popular type of the day, which were large full-bosomed blonde women. As always, Gentlemen Preferred Blondes then too. [Editor's Note: This is a reference to Anita Loos' book and 1953 film, *Gentlemen Prefer Blondes* with Marilyn Monroe and Jane Russell]

There must have been an emotional content that made her approach so vivid. I can hear the rustle of taffeta coming down that long hall—it was black taffeta with ruffles on the bottom. That sound brought joy. The picture of black taffeta was probably all I saw from my point of view on the floor. I don't remember her face, actually. I have a photograph or two but no recollection of the likeness to my mother. My mother became an ideal made of the fabric of a child's longings. She was warm and emotional one moment and the next we would be left alone for hours. I remember one time looking into the contents of a store window with my mother by my side and the next moment when I looked about she had disappeared. A panic rushed over me—I was lost, only to find that she had moved around the corner to another window!

I can hear a song my mother used to sing as she stood in a little clothes closet selecting a dress to wear:

> All I want is fifty thousand dollars,
> Sealskins to protect me from the rain,
> Vanderbilt and Pierpont to escort me —

(I can write the notes of the melody if I were near a piano). There, memory of the following words stops short—but the melody continues to finish the fourth line phrase. With much research, I have not been able to find that song. It seems to me to tell so much of the times. Fifty thousand dollars was a fortune. Sealskins were the luxury fur, and Pierpont Morgan and Vanderbilt were the millionaires of the day.

At night, jumping up and down in the middle of the bed with my brother, I was singing:

> Yankee Doodle went to town
> A ridin' on a pony
> Stuck a feather in his crown
> And called it maca-ro-ni.

Hilarious laughter—then prayers.

> Now I lay me down to sleep.
> I pray the Lord my soul to keep.
> God Bless Papa. God Bless Mama.
> God Bless Davey and me.

Street scenes looking out the window:

A Chinese man in black coolie suit and large straw hat with two large heavy baskets, three-feet deep and a foot-and-a-half across, filled with vegetables and hanging from the ends of a pole arched across his shoulders. He moved with short steps that gave the impression of running. I remember feeling it was too heavy for his frail little body. Next a curly black-haired Italian vendor, swinging up the street, with a stocking cap pulled to one side and singing lustily his wares—white plaster casts

**Chinatown pharmacy in San Francisco, c. 1900**

sticking out above the basket he carried rakishly on one shoulder. I remember these rather awful bits of sculpture sitting on pedestals in the parlor of many houses.

The tamale man was always a pleasant sight. He came along at night when darkness outside seemed a bit formidable. First his voice calling, "Tamales—nice hot tamales!" It was the little bright flickering light from his charcoal burner swinging by that gave off warmth and life.

The messenger boy with dark blue uniform suit and a square patent leather visored cap seemed to be a theatrical bicycle performer. He went by balancing a huge tray of food covered with a white napkin on his cap, with both hands on the handlebars; at least he never hung onto the tray. When he came to be the symbol of clandestine suppers, I do not know, but he did.

The dark black figure of the lamplighter was there too. His movement was never hurried. He lit the lamp at the corner with a long stick that turned the gas key and also carried the lighted match. He became a work of art in that golden light. With unhurried rhythm he crossed the street to the next lamppost.

All seemed orderly and intent upon their very individual enterprises until the Chinese laundry wagon would pass. Then there was commotion! Dogs barked—boys shouted, "Chink—Chink—China man. Go back where you came from!" and rocks were thrown at him. The excited Chinaman with long queue flying stood up in his one-horse covered-wagon and whipped his bony horse into a gallop through the shower of rocks, then yelling in a high-pitched voice Chinese swear words and pointing at the boys as he disappeared down the street. I had been told a legend that if a Chinaman pointed his long finger at you, you would turn to stone; so there was always a scampering for cover on my part.

Now came the beginning of drama. I seemed to be the observer of myself and the incidents. I was lying on a double bed crying lustily as a bottle crashed into a mirror above a sideboard covered with glasses. My mother had thrown that bottle.

A little girl sitting between pointed standards of an iron rail fence watching older girls at play. I played baseball and this seemed to separate me from them.

Sticking my head between the roundels of a decorative fence rail trying to get into where some other children were playing, my head got caught so that I could go no further nor back out again. I remember the fearsome thought that I would have to stay there forever or have my head cut off.

I was playing with shiny green-mottled tile that was scattered about in the process of being a new fireplace mantle, and also repairs were being made in the basement to house a very large billiard table. The billiard table was the indication of prosperity coming into the home such as the cocktail bar in present-day homes.

8579. SAN FRANCISCO, CAL., AND BAY, FROM FAIRMOUNT HOTEL.     COPYRIGHT, 1905, BY DETROIT PUBLISHING CO.

I can see the great beer wagons loaded with kegs, being hauled up the cobble-stoned hills and every sorrel muscle bulging from the magnificent horses of great bulk.

The clanking of bells from the fire engines—I rushed to the window to see the fire horses as they passed. They, too, were great shiny animals putting forth every effort from their great hearts for speed.

I climbed on the edge of my doll's bed, then up on a ledge of the wainscoting, but I slipped and smashed the doll's head in. The doll was blonde and brown-eyed and my biggest and best doll. Oh, I had dolls. Naturally I was given them. I was a little girl, but they were just things that had to be taken care of. I hauled them with me for many years but always they sat in corners neglected.

I only remember one Christmas during those first years. "It was the night before Christmas and not a creature was stirring." When suddenly from my darkened room into the light from the hall I saw the fleeing figure of my brother with my little black stocking in his hand. I had hung it at the foot of my bed. In that instant, I knew Santa Claus was a fake. I don't remember when I believed that he was real. I only remember the moment of full realization that he was not real.

Christmas Eve drops in on quarreling words between my papa and mama. Nothing violent, just words of dissention. This is followed by long days of being left alone and left with other people—a tobacconist and his wife. I used to love to watch him roll the large leaves into cigars and cut the ends. Sometimes he would let me push the cutter. There was a life-sized wooden Indian outside.

A strange family with strange children. I met one many years later. She was a fortuneteller, from cards. All I can remember is my reaction to dirt and disorder. A piece of flannel was given to me as a handkerchief; that bothered me most of all. I was crying for my mother, which I did the whole time I was there. Then one evening she appeared like a dream princess and I was saved from the ogres and villains. As I look back, probably the only villain was dirt and a kind of disorder that exists with too many children and not enough money.

I was also left with a policeman's wife, a little precise woman with a tight black dress buttoned up the front to her neck and black rushing about the collar. Everything seemed black and rigid. On the wall was a picture of her dead husband, a formidable man in uniform, and a wreath of brown "immortal leaves" hung round it. Death seemed to be in the house. She was kind but I didn't like the pictures I saw.

I also remember a large color picture of my brother on a white easel. He was about five years old and had long golden curls to his shoulders. He was dressed in a black velvet Lord Fauntleroy suit with a large white collar and a ruffle on it. That picture was the bane of his existence even though he had long since had his hair cut. It was the style for little boys to have long curls if they had them. It must have come from the aping of the English aristocrats.

Now my brother and I seem to exist in a house alone.

The parlor satin cushions and a sick kitten lying on one of them while we watched it breathe its last breath.

Playing train with the parlor chairs in a row.

A wooden sled—greased runners—a wooden box—and me in it, one slide—and I was thrown on my face as it landed at the bottom and the scene blacks out of my memory.

Storm outside—we were alone again—another glass door, to the basement. Tagging behind my brother. He was struggling to get the door open against the storm when a gust of wind slammed it shut on his arm and broke it. Neighbors running in. Doctor called. Watching—waiting for the doctor. Then splashing through the mud down the street I saw the familiar one-horse shay.
Such relief! Such great, kind friends—the doctors of those days. The one-horse shay on a rainy day was unmistakably a doctor.

That break in my brother's arm seems to have been the beginning of what later was a frailty—broken several times playing baseball and football, and it undermined his strength.

A trip downtown with my father—this was an unusual occurrence. As we entered the lobby of the Palace Hotel, I saw my mother sitting in the corner. I thought she looked beautiful. She was dressed in a sealskin jacket and wearing violets. I rushed toward her—my face was crushed into the violets and fur. She started to cry and so did I. Then a pulling apart. That was the last time I saw my mother except for one brief glimpse a few years later. I was five years old. Now my brother and I were "children of divorce."

## PART II
## JULY 5th, 1955

There was no problem to readjusting to a new environment. Evidently, everyone was kind and made an effort to entertain a lonely little girl. At least there were people about and that seemed to be interesting. There were five in my uncle's family—my brother and I added made seven.

The house was a white Victorian wooden house, one floor sitting above a basement. The front had a lawn with a white picket fence around it and a gate that led to the front entrance. But it was a view from the rear that seems to have been my approach. I believe it was through the back gate that one came from the railroad station. Everything must have been within walking distance because I have no recollection of vehicles, only bicycles, and walking on wooden sidewalks.

There was a long stair against the rear of the house that led to a little landing and a back screen door that led into the kitchen. The kitchen was dining room and kitchen and living room combined, though there was a front parlor and a back parlor, along one side, and three bedrooms and a bath with a galvanized iron tub on the opposite side. In the front parlor was an upright piano and on it was the first piece of sheet music I had ever seen. It was "The Rose of Killarney" and a colored picture of a lady's face in a large red rose on the cover. In the back parlor was an organ and a formal dining table, which was never used except for Sunday dinners and in a bay window was a couch where I eventually slept.

The backyard was fenced with a gate at the rear. A chicken house with chickens. A large windmill with a water tank, where I used to make mud pies and the base served as a counter from which to sell mud pies to my aunt. There was the outhouse with two boards, A walk from the house that led to it from the rear stairs. I remember the board was new and there were two big holes in it and one little one made especially for me. Also hanging on the wall was Montgomery Ward's catalogue.

The detail of the period is familiar to most, so I will not go into it all. Oil lamps to be cleaned every day. All hot water was heated on a wood stove. Three meals to cook—chickens to be fed, and all the rest of the household drudgery that a woman had to assume. The Saturday night bath was a real routine. Hauling water to the bathroom and heating it on the wood stove was a chore.

My uncle was a tall, typical Scotsman. Handsome, ruddy, with curly iron-gray hair, and a rather large head that sat erect on his shoulders. My aunt Lena was small, thin and frail, a gentle little woman, with all the signs of hard work imprinted on her face and form. She wore gray gingham dresses that buttoned to the neck and long sleeves. Her hair was pulled back into a tight knot at her neck. Her face was sweet but thin and lined. I remember sitting on her lap and being a healthy plump little girl. I would say, "Here I'll give you some of my cheeks" and I'd pull at my cheeks and place them imaginatively onto hers. I can see her sad sweet smile. I would be up in the morning with her, making the mash for the chickens and soon I was also helping with the making of butter, pushing a plunger up and down in a tall wooden bucket. There was an older boy Willie, who was away all week in San Francisco working and Johnny, a younger boy about fourteen, who went to school and worked at night in the telegraph office. Polly the girl was fourteen and starting in high school.

When I first arrived I was to sleep with my cousin Polly. She would wait until the lights were out and then start telling ghost stories until I would cry with fright. Aunt Lena would scold her but it did no good. Finally they set up the couch in the back parlor and there I slept in peace. I remember liking that little place to myself. My cousin Polly evidently was not too happy having me usurp her privacy and used this method of revenge. I guess I tagged about after her, because there is an incident that stands out vividly. She was sitting before a mirror brushing her hair and the next thing I knew I turned and found that she had disappeared. I looked all over for her. Then when I finally found her back, sitting before the mirror and asked where had been, she said, "Why, didn't you see me. I turned into a little flea and was sitting on the curtain there." That was frightening to me. I guess I believed her and it was frightening.

This period in my life seems to have so many firsts in it. The first time I was accused of a lie. My cousin Polly and I each had been given what was called "tick tac toes." If you squeezed the metal bug it gave off a tick-tac sound. Mine seemed to go out of commission and wouldn't work at times, then would work. My cousin lost hers and mine seemed to be working at the time I was accused of having taken hers. To my knowledge I had not taken it. But my kind aunt made a point of the fact that my cousin said I had lied. I remember the effect on me, of my aunt thinking that I had lied. My best friend had gone against me. My best friend had called me a liar!

452 RUSSIAN HILL and BAY as seen from Nob Hill in 1908. SAN FRANCISCO, California.

I remember sticking fast to the fact that I had not taken my cousin's toy, that the one I had was mine. I was crying copiously and the impression left was that I had been unjustly accused. I was made to give mine to my cousin. This injustice stayed for years.

Many times I have wondered about that incident. Knowing how unaware children are of these rights and wrongs and how eager to have what they want, I hope it was true that I had not lied. Though whether I had lied or not is of little significance unless I knew what was a lie and what was the truth and then went against the truth. And I would only ask that from a more mature person than a five year old. Especially when we know how much subterfuge and untruth seems to be rampant in the world. The statement of simple fact is very rare. Perhaps Mr. Shakespeare comes nearer the truth, "If you believe it, it's true."

Another first. My uncle and a friend of his who lived across a field used to play cribbage in the evening. He too was a Scotsman, a friend from "the old country." He seemed to be a very well-educated man because he was so interested in teaching me things. I learned to tell the time from a clock that hung on the wall. I learned the name of cards. I learned to play casino. I was also told wonderful stories about castles and knights in armor and queens and kings and princes and princesses—all rather tied up with those little square cards that were so important to the evening's entertainment.

I found out that things that did not look hot could burn. My aunt was placing the lamps in a row on the table and because the glass upright shade over the wick looked so slick I put my little hands around it and with instant excruciating pain I had seared the palms of my hands. I went around for days all done up in bandages. This was the first time I remember being hurt very badly.

I had my sixth birthday and that meant I could go to school for the first time. There was always much to do about curling my hair on rags for Sunday, and lovely clean white dresses and ribbons and bows. I guess my mother had established the curls. From pictures both my brother and I dressed and looked like the wealthy children of the era. My father also was by now known to be reasonably successful. He paid for everything we had and gave us most everything we wanted.

My recollection of that first day in school was mainly associated with having learned to raise my hand before speaking, because I remember gales of laughter at the dinner table when I raised my hand to speak from habit so quickly impressed during the day. Also we were told to raise our hand with two fingers up when we wanted to go "out."

My brother did not play a very important part in my life during this period. There are pictures of him with larger boys with baseball mitts, so I was no longer included in his baseball playing—he now had boys to play with. I was busy having my sweet little aunt for a companion, being given little pieces of pie dough and filling to mold a little individual pie for myself. Making mud pies and having my aunt come by the counter as a buyer of them. Then there was a little boy I played with—Willie Parrot. He used to haul me everywhere on my tricycle. He had a little harness and I drove him.

I also had a black kitten I was very fond of. One day my aunt had made a berry pie and it had strips of dough on top—very fancy. Guess she baked it for a special occasion. She put it out on a little shelf to cool. The next thing I knew she flew out of the kitchen door with a coal shovel and I saw that shovel go flying down the stairs after the black cat. It missed him. But in spite of the top of the pie having been eaten off, I was shocked at the violence. She was so mild and gentle and kind and long suffering. I had such a love of that little kitten. I remember defending him. But it was too much for my aunt. Now as I look back she well deserved some outlet.

Uncle Johnny was a good man when he was sober but on Saturday night he would hold back some of his pay and Sunday night after being away most of the day he would come home actually roaring drunk. We could hear him coming, singing, usually, at the top of his voice and sometimes falling into the honeysuckle house, a kind of little shady summerhouse formed by thick honeysuckle vines. Other times he would be in the house. He was very funny to all of the children—full of wit and loud laughter, tossing nickels and dimes about for us. But my poor little aunt saw no humor and only suffered deeply. She would have to get him to bed. He did not always want to do what she wanted him to do and he would throw her off with a deadening thud against the wall or the door. His language was not what it should be at those times and I'm sure she was fighting to protect the children from exposure to his drunken outbursts.

Monday morning all would be as usual. But these violent Sunday nights became kind of nightmares. There was a story about my uncle. There was a roll-top desk in the back parlor and it was the place of valuable possessions. I had a little diamond ring my father had given me for Christmas and I remember there was a little secret drawer that I could put it in when I was not wearing it. Also in another one the savings were kept. There were no banks near. One banked any great amount in San Francisco. But here all my aunt's savings were kept in that desk.

This story of my uncle happened before I went to live with them. It seems my aunt had the four children and all were little. One day Uncle Johnny did not come home. She discovered that savings had been taken from desk and only a small amount left. Weeks passed—and when she had become desperate not knowing what to do for money a letter came from him saying he was in Scotland. I have always thought about him a lot. He had a good mind. He had pride and was one of the finest tool men in the shipyards. After I grew up and was walking beside him he used to remark that I stepped out like an aristocrat. That was revelatory to me. He longed for a life beyond just laboring. I think in desperation, after years of laboring for others. he decided he would close his mind to all responsibility and leap into freedom from it all for a "fling." He did—but it was hard on my aunt and evidently something that was not to be easily forgiven. But he returned after his trip and settled down to the hard work he'd always know "dressing tools."

One day my aunt was busy getting all dressed up. This was unusual for her. The house was all in order and so quiet. There was an air of strangeness about it all. She never went out. I had never seen her in a black suit and a hat and veil and her hair dressed a little bit by being curled in front but the same simple knot in back. She informed me she was going to San Francisco for a week—for me to be a good girl and she would be back soon. But this seemed a tragedy to me. I cried. I could sense that she was not happy. We went to the train to see her off. On my way home, when I was still crying, I looked down at my hand and the little diamond from my ring had been lost, tragedy upon tragedy. Then I found out that my aunt was going to the hospital to have an operation. They had to tell me since I was carrying on about the whole thing to such a degree.

I remember this rather calmed me down because I realized this was something that she had to do, that she was not just leaving us. Somehow I felt nothing but doom about this absence. Most unhappily I was sitting on the floor trying to button my own shoes the second morning when my cousin Polly came in and told me Aunt Lena had died. This came as a climax to my feeling from the day she left.

The funeral was in our parlor. Death has never seemed to me to have been marked by any early fright because when I was lifted up to look into the casket I remember seeing that little face looking so peaceful, There was not anything frightening about it. I remember wanting to see her. It was not forced upon me. I loved my aunt. She was so kind and loving and the only incident that was not the most gentle was the incident of the little lie. But I'm sure that came about from her love of me, and not wanting me to lie. There was no violent scene about it, just an administering of justice. But she has become a symbol of the hardship and painful long-suffering of many of the women of her time. So if women today seem to be useless and spoiled it must be an accumulated credit they have been given by their pioneering self-sacrificing mothers and grandmothers.

It seems to me I did a great deal of crying in those days but also they were happy days, contented days. I was not lonely. Now my friend had gone and there was another adjustment to be made.

It was Sunday—everybody was dressed up including me. I was told my father was coming for me. I loved my father, although I did not see much of him. I was looking for him. The back gate opened and there he was, looking very different from other men. He was dressed in extremely well-pressed clothes. He wore a large fine Panama hat.

He always had fine eyes and they shone more than ever this day because they were serious. I remember being allowed to rush out to meet him. He was always businesslike but kind. He never had much time. Things moved fast. All three dolls and my belongings had been packed in a straw telescope basket and the whole family saw us off on the train that very night. My Papa had come to take us away to Los Angeles.

Only one year had passed since we had left our mother. Now we were on our way to a new world. A train was a new experience, a bit frightening at night. I was unhappy and cried. My Dad was clumsy about getting me undressed. I can imagine what an ordeal it must have been for him. I insisted upon sleeping with him in his berth. I guess I was just scared. It must have taken a night and a day on the train in those days to go from San Francisco to Los Angeles. At any rate, I know when we arrived. It was at night. I must have been asleep because all I can remember is insisting again that I sleep with my father, but when I woke up in the morning I woke up alone. I remember this little girl getting up and wandering about looking for her father and finding him in bed with a strange woman! That was a shock!

I was told that the strange woman was my stepmother. Not a very good introduction to my stepmother. Hard on her and hard on me! It was as simple and natural as that but to me most unnatural to find my father had disappeared and now a strange woman was sort of forced in my life. She tried to be nice, but we knew my father was going to go to work and both my brother and I insisted upon going with him. We did not want to be left with this strange woman. In desperation my father took us with him.

All seemed to be fairly calm downtown with him until the woman who was now known as my stepmother arrived on the scene and literally dragged me away from my father. In retrospect it is understandable. My father's business was a restaurant in back of a saloon and in connection with a theater: "The Grand Opera House," one of the oldest theatres in Los Angeles

**The Grand Opera House**

located at First and Main Streets [Editor's note: sources list the address of the Grand, built in 1884, as 110 S. Main Street]. I screamed and yelled my lungs out, threw myself down on the sidewalk and was dragged bodily through the streets and up a long flight of stairs to a hairdressing parlor.

There were two very nice women, sisters. They proceeded to placate me. They finally calmed me down by making designs with hairpins, ordering an ice cream soda to be brought up to me and constantly reasoning with me. I finally calmed down. But this introduction to my stepmother was the beginning of what was always a strained relationship, full of misunderstandings and oppositions.

I do remember before I left that I, too, had my hair dressed by one of the very pleasant ladies and I thought I looked rather nice. They did it so carefully without pulling it. It was softly curled and trimmed and a round comb was placed on my head like a little crown and the hair was softly held away from my face. I thought I looked rather pretty for the first time. I guess the hairdresser had diverted my misery with flattery and it must have worked. Also, my stepmother complimented me on my lovely hair. As I look back on this incident, I must have been a pretty tousled-looking little girl by the time I was dragged into that hairdressers. Also I doubt that my hair had been combed since I had left except as my father might have struggled with it. I'm sure I wouldn't have let my stepmother touch me.

My brother had stayed with my father. He probably had his own problems in making the adjustment, but I was too full of my own miseries to know what was happening to him. Only after I had matured a bit did I develop a real sympathy for all concerned. It must have been just as difficult for Dad and for Mabel, my stepmother. But somebody should have some wisdom about those things. I often wonder how long it will take for man to have any wisdom at all.

The next I knew we were to be boarded out. Living in a boarding house is a special kind of experience for children.

## PART III

In one year my brother David and I had been transplanted twice, cut off from our mother and father, then from a loving aunt and uncle, taken to an unknown land, Los Angeles, introduced to a stepmother, and now taken to call on some strange people: Mrs. Dunlap and her two daughters. One was a nurse

Main St. looking South from 1st St.,
Los Angeles, Cal,

went. There were outside people, who came in to dinner. On Sunday I remember I always got the neck of the chicken. For many years after I thought that was the part I liked best because I hadn't been given the other white meat.

This was a boarding house. There were many little disharmonies. I saw Mrs. Dunlap whack her son with a butcher knife. I suppose she was careful and happened to have it in her hand, but she was always taking a leap at him. My brother made his own friends and I tagged along. There were often words about us being gone so long or being late or staying away too long. I would want something and he would stand up for me to get it. No one dared correct us too drastically because when my father left us he had taken us aside and told us not to let anyone raise a hand to us. If so, "you tell me" he admonished to my brother and told him to take care of his little sister. He did as best he knew. I tagged along wherever he went, chasing after a gang of little boys or playing baseball. I was never comfortable in the house alone. The people were strange to me. The sleek man was too affectionate. The older daughter, engaged to him, was not friendly. He was always showing off his strength. When I would run from him he would catch me by the waist of my dress and pick me up at arm's length and hang me over the banister while I screamed. Between that and forcing kisses on me I was not happy.

Every afternoon there was a time that Mrs. Dunlap disappeared into her room and locked the door. Although I called and knocked, she would not answer until she was ready to see me. Up to that hour she wore a boudoir cap and I didn't think it was very pretty. The ruffle flopping around her face bothered me. One day when I was looking for her, I tried her door and it was not locked. The door opened wide and to my surprise there she sat directly facing me and completely bald! She was dressing her wig on a wooden head. Just one frightening flash picture and I slammed the door and scampered away. Now a definite barrier existed between me and Mrs. Dunlap. This I had to keep a secret. It was too odd to tell to anyone, not even my brother. It was her secret and I had stumbled onto it and somehow I knew I must keep it to myself.

One rainy day not long after, I wanted my table and chairs up in my own room. I carried them from the base-

named Emma and the other, Jeanette, was pretty and cashiered at Jevne's Candy Store. There was Fred, a son, about my brother's age, and a young man boarder, a plasterer by trade. He was rather handsome in a slick way, with greased hair, and very sure of himself. Mrs. Dunlap seemed kind enough but there was something about her that was strange; her hair sat on her head like a cloche cap, rather too reddish-brown and always shiny and too perfectly wavy.

We sat in the parlor. A few words were exchanged with us, then Emma, the nurse, came in to look us over and Fred, the tow-headed rather disheveled boy, came in barefooted and he was introduced. My brother and I were always dressed very well and I noticed these people looked different. Mrs. Dunlap and my father exchanged a few words that sealed the bargain that Mrs. Dunlap would take us on and we left.

The next day we were given all the things we had wanted. My brother had a new bicycle and a gun and I a new tricycle and a new French doll with a lot of luxurious clothes in a little trunk, and a table and chairs. This seemed to represent a home of my own to me, which I could make for myself. It was white with blue flowers painted on it. My stepmother was the instrument of this generosity and I realized than how very giving she was but somehow there was no harmony in our natures.

We arrived at Mrs. Dunlap's with bag and baggage. Me with my little telescope basket full of dolls and clothes. I was to room with the younger daughter, who was nice and was away most of the day and into the night. I rarely saw her. We started to school and soon played with the neighborhood children. This life had very little personal affection in it, just the business of living. People came and

ment where I had been told I should keep them. Mrs. Dunlap didn't want them upstairs so she hauled them down again. I confided this injustice to my brother. I suppose I was crying because I could not have my own way. My brother took the incident into his own hands. He carried the table and chairs back upstairs to my room, got his gun, and locked the door. We heard the voice of Mrs. Dunlap calling and saying, "Open that door! Open that door or I'll break it down!" Then my brother called back, "If you do, I've got my gun and I'll shoot you." The next day my father came and we were packed up bag and baggage and taken away.

My brother was sent East to Cleveland, Ohio to live with one of my mother's sisters, Aunt Annie. I was sent north to Oakland for a trial visit with my stepmother's mother.

A very sweet little woman whom I had never met before was to take me North on the train. She was the mother-in-law of my stepmother's brother, who was employed by my father. She seemed to have good sense about a child. She lived in a tiny apartment and gave over the entire day to entertaining me with making paper flowers. The next morning we left on the train, sitting up all day, but she had a wonderful basket of food, all the things I liked and she was so much fun.

I now have the deepest sympathy for my father and what he must have gone through trying to find a place for his children. My stepmother never tried to force herself upon us. She gave us wonderful presents and was always with my father at his place of business. He owned the saloon and restaurant next to the Grand Opera House, one of the oldest theaters in Los Angeles, until it was torn down a few years ago. The actors and actresses were the main patrons of my Dad's Café. While we boarded at Mrs. Dunlap's, Dad used to come every Saturday morning and take us downtown to be with him. My brother and I played hide and go seek in the theatre, then went to the matinee. They were playing good old melodramas. I can't remember any of the subject matter, only the look of the people. It was a stock company. The villain by the name of MacKaye, had typical black shiny hair and a black mustache. He used to come into my Dad's restaurant and I liked him best.

William Desmond

He was always so much fun, just the opposite from the parts he played and he didn't have the mustache when I would seem him after the theatre.

Then there was the matinee idol William Desmond. He was dashing and handsome. He came in followed by several women whom he had to dismiss one way or another, because his wife, a very powerful [woman], was always there waiting for him to come from the theatre. These women used to wait at the stage door and follow him wherever he went, very much like the movie fans of today, except that he could not step into a fast automobile and escape. The actor in those days was on foot mainly and therefore vulnerable. His wife Lillian Desmond was my mother's best friend, and also the sister of Nance O'Neill, a famous actress of the day. All these theatre people passed by pleasantly and patronizingly, and were the bright spot of the week.

There were little incidents of my stepmother observing that our hands were dirty, nails not clean, hair unkempt, which made me uncomfortable. My Dad, with his soft heart, only knew one way to treat a child — give them what they want. So we had candy and ice cream sodas and the food we wanted. The combination of emotional sensitivity and the sweets usually ended my day with my being sick to my stomach.

By the time I arrived in Oakland to live with "Mam," and having been happy on the trip, I was now an experienced person in making quick adjustments. I also was alone to make my way in this new trial. Everything went smoothly. Mrs. Holmes seemed to know how to receive a child. My own room was in readiness. Little things were done for a child. I remember there was a tiny vase with a geranium in it. There was a place for all my things. She showed me around like a grown-up. There were lemonade and cookies that first afternoon.

I was introduced to a very nice boy, who looked very handsome in a white sweater with a red stripe across the middle of it. He was about the age of my brother and he asked me if I wouldn't like to see his domain. He had a little house of his own in the backyard. There was a skull and crossbones on the door and a big S.S. underneath, meaning Secret Service. There were pictures on the wall of ballplayers. I knew somehow this was an honor being bestowed upon me. I was told that no girl had entered this Secret Service room before. But that I could be an honorary member! He showed me his bicycle and told me I could ride it if I wanted to. Everything was to my liking and I reentered the house to ask if I could change my Sunday shoes to everyday shoes. I remember the comment made that it was wonderful how grown up I was and that I was such an intelligent little girl to want to change my shoes. I think that gesture made everyone comfortable because they knew I had accepted my new home happily and, being good people, that was what they had not dared to hope. And they made every effort to win the heart of a child. Mrs. Holmes, whom I later called "Mam" because this boy Burt called her that, was a real mother. She understood children. She adopted this boy after bringing up her own two children. This was the beginning of a rather involved array of relationships that later became always cumbersome, when trying to explain who was who in my family.

Now there was Tom, Mam's second husband. He was a Welshman, small, gnome-like, with a twinkle in his eye and song in his heart. He came in toward the end of the first afternoon. I've always wondered if he stayed away and came in at the end to pick up the pieces if there were any, knowing that a child should not have too many strangers to meet up with at one time. He and I struck up a friendship right off. He had the heart of a child and after dinner the first night away we two went hand-in-hand for a walk and to a candy shop. We bought licorice whips and jawbreaker jockey caps and peanuts and sang amusing little rhyming songs. He was a miner and when the mines shut down periodically this was the only time he was home. Fortunately for me, this was one of the times. I don't know how I got there but when we arrived home I was being ridden on his back piggyback. Everybody seemed to be so happy that I was happy.

Just before going to bed, Burt and I got into an hilarious game leaping off a couch onto many pillows that we had thrown onto the floor. When were finally quieted down and told it was bedtime, I realized this activity was one not to be repeated, because Burt was admonished for starting the game. However, it was made clear that it was all right this time but not to be a usual habit. Life now was full of normal procedure. No hidden corners. All was open and healthy. Wrong things were never harshly corrected. School days started again. Neighbor children were invited in. Candy pulls were Saturday night celebrations. Books were brought from the library regularly and Mam read them aloud to us. Many times five or six neighbor children would come in and we would all lie around on the floor in front of a warm coal fire burning brightly in an oval topped fireplace in the dining room.

Going to the library on my bicycle, returning a book and getting another became a regular routine. *The Wizard of Oz*, Louisa May Alcott—one after another from *Little Women* to *Joe's Boys*. There was *Black Beauty*, the wonderful horse, and later my own favorite private reading was the Alger Boys' stories. This was my first introduction to books. The Alger Stories had a picture on the cover of the books of a little boy with all of his belongings tied in a bandana handkerchief hung onto a stick over his shoulder. This somehow related itself to me. There was always the longing for my mother and an inner secret dream that I would leave home like the Alger boys and go looking for her someday when I grew up just a little bit more.

Apparently there had been the warning that my mother would try to take us away. Even at my aunt's there was a day the doorbell rang and instead of opening the door, my aunt rushed to all of the windows and drew the blinds. Then I heard my mother's voice calling my name. Of course I wanted to go to her but I was held with a hand placed over my mouth as I tried to cry out to her. All around the outside of the house I heard her voice calling me but no sound was allowed to go out to her. She soon went away. There may have been a reason for not letting her see me but it all seemed wrong and mysterious then and no one ever said anything against her and there were no explanations so the mystery grew. Soon after, there were rumors that my mother had died. But in reality she had not died until eight or ten years later. I discovered that by visiting her grave long after I had grown.

For many years, I used to imagine that when I grew up I would romantically find my mother, very

much like the storybook experiences of which I had been reading. She was always beautiful and like a storybook princess to me. Many of the early novels dramatized such situations. The play *Madame X* is a good example of the period.

Peculiarly that child imagery became a melody that played a reprise. Many years later, after I had become a motion picture director, Ruth Chatterton was brought to Hollywood to play in *Madame X* with Lionel Barrymore and Paramount Studies signed her to be starred. I made her first starring picture, called *Sarah and Son*. It was the story of a mother who had been separated from her baby son. After she had attained wealth in a career, she searched for her son and found him.

**Dorothy Arzner poses with Ruth Chatterton**

Pretty fundamental plot. It was an enormous success. By that time I thought I was sophisticated and was afraid the story might be too "corny," but I knew the story down to the ground as far as emotional content, and with my many early theatrical incidents it evidently had a living quality that was unique and fresh. It is from such incidents that I have the thought that all we can ever do in our work is write our own biography. There we are, and our work is limited and enlarged according to how much we have been aware of our own biography and all its details and make some effort toward evaluating them, not always relative to ourselves but in relationship with the whole of life.

However, this inner longing for my mother was balanced by a very healthy, active life at Mam's and I can't imagine a better person for me to have been with under the circumstances. It is interesting to note how easily we blend with one person and how difficult with another, her very own daughter. Everything went along smoothly and contentedly. Just once, when I was coming out of the door of a neighbor's house, I saw a very bleached-blonde woman leaving our house. I didn't recognize who it was at first but later realized it was my mother—I had just a glimpse of her. After she had gone, I rushed into the house and asked if that was my mother! And I was told it was mother, demanding to see me. Evidently the orders from my father were not to let her see me, if she came, so she was sent away again. I was told that she left with the threat that she would get a lawyer. But I never saw or heard of

my mother again until many years later when I made inquiry and have gathered bits and pieces of a sad life.

I went to a fortune teller once for amusement and, I suppose, curiosity to find out if someone could tell me something I would believe about my life. She told me every detail of my early life and all about my mother. I was a bit amazed because by then I didn't think anyone could know anything about my mother. Then she said, "I have watched your career constantly because I knew your mother." It seems her mother and mine were friends and it was to their home my mother went when she was first divorced. Of course this woman was only a few years older than I and would have been a young girl then. She had great sympathy for my mother and, of course, told me another side of the story—how my Dad had been taken away from my mother by this other woman, my stepmother. However, by now I think I know all sides and see the inevitability of many things being just as they are. It's a long road to wisdom.

**Part IV**

I found peace, at last, with Mam. I made my first girlfriend in spite of the fact that I always played with boys. She was Burt's best girl. She was enough older than I to know how to win my friendship at the same time I was living in the same house with the boy she admired. I now began to feel I belonged. Everyone was my friend and I loved everyone. Life was pleasant. There were no more tears. Reports of contentment and good conduct must have gone out to my Dad and stepmother. Letters were exchanged and great five-pound boxes of candy and presents arrived periodically from the South. Mabel was very devoted to her mother and my father's constant devotion to his children made for many indulgences in the luxuries of life.

The day I was about to start to school again Mam asked me if I had another name than Emma. "Oh, yes," I said. "My real name is Dorothy," but because my father's sister's name was Emma he wanted me to be called that. He had a deep affection for his sister. In fact all his life he took care of her. He never missed sending his mother part of his earnings and when she died he continued to

119

send money to his sister. Until the day she died he sent one-hundred dollars every month and sometimes more. At any rate my real name was Dorothy and Mam thought that a much prettier name. I liked it better too. Emma, the nurse at The Dunlaps, had turned me against the name and I was glad to have it changed, although I corresponded with Aunt Emma and always signed Emma. I didn't want to hurt her. She lived in Switzerland and constantly sent me religious postcards and spoke of God and Jesus. My father was not too sure he liked the changing of my name. I believe he was afraid his sister would be hurt. That beginning of subterfuge because of the fear of hurting someone became a subtle poison, which later had to be met head on in my life. He continued to call me Emma until later years and then he called me Dot.

Stability began to grow, and courage. My stepmother came from pioneer stock. There was a grandmother too, Mam's mother. She lived on the other side of the tracks. She had recently married a Portuguese street cleaner, to the family's consternation! I used to ride my bicycle over to see her. She was a real pioneer woman, stalwart and strong, built straight up and down, and stood straight as a column. I usually found her sitting on the back steps with a weezy little black-and-tan dog and she was smoking a clay pipe. She used to tell me stories of crossing the plains. At sixteen she rode a pony all the way from Pennsylvania to San Jose. They were Pennsylvania Dutch. Her grandfather was John Carroll, one of the signers of the Declaration of Independence. Mam was the third white child born in San Jose. And Mabel, my stepmother, would ask for the wildest horses when going out for a drive. These were strong women. Mam's father had come to California in 1847. It took him six months to get here around Cape Horn in a sailing vessel, bringing the lumber with him to build his house. These were brave people.

There was a dark alley between our house and the next neighbor's house, and a large clump of dark bushes on both sides of the entrance to the alley. One night as I rode my bicycle by I heard something in those bushes and saw them move. I raced to the back of the house, dropped my bicycle and flew upstairs and rushed into the house breathless, and exclaiming that there was someone in the bushes as I passed. Calmly, Mam took me by the hand and led me to the spot to investigate. She pushed the bushes and there in the corner was a frightened kitten, meowing. She explained that he had probably been on the branches as I passed and I had frightened him as much as he had frightened me. She seemed to impart to me in that experience that there were usually rational explanations for things that seemed frightening and if we know what they are many of the incidents will not be frightening.

This idea of knowledge eliminating fear made a deep impression upon me.

If a report card had a low mark she would say, "You did the best you knew how, didn't you? That's all you need to do. These marks don't matter—they will improve." With that faith in us, of course we tried to do the best we could. Mam was a woman with little or no formal education but she read constantly and every morning she read the newspaper from cover to cover. It was through this that I realized the power of the press. If she read something in the paper, it was true. In later years she would tell me what the paper had said I was going to do and I would say, "No, Mam, I'm not going to do that. I'm doing this." She would come back with, "I guess they just haven't told you yet." This of course was during her later years. One's family of that other generation doesn't always comprehend that their children have attained a kind of authority of which they never dreamed. There were powers that they had been trained to think were beyond them.

These peaceful days were not to last long. One morning I was awakened with a violent shaking of my bed, as if the giants of all stories had been let loose and were about to destroy humanity. The roar came from the bowels of the earth and as far as I was concerned the world was coming to an end! I had thought about such a thing happening and here it was. I rose from the couch where I had been sleeping and just as I did a tall glass bookcase was hurled down upon it. Then bricks started to come crashing through the window. I looked out and telegraph poles were swaying like trees and a huge chimney built on the outside of the house across the street was thrown to the ground.

I tried to get to my grandmother's door but it was uphill and I couldn't make it. Then suddenly I was hurled through the door right into the middle of my grandmother's bed, screaming above the roar. "Mam, what is it?" "It's an earthquake," she said, at the same time grabbing me and pulling me under the covers and piling pillows on top of me. All I was aware of after that was being rolled from side to side and almost smothering to death. It was only a matter of moments until it was over. I crawled out to see a house in shambles. But my grandmother calmly proceeded to put things in order and started making the familiar movements toward getting breakfast.

Then we went out to investigate the damage about us. The old man who lived next door to us was on his front steps in his nightshirt with a vase of carnations in his hand. Great churches on the opposite corners of our block were half-demolished and their steeples tossed into the street. Immediately news of the quake reached Los Angeles and my dear vulnerable father came North

The 1906 San Francisco earthquake's massive devastation was felt all over California, including Oakland.

by whatever vehicle he could command. Trains were not running into the city and no one was allowed in or out except through the National Guard's okay. All men were commandeered to clear the street of brick and search for bodies. Two days after his arrival he found us intact except for the chimney down, windows broken and the eaves torn off where our house bumped against the next about eight-feet away.

The red glow from the burning city cast a fearful glow on everything and the booming from whole blocks being dynamited in order to check the blaze were ominous. My father stayed a few days, making the decision that we should all be moved to Los Angeles as soon as he could find a house for us.

For weeks the earth shook intermittently until our nerves were at the breaking point. We finally got to just sitting and waiting for the quakes to come.

Schools were condemned—soldiers everywhere and constant lines of refugees passed our house dragging their worldly goods in sheets and trunks and carts. Our house was filled with several of Mam's San Francisco friends, who had been burned out. We set up kind of a canteen. We had water, which was rare and we all helped to serve

some food to people who were hungry. This went on for weeks until finally the earth subsided and the refugees were cared for; then the preparations for moving started.

A large house was bought on Wilshire Boulevard and Union Avenue. It was just a residential street then, as far as Mac Arthur Park, which was then called Westlake Park. From the park on out to the beach were mustard fields. My brother Dave was brought from the East. Burt, Mam, Mam's mother, my stepmother, Dad and Tom (who visited us periodically)—all of us were to live under one roof. Four generations, four separate and distinct families, all joined together. I managed to harmonize myself in the situation. But my brother had difficulty making his adjustment to so many people belonging to my stepmother's side of the family. He was never happy there and soon left home to board out near the college he attended. I went through grade school with one accomplishment. I was one of the best baseball players on the boys' team! I rarely played with girls. And girls did not play baseball at that time. How I know I was a good player was the fact that at recess or lunch hour or after school the moment I would appear I could hear the yells go up, "First Chooser! Second Chooser!" and then my name would

West Lake Park, Los Angeles, Cal.

be called next! I was a crack first baseman. They could burn the ball into me and I never missed putting my man out on first. I could bat the ball out farther than most and run faster than any boy except one, Donald Lingle, who was my beau at the time. I rode his bicycle and wore his stickpin. These were the special insignia of a bond. Those were happy days of just pure healthy activity. I never even knew I had a face or a body. My mind was filled with the joyousness of competitive play. I was a reasonably good student. I jumped one grade, B seven, and for years have blamed my lack of knowledge of punctuation on the fact that it must have been missed then. I have no knowledge of having studied it.

The eighth grade was the year I seriously took up tennis. Most of the ballplayers turned to it also. We built our own court on a vacant lot and learned on the roughest and bumpiest ground. I continued to play with boys. The only girls I knew were friends of my brother or Burt's girlfriends. They were always about but looked upon me as a little girl and mothered me somewhat. At least that was my interest in them. They were not interesting to play with.

There were very few automobiles seen in those days. But down the street from us there was an apartment house. It had just recently been built and there was a very pretty lady who came from the apartment house every day and got into an electric automobile. I remember thinking then that they were rather like a glass showcase. She was very blonde and very dressed up and all the kids on the street thought she was very nice because she would smile so pleasantly at us and we would pause in our games to let her go by. Sometimes she would give us candy as she

passed returning home; they were big bags of it. We thought she was quite a wonderful lady. We used to call her the pretty lady. One day she asked all of us if we would to come up to her apartment and have ice cream and cake. We all trailed up, a bit shy, as I remember and we were a pretty grubby looking troupe. We were standing about the dining room table and she was telling a Japanese boy to get plates when suddenly from a very low sweet voice giving directions it rose into a harsh hard shriek of words I had never hear before! The boy had left the electric coffeepot on and it was dry and this what had brought on the change of character. We were shocked! And as I remember we didn't even wait for ice cream. We all got out of there as fast as we could. We said very little to each other about it. I can remember the effect of disillusion on the part of all of us and our balance was only regained when we immediately started into another game in the street. The pretty lady passed many times afterward but there was always a shy response from us all. She was no longer the "pretty lady" as far as we were concerned. It was several years later that I realized she probably was a "kept lady." Certainly she had all the traditional characteristics, even to a very fluffy feather boa that she wore, and rather too much makeup for those times.

By the time I graduated from grade school I'm sure my family had some concern as to what to do with me. I'm sure they decided I needed a little feminine polish because it was decided I should go to a girl's school. So I was sent to the fashionable Westlake School for Girls. It was a very large house on Alvarado and Sixth Streets. My first days have always made me think of Jack London's *White Fang*: the white wolf that had such a difficult time adjusting himself to the world, because he was different from the other wolves. I thought all the girls at school were such sissies. I would stand at a distance and throw rocks while they greeted each other in the morning with such affection. Very soon came the day for the seniors to properly subordinate the freshmen. They dressed in long white robes and we were called before a solemn ceremonial and were told what our conduct should be.

I thought this was all pretty silly. They were just "other girls" and what were they doing dictating my conduct. Then we were told to kneel, to them! That was too much for me. I stood alone as the others kneeled and gazed out the window. There was no attention paid to me. Soon everyone rose and the meeting was dismissed. A few weeks later the seniors ganged up on me to haze me. They caught me alone and the whole class was about to rush me off into a car and take me to one of their homes. What their plans were for me I have no idea because that was a signal for me to let loose with all my boyish strength and know-how. I went down in the skirmish grabbing legs and throwing girls down, punching and fighting to get free from them when the principal appeared on the scene. Lifting me from the midst of them with torn clothes and a generally pretty disheveled appearance, I was told to report to the office for an explanation of this disgraceful and unladylike episode.

I told my side of the story quietly and unemotionally, I remember. I think I enjoyed the skirmish. I think I was prepared to be rather happy if I was told I could not come back to school. However, I remember making a point of the fact of the injustice of thirty girls against one. That wasn't cricket from my point of view. I had been used to very fair play with boys. Then I began asking questions. Why should I be asked to kneel to anyone and why should I allow anyone to rush me off anywhere. I had never done anything to them. I remember the wry smile that played around the corner of that fine woman's mouth. And all she said was, "I shall see that it doesn't happen again. You may return to your

**A young Dorothy Arzner, courtesy Sally Sumner**

classes." Nothing more was said. There were no further references to the incident. It had been completely dropped by everyone. I've often thought that if nothing more were learned than that, much of the human relationship troubles would be eliminated. Everyone dramatizes things so much and builds small incidents into major differences. I later became friends with most of those young women. I played tennis on the team with the seniors and for three

years held the school tennis championship cup and won the girl's school championship pennant for Westlake.

There was always much discussion of preparation for college: what course to take, what college to go to, what career to aim for. I'm not sure how I arrived at the decision that I wanted to be a doctor. Possibly it was a combination of religious influences from my aunt. In reading the Bible I was imbued with the idea of Jesus

**Dorothy Arzner at age 20. Courtesy Mildred Sumner © 2001**

healing the sick and raising the dead. I wanted to heal the sick and raise the dead. I had made friends with a young married couple who lived across the street from us. He used to play catch with me in the evenings. His wife was going to have a baby. They used to say that they would be perfectly content if they had a little girl who would grow up to be just like me.

They were a very loving couple and included me in their affection. I was with them constantly. Mam had her aged mother to care for and my Dad and stepmother were away all day and into the night. I was on my own to some degree. That baby coming was of paramount interest to all of us. Then one day came sadness; she lost her baby. There were weeks I saw those two people suffering. She was months getting well and my dear friends were so deeply grieved that I was fired with the idea that there

should be no such thing as pain, sadness or death. I would learn how to prevent this pain and sorrow. So my studies were directed toward that end: four years Latin, two years German, chemistry, biology and all the rest. No tennis my fourth year—just study at U.S.C. premed for two years. War broke out! The First World War. I left school and joined an ambulance corps—the Drake Section Sanitaire. I was too young for the Red Cross, but the French government would take us at eighteen and at twenty-one I could go overseas. I wanted to get over and drive right up to the front line trenches. Adventure! Instead I merely transported medical supplies to the base hospital and delivered messages for the Intelligence Corps. [Editor's note: This was apparently the Los Angeles Emergency Ambulance Corps and not an overseas corps. The time of her entry in the corps was 1917 and she continued to the war's conclusion in 1918. Her dates at U.S.C. are sometimes said to be 1915 and sometimes slightly later].

In one year the war was over and I was looking into space. I had had a taste of the outside world and I didn't want to go back to school. My family was not very friendly about my ambulance corps duties. I think they would have preferred to have me stay home and help with the housework. I don't know what was in their minds but a tension and dissension began to grow. My stepmother didn't approve of my friends and I stayed away more and more from home. I came in late at night and left in the morning. I went to parties with soldier boys and I don't think they quite knew just what I was doing or who I was with. But I knew. Commander Starkweather and his wife were very fine people heading the corps.

I was having dinner with them, a farewell dinner. The war was over in eighteen months and we were being disbanded. I passed the remark, "Well, where do we go from here?" I had had a taste of independence and being out in the world on my own. I didn't want to go back to school. The two of them started conferring as to what I should do. It was Mrs. Starkweather who made the remark, "Dorothy is a modern girl; she should be connected with modern things. I think she should be in the motion pictures." I have no idea why she associated me with the motion picture business unless it was a field she would like to have been in if she were younger and wanting activity. She was an artist and a writer. I saw some of her writing in rather obscure magazines.

Our corps was smartly uniformed. Coats were like the French Air Force, buttoning across to the shoulder and we had short skirts and high leather riding boots. We made quite an impression with whomever we met. I had met William De Mille, who was in the intelligence department for the studios during the war. Mrs. Starkweather made an appointment for me. He was a director along with his brother Cecil B. De Mille at the Paramount Studios on Vine Street, which was their original location. These two men had pioneered the beginning of the Paramount Studio. It was then called Famous Players Lasky Corporation. William De Mille had organized many of the departments including the scenario department.

I was shy about applying for work and would never have followed up the suggestions except that one day Mrs. Starkweather drove me out and dropped me off at the studio, saying, "Go in and see Mr. De Mille; you have an appointment with him." Then she drove off leaving me in the middle of the street wishing I had never opened myself to this ordeal. But I went in. I was not in uniform and not nearly as attractive to Mr. De Mille. He commented on the fact that young ladies should always wear those uniforms. He then said: "Let me see

**Dorothy Arzner as a bridesmaid at the Mildred Rivers' wedding in 1916.  Courtesy Sally Sumner.**

your profile." "Oh, I don't want to be actress!" I said. "What do you want to do?" he asked. Hesitantly I grasped at a straw. "Well, maybe I could dress sets." That seemed easy enough to me, but he asked what the period of the furniture was that he had in his office. I did not know. "Franciscan," he told me rather sternly. I remember then having the impression he was like a professor in college. He also looked like the engravings of Shakespeare I had seen. I sat silent. He was quite formidable. Then with a drawl he said, "I think you'd better spend about a week looking around the lot. I'll arrange for you to observe all the departments and go on the sets and watch them shooting pictures."

I'd seen pictures being shot. D.W. Griffith, Mary Pickford, Mabel Normand, Mack Sennett, and all the rest of them used to eat at my Dad's restaurant, and seeing actors was not particularly interesting to me. He then told me to come back

in a week to see him. That last request was what made it imperative that I observe so I could at least make an intelligent report. I did just what he told me to do. In addition I talked with his secretary and found out how she started. "Typing scripts," she told me and now she was in the very important job of being William De Mille's private secretary. I was impressed with that.

I went in to cutting rooms, projection rooms, and I visited the Cecil De Mille set. He was making a picture called *Male and Female*. [Editor's note: This was made in 1919 with Thomas Meighan, Gloria Swanson and Bebe Daniels.] There I saw the personification of directorial au-

125

**Joannes Brothers building**

thority and I remember thinking "well, if one were going to be in this business the thing to be was the director. He was the one who told everyone what to do. He was the whole works!"

I returned to William De Mille's office at the end of the week eager now to be connected with this very colorful activity. I opened the conversation after Mr. De Mille's questioning "Well?"

"I think I'd like to be in the picture business," I said.

"And where do you think you'd like to start?"

"At the bottom," I said.

"And where do you think the bottom is," he said grimly.

"Typing scripts," I said.

"For that answer I'll give you a job." And Mr. De Mille took me right off to the stenographic department and introduced me to Miss Miller, a precise and rigid little English woman. She was told to give me the first opening in the department. Miss Miller took down my name, address and telephone number. Today I have been told that that is the way one is sure they will never get the job. But I was too young to think anything but that what people said they meant.

Days, weeks, a month passed and one day I ran into one of my Westlake student friends on the street. To my surprise, she was working. "Where?" I asked. "At a wholesale coffee house on the East side of Los Angeles down in the wholesale district." This seemed like adventure to me and I must have expressed a desire to work. I knew I had grown to be a problem to my family. I didn't want to stay home and learn to cook and do the things that all young women should know how to do. Also there must have been a financial pinch after the war and a very severe influenza epidemic had taken off many people. I was told one day that my allowance would have to be cut

in half from $60 a month to $30. Thinking this had only to do with a disapproval of me, I rose to my most adolescent independence and announced to my father: "I don't want any money from you. I have friends. I'll manage, somehow, on my own." Of course I contemplated leaving home but I had no place to go. I saw only one way — go to work and be independent. When my friend expressed an enthusiastic assurance that she was sure there would be a job for me and that she would speak to the boss, who was one of the brothers of the Joannes Brothers Wholesale Coffee House [Editor's note: here Arzner has called them the Johanes Brothers, but she often misspelled names so it may have been the Joannes Brothers whose five-story building was put up in 1916 in Los Angeles]. There were several openings, filling orders or working the switchboard. I was more than happy to accept. I went to work. I filled orders and ran the switchboard. For this I was give the large sum of $12.00 a week.

When I told my Dad about my job he seemed to be pleased. He would give me a dollar for every dollar I earned. From then on my financial independence was assured. There were things about working that I had to get used to. I rather resented the brusque way salesmen came in to the office and would speak to me. I'm afraid I felt a little superior to the people about me but I tried not to show it. I was a working girl now. I liked the atmosphere of coming out at night with all the others after a day's work. There was something particularly interesting about the city downtown at night when everyone was on his way home and the streetlights were lit and it made me feel a part of a very vital life I had not experienced before, mixed with the feeling of independence.

Not three weeks had passed when I plugged into an outside call and over the switchboard the voice of Ruby Miller said, "There is an opening in our stenographic department typing scripts. Would you like to have the job." My next question was "what is the salary?" "Fifteen dollars a week to begin with," she said. That was three dollars a week more than I was getting and that three dollars was the deciding factor. The motion picture studios held no attraction for me. I'd been brought up with actors all my life. In fact I was just about to make a special place for myself, I thought. I had made a color sketch for a poster advertisement for the Joannes Brothers Coffee and Mr. Joannes' wife, who was a painter, liked it and had asked to meet me. I was going to have dinner at their house. When I announced that I was leaving to accept a position at the Famous Players-Lasky Studio the invitation was forgotten and with courteous regret I was allowed to leave as soon as I could train another girl to take my place.

I had one moment of regret that I was leaving and that came when I said goodbye to Spencer, the accountant. He was known as a disgruntled little man. When I first met up with him all I heard was complaints from him, not anything directly but just a general muttering all the time of things that were wrong in the office. He had been with the firm a long, long time and no one paid much attention to him. His complaints didn't seem to count with anyone but he was a fixture and a thorn to everyone. He looked undernourished, with narrow shoulders and a very shiny suit, worn thin. It had been cleaned and pressed too many times. His collar was a little too high in order to cover his thin neck. It was always immaculately clean.

His shirt was worn too many days and always looked mussed. I felt that he had made a brave attempt to be as well dressed as the others. One had the impression that he had been at those accounts ever since the firm was established and that date was obviously stamped on all correspondence: Est. 1886. Spencer learned that I was leaving from Mr. Joannes. He must have been told immediately after I announced my intention because I had planned to tell him myself. I had grown to have an affection for him; we had become friends. I made a point of winning his favor, mainly because of my own sensitivity in being in the presence of anyone who would be unpleasant with me. It would have been impossible for me to work with him. I used to help him with his account filing after he had made his entries. This was not my job but he seemed to be inundated constantly with work and things to be filed. No one seemed to like him. He was crisp and staccato and the others thought him grouchy. I had the urge to help him, lighten his burden, and that seemed to soften his general conduct. There were rumors to the effect that at last old Spencer had met up with someone who could gain his respect enough to make him human.

I had just arrived at my desk when I heard Spencer say, "That's the way with these society girls. They just begin to be of some value and then they up and leave!" I looked over at him but he never raised his head from making his entries. I knew someone must have told him before I could. I tried to explain to him that I wasn't a society girl but I did think I would never be very good at office work and it would be just a matter of a short time until I would leave anyway. I explained how appreciative I was of his kindness to me in letting me learn so much and he was the one real gentleman in the office. He never looked up at me the whole time. A day or so later was my last day and he had not spoken to me. When it was time for me to say goodbye to everyone he was the last one I went to. I put out my hand right under his nose said, "I

Lasky partners in 1916: Jesse L. Lasky, Adolph Zukor, Samuel Goldwyn, Cecil B. DeMille, Al Kaufman

do want to say goodbye and thank you for your kindness to me." My hand was extended for a moment without response from him, and then suddenly he was on his feet, grumbled once, gave my hand one down shake and let it drop. Then the saddest blue eyes I have ever seen looked straight into mine for a moment only and he sat down as abruptly as had risen and went back to his entries. There was nothing more I could say. I stood for a moment, then left. I had to stop thinking about him because he offered too many complexities [Editor's note—Miss Arzner has written "characters" here instead of complexities and I have changed it] to me and I would never know why he was as he was. But he was a gentle man and the grumblings somehow were a cover that probably made it possible for him to go on.

With trepidation I faced a new job the next day that I knew entailed typing. I had only typed college notes with two fingers on each hand. To this day I type the same, but with a little more speed than I did that first day and if I am careful, with a great deal more accuracy. Fortunately for me it was Miss Miller's day off. I was greeted by one of the other typists, Mike Leheigh, a tall, freckle-faced girl with glasses. She was in charge. She directed me to a desk opposite hers in a small office. Miss Miller had left a pile of copy with my name on it. All I was supposed to do was to copy the handwritten pages for one of the scenario writers whose office was down the hall, but I was informed by Mike Leheigh that the one thing Miss Miller was a stickler for was letter perfect copy.

All day I struggled, hitting wrong letters, erasing, and hearing the rat-ti-tat-tat of the typewriter just across from me. Her pile was done hours before the end of the day and I was left alone to hear my own mind repeating, "You aren't a typist. Listen to how fast the other girls type. You'll never hold down this job. Why did you want to leave a job that you had learned to do so easily and come to this one that is something you don't know how to do? What are you thinking of? Better quit before you get fired. You couldn't stand to be fired. Better quit before you get fired." I was in this state when Miss Leheigh came in and informed me it was time to go home. I wasn't half through. I asked if it would be all right if I finished the work at home. Without revealing her superior wisdom about me, she said, "Oh, sure. Just be careful not to lose any of the original." And off she went leaving me to my misery. I saw her beautiful, clean, expert typing, laying on Miss Miller's desk before I left.

**C.B. DeMille in his office on the Lasky/Paramount lot.**

That night I spent the whole night retyping everything I had done through the day and all the balance that had been given me to do. I hardly took time to eat dinner. Carefully, surely and solidly, I pounded the letters out one after the other. I proofread it carefully, made a few unseen corrections and retyped a few pages. All was in readiness by the time eight o'clock arrived and I had to leave to face another day of the same. However, the eagerness to make good somehow sustained me.

Miss Miller was at her desk when I arrived. I handed her my copy. A few pleasantries were passed. "How did I get along?" "Oh, fine," was my answer. "I'm awfully slow, though." She assured me I would pick up speed quickly each day. It was a good thing for me that the flu epidemic had made a shortage of typists or I never would have been retained, I'm sure. Entering my office I saw the usual pile laying on my desk. Miss Leheigh was hard at it, dashing out copy, greeting me and inquiring after my welfare without pausing to look up. I had made up my mind I would do this day's work more carefully. At least I wouldn't have to do the pages over that I had done. Each one of us put our initials at the bottom of the page so it would be known whose work it was. Hours passed and my pile showed little evidence of being half finished when Miss Leheigh picked up all of her work and took it into Miss Miller for proofreading. She came back immediately, picked up half of what was left of mine and said, "Miss Miller thinks your work was very well done for a first day."

It was then I confessed to Mike what I had done, how little of typing I'd ever done and how much I wanted to make good at this job. Did she think I would make it? "Oh, you'll be okay. Just keep at it. You can't help but gather speed. I'll just knock out these few pages for you and nobody need ever know the difference." She did knock out those pages in no time at all and dropped them on my desk with my initials at the bottom. She took up some more that were remaining and soon I had finished my day's work! What a friend! And the kind of a girl I admire tremendously. Just a grand girl. I haven't met too many. But they are the shining lights on one's path. This procedure continued until I could hold my own. Later, to my satisfaction, when work was slack, the four of us, who typed all the scenarios for the studio, used to race to see who could finish with letter-perfect copy. I was not the first, nor was I last. At the end of three months a typist was either fired or received a raise of one dollar and a half. I got the raise. My salary would now be $16.50 a week.

Naturally I began to hear of the big salaries people received as actors and directors but I remember my thought was, if I ever make as high as $30.00 a week that will be all I shall ever want. That will buy everything that I want. Of course I was living at home and had no consciousness of what it meant to have to really pay for one's living needs. This was spending money for me and besides I had only been working all together about four months and I had not even needed to buy myself clothes.

I was kept pretty close to the typewriter those first few months but there still remain a few outstanding impressions.

Things about me began to take on speed. Boys in uniform were returning to the studio from overseas. It was 1920. The four companies that made up the Lasky studio now expanded to six. Mary Pickford and Douglas Fairbanks were leaving to start their own company. The Big Four were D.W. Griffith, Charles Chaplin, Mary Pickford and Douglas Fairbanks. Mary Pickford's bungalow, the mark of a "Star of Stars," stood empty. Not until Pola Negri came onto the lot was it occupied. The "Lasky Studio" was located at Vine Street and Sunset. Huge pepper trees lined the oiled [Editor's note: "old?"] street. A narrow strip of sidewalk ran between the trees and a row of low gray wooden buildings, which were the offices for executives, writers, directors and business personnel. They were little wooden cubbyholes, except for the four or five belonging to the De Milles, Mr. Lasky and Charles Eyton, Studio Manager. These were relatively more luxurious. Cecil De Mille's was the most pretentious, with a white bear rug and all.

There was an opening in the buildings that led to "the lot" where the stages were located. There was a guarded spring gate at that opening into the casting office. The assistant casting director stood there and saw that everyone going through was eligible to pass. There were no policemen in those days to keep you out. Everyone could go to the casting office window and make himself known.

Famous Players-Lasky Corporation was the latest letterhead for correspondence. We could have for personal use the old letterhead Lasky Feature Play Co. That meant that Jesse Lasky, who was president had negotiated a combine with Adolph Zukor who owned theatres, and his company was known as Famous Players. This was the beginning of the growth of Motion Picture theatres and production in Hollywood.

Cecil De Mille presented a formidable and unique character to the studio. He would drive up in a grey Pierce Arrow roadster, with red leather seats. There was nothing like it about. He was at the wheel and beside him was a uniformed Japanese chauffeur, who jumped out and opened the door for him and then followed just a few steps behind as De Mille strode through the gate speaking to no one, and dressed in a well-tailored gabardine Norfolk suit with leather puttees. (Editor's note: a puttee or cloth piece was worn by riders wound spirally around the leg between knee and ankle for support and protection). It looked a little odd to me at that time but now I realize it was showmanship. No one else dressed like that but I soon learned they did wear puttees on location because

Dorothy Arzner received her first editing credit for *Too Much Johnson* in 1919.

there were many outdoor pictures and they had to work in rough country.

Very few people had their own cars in those days. They lived near and walked. But my Dad had given me a car the year before. We had cars from the time I entered high school through my persuasion. There were no No Parking signs, no need for them. One day I had parked my car just in front of the entrance when Mr. De Mille's Japanese chauffeur rushed up to me before I could get out and informed me I would have to move. That place belonged to Mr. De Mille. I looked about and he was sitting in his car waiting. I realized by his expression that I had made an intolerable mistake. I noticed on the curb then, "Reserved for Mr. De Mille." That mark of distinction has grown in the studios. For the first time I came up against class distinction or as I prefer to call it "Power Distinction." This was no problem for me. I don't believe I had any sense of inferiority or superiority. I was brought up to bow to certain customs and there was always a sense in me of social sureness. I've always known no one was really so very superior and that there is a great

**Dorothy Arzner poses for a studio portrait in the 1930s. (Photofest)**

Dorothy Arzner directs *Get Your Man* in 1927. Cinematographer Alfred Gilks is behind the camera. (Photofest)

deal of whistling in the dark when actions seem to have a false superiority.

As I look back, I think Cecil De Mille was having a great time for himself, dressing and acting a part he reveled in. He had attained the position of a top movie director then, but he wasn't mature enough to wear the mantle with simplicity and besides he was and is a showman. I have heard since that before Cecil came to Hollywood to look the field over, he was an actor out of a job. He was going to join Teddy Roosevelt's Rough Riders in the border warfare. Jesse Lasky, his friend, was so concerned over what might happen to him that he, together with Sam Goldwyn, sent Cecil out to Hollywood to see what was going on. They had heard that the motion pictures were beginning to take hold and most of them were starting up in Hollywood. Jesse said, "Go out and look the place over and tell us what you think." Cecil did and sent back enthusiastic reports. Lasky raised some more money. Cecil rented a barn and started to make pictures. *The Squaw Man* with Dustin Farnum was the first. It was so successful that he then started to make one by day and one by night.

This was the beginning of a business in which I was to spend my life. Again I found myself feeling strange, out of synch with the people, having to make adjustments constantly, not really at one with them but still in it.

I cannot cover the rest of my biography but I shall try to set down the incident from which I have attempted to write a short story.

Editor's Note: The autobiography ends here and nothing else was submitted to Dorothy's friend Bunny Sumner who wrote on the manuscript in 1955:

> Miss Arzner, it will be a shame if you don't develop the 1920 recollections into either story background or a sort of auto-biographical novel. It is invaluable stuff.

We can only agree with this assessment and lament the fact that apparently she never wrote any more.

# INDEX

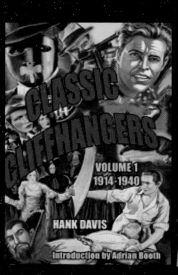